Radical Reconciliation

To: Vicky,
with prayers for God's blessings
in your life + work.

Allan Boesak

Radical Reconciliation

Beyond Political Pietism and Christian Quietism

Allan Aubrey Boesak

and Curtiss Paul DeYoung

ORBIS BOOKS

Maryknoll, New York 10545

Founded in 1970, Orbis Books endeavors to publish works that enlighten the mind, nourish the spirit, and challenge the conscience. The publishing arm of the Maryknoll Fathers and Brothers, Orbis seeks to explore the global dimensions of the Christian faith and mission, to invite dialogue with diverse cultures and religious traditions, and to serve the cause of reconciliation and peace. The books published reflect the views of their authors and do not represent the official position of the Maryknoll Society. To learn more about Maryknoll and Orbis Books, please visit our website at www.maryknollsociety.org.

Library of Congress Cataloging-in-Publication Data

Boesak, Allan Aubrey, 1946-
    Radical reconciliation : beyond political pietism and Christian quietism / Allan Aubrey Boesak and Curtiss Paul DeYoung.
        p.   cm.
    Includes bibliographical references (p.   ). and index.
    ISBN 978-1-57075-976-5 (pbk.); eISBN 978-1-60833-211-3
    1. Reconciliation—Religious aspects—Christianity.   I. DeYoung, Curtiss Paul.
II. Title.
    BT738.27.B64 2012
    261.8—dc23

                                                                    2012008146

Contents

Foreword—Archbishop Desmond Mpilo Tutu   *vii*

Introduction   1

Part I: Reconciliation Redefined   **7**

1. Reconciliation in the Empire: Real, Radical,
   Revolutionary (*DeYoung*)   9

2. Reconciliation, Risk, and Resistance:
   The Story of Rizpah (*Boesak*)   25

Part II: Jesus Christ Reclaimed   **41**

3. Jesus the Radical Reconciler:
   Two Takes, One Perspective (*DeYoung/Boesak*)   43

4. "Just Another Jew in the Ditch":
   Incarnated Reconciliation (*Boesak*)   57

Part III: Beloved Communities Restored   **75**

5. Reconciliation in Diverse Congregations:
   Restoring the Beloved Community (*DeYoung*)   77

6. Between Reitz, a Rock, and a Hard Place:
   Reconciliation after the Reitz Event (*Boesak*)   93

Part IV: Just Societies Realized   113

7.   When Prophets Are Silenced, Injustice Prevails (*DeYoung*)   115

8.   Subversive Piety:
     The Reradicalization of Desmond Tutu (*Boesak*)   131

Conclusion: Beyond Political Pietism and Christian Quietism   151
(*DeYoung/Boesak*)

Acknowledgements   159

Endnotes   161

Bibliography   183

Index   193

Foreword

Desmond Mpilo Tutu

Since the completion of the work of South Africa's Truth and Reconciliation Commission, our reconciliation project has become a worldwide discussion. That is very gratifying indeed. Even more gratifying is the publication of this important book. There has been much collaboration by persons from different contexts about reconciliation in general, and South Africa's reconciliation process in particular, but here, for the first time, is a dialogue between Allan Aubrey Boesak, a (black) South African and Curtiss Paul DeYoung, a (white) citizen of the United States. The realities, challenges, and opportunities of and for reconciliation from both contexts are discovered, examined, and confronted in this compelling, scholarly, yet passionate, collaboration. Their point of departure and central argument is that reconciliation, if it is to mean anything at all, has to be radical.

A Christian understanding of reconciliation, often dismissed as romantic obscurantism, political naiveté, and hopelessly out of touch with the socio-economic realities that govern our world, is placed at the center of the argument Allan Boesak and Curtiss DeYoung are putting forward. For them, Christian reconciliation *is* radical reconciliation. This radicalism, they argue, is the very root of all genuine reconciliation. Without it, our processes and practices of reconciliation cannot avoid the temptation (or the trap, if you will) of cheap grace, on the one hand, and political expediency, on the other—what the authors call Christian quietism and political pietism. What that means is unpacked in the captivating chapters of this book.

The book has several strengths that make it stand out among recent publications. Firstly, it takes the debate on reconciliation and its central

elements significantly further. Without in any way diminishing the importance of "political reconciliation," it makes the strong argument that reconciliation should be more than just political accommodation, the result of
successful negotiation, or the achievement of an equilibrium of interests—a
position I personally hold as strongly as the authors do. In *No Future without
Forgiveness,* I place strong emphasis on forgiveness as not just a crucial but,
in fact, indispensable element in the process of reconciliation, political or
otherwise. Secondly, in reading this book one is once again impressed by
how radical a book the Bible itself is, and what it might mean to bring
those radical demands to bear on the processes of reconciliation, within
contemporary socioeconomic, political contexts. The biblical insights are
fresh, and the retelling of biblical stories are delightfully enlightening, helping us to understand that reconciliation is radical *because* it is biblical. Third,
this book helps us to understand the difference between "political pietism,"
"Christian quietism," and "radical reconciliation." It makes clear the dangers and consequences of not understanding those differences, both for
the political processes where reconciliation is sorely needed, and for the
spiritual, personal responses without which reconciliation remains shallow
and unfulfilled. Fourth, *Radical Reconciliation* offers the reader a truly powerful blend of theoretical reflection, biblical exploration, social, political,
and economic analysis, as well as activist experience from two theologians
who have worked both in the academy and at the coal face of political and
church activism for many decades. Fifthly, central to every chapter is the
inextricable intersection between reconciliation and social justice. In many
ways, social justice is the centrifugal power at work in this book, as it must
be in every reconciliation effort. And lastly, almost every chapter offers
invaluable "lessons" for practitioners of reconciliation, lessons drawn from
the biblical stories as well as from contemporary experiences.

In chapter after chapter this book presents the reader with creative
and thoughtful insights that compel us to think again, or differently, about
reconciliation and what it might mean for our societies and the life and
prophetic witness of the church. And so, in sequence, we are invited to go
on a journey to discover the meaning of reconciliation within the realities
of empire and in confrontation with political powers. Then we meet Jesus,
in the words of New Testament scholar Marcus Borg, "again for the first

time," as the radical reconciler. But meeting Jesus makes clear that radical reconciliation means radical transformation of persons and societies; so, in section three the authors think about how reconciliation can restore beloved communities after, despite, and beyond realities of oppression, exploitation, division, and alienation. Here we encounter the challenges for genuine reconciliation in the efforts to establish open, multicultural, and multiracial communities of worship in the United States. In the South African context, we encounter the shocking, yet moving and even inspirational reality of the search for reconciliation in a university community in South Africa rife with historical, racial, and cultural alienation and tensions. What does radical reconciliation mean in these so-called post-apartheid, postracial situations? In the last section, the reader is confronted with the crucial question: what happens in and to a society when the prophets are silenced? How can prophetic truth-telling, an essential ingredient of genuine reconciliation, enable the realization of just societies?

This book is a welcome, essential addition to the growing literature on reconciliation, and it is required reading for students of the Bible and theologians interested in the interface between the biblical contexts and the contemporary contexts in order to give meaning to our existence now. To pastors and preachers the book illustrates how to dialogue with the text in order to extract from it the fullest potential and enormous wealth of the meaning contained within it. To politicians and practitioners of reconciliation in search of reconciliation with integrity that leads to genuine restoration in contexts of social and political conflict, this provides insight into biblical values that are truly universal and humanistic in the best sense of the word. For ordinary readers of the Bible, it confirms the power of the biblical message and its applicability to situations where struggles for justice call for creative, authentic responses of solidarity, justice, and transformation.

None of us get to see ourselves quite as others do, and I might be peeved that I might have seemed other than radical at any period in my life. I do not think the gospel allows us that luxury. I would be guilty of crying peace, peace, where there is no peace, trying to heal ever so superficially.

In *Radical Reconciliation,* Allan Boesak and Curtiss DeYoung take us on an exciting, sometimes perhaps uncomfortable, but certainly life-transforming journey. This is a prophetic book, thought-provoking in its imaginative, evocative, and provocative content, and in the thrust of every single chapter, challenging us all to rethink the meaning of our call to become agents of reconciliation.

Desmond Mpilo Tutu

Introduction

Allan Aubrey Boesak and Curtiss Paul DeYoung

This book is a call for reconciliation in society that is radical, that goes to the roots. We believe that unless we remove injustice at the roots, the weeds of alienation and fragmentation will return and choke the hope for reconciliation. Far too many initiatives for reconciliation and social justice stop short of completing the work required. In our work and engagement with reconciliation, we have discovered how often reconciliation is used merely to reach some political accommodation that did not address the critical questions of justice, equality, and dignity that are so prominent in the biblical understanding of reconciliation. Such political arrangements invariably favor the rich and powerful but deprive the powerless of justice and dignity. Yet more often than not, this "reconciliation" is presented as if it does respond to the needs for genuine reconciliation and employs a language that sounds like the truth but is, in fact, deceitful. This we call "political pietism." Christians measure these matters with the yardstick of the gospel and therefore know better. When we discover that what is happening, is, in fact, not reconciliation, and yet for reasons of self-protection, fear, or a desire for acceptance by the powers that govern our world seek to accommodate this situation, justify it, refuse to run the risk of challenge and prophetic truth telling, we become complicit in deceitful reconciliation. We deny the demands of the gospel and refuse solidarity with the powerless and oppressed. This we call "Christian quietism." Therefore, reconciliation must be radical.

A biblical vision of reconciliation and social justice activism guides the writing of this book. In other words, this book is biblical, theological, and contextual. It celebrates faithful activism and the witness to reconciliation as seen in and shaped by the biblical story. Each chapter is anchored by scriptural texts. We bring together insights culled from activism and reflection in South Africa and in the United States (and refined by interaction with other global activist theologians), therefore giving the book a powerful blend of narratives, histories, cultures, and perspectives. We look for the intersection of reconciliation and social justice. We are informed by grassroots realities, reconciliation reflections, postcolonial critiques, feminist insights, and liberation theologies.

We form a unique team for this volume—one a black citizen of South Africa and the other a white citizen of the United States. We have both been academicians as well as activists. We have lived on both sides of this dynamic and creative tension of reflection and action. Beginning in the late 1960s Allan Boesak served in pastoral roles at congregations facing the brunt of apartheid and its lingering legacy. Beginning in the early 1980s Curtiss DeYoung served in pastoral roles at congregations in urban African American communities and multiracial settings. By the 1970s Allan was an active participant and leader in the antiapartheid struggle. He emerged in the 1980s as a primary leader and the voice of the United Democratic Front, the largest and most significant grassroots movement during the final days of the South African struggle against apartheid. By the early 1990s Curtiss was leading the Twin Cities Urban Reconciliation Network and emerging as an important voice in the reconciliation movement in the United States. During the apartheid era Allan Boesak served at the University of the Western Cape. In post-apartheid South Africa he has had appointments at the University of Stellenbosch, University of the Free State, and University of KwaZulu Natal. In the early 2000s Curtiss DeYoung joined the faculty of Bethel University and designed its bachelor of arts in reconciliation studies. Allan is a liberation theologian. Curtiss has been called a reconciliation theologian.

In the past few years we have been writing with each other's work in mind and even partnering in the process. Allan Boesak's 2005 book *The Tenderness of Conscience* used portions of DeYoung's 1997 book *Reconciliation*.[1] In Curtiss DeYoung's 2007 book, *Living Faith*, he used portions of Boesak's work on Dietrich Bonhoeffer and sections of *The Tenderness of Conscience*.[2] Allan asked Curtiss to read and comment on his manuscript for his 2009 book *Running with Horses*.[3] And Allan wrote a section in Curtiss's

2009 book *Coming Together in the 21st Century*.[4] Both personally and professionally, we have developed an easy spirit of collaboration, mutual respect, and creative synergy.

Radical Reconciliation: Beyond Political Pietism and Christian Quietism brings together our central passions biblically and socially as well as our heartfelt concerns. The book has four sections with two chapters each. In Part I, "Reconciliation Redefined," we reexamine the meaning of reconciliation in the biblical context. This section is essential reading because the remainder of the book hearkens back to the definitions forged in the first two chapters. Part II is, "Jesus Christ Reclaimed." Here we place Jesus of Nazareth in his first-century context and show him to be a radical reconciler and prophet of social justice. "Beloved Communities Restored," Part III, begins the second half of the book, and we move toward the reality of what it means to live out radical reconciliation in our lives. In these chapters we look at congregations and institutions and the need to restore in them a sense of beloved community. Part IV is "Just Societies Realized." We proceed in the book from the individual to the communal and in the final section to the need for reconciliation in broader society. We pay particular attention to the role of the prophetic voice as a way of ensuring that our attempts at reconciliation are indeed radical.

The opening chapter, "Reconciliation in the Empire: Real, Radical, Revolutionary," addresses definitions of reconciliation coming from New Testament texts. Fresh biblical definitions are introduced using the life of Jesus and the theological lens of the apostle Paul. This process of seeking biblical definitions of reconciliation takes into account the context of the writers of the New Testament, which is the colonial context of the Roman Empire. The discussion is enriched by engagement with the biblical and theological work on empire. A deeper understanding of the effect of a colonial context on the first-century church's definition of reconciliation is found through inviting the insights of postcolonial theorists and activists from the 1950s and 1960s like Steve Biko, Aimé Césaire, Frantz Fanon, Paulo Freire, and Albert Memmi. Also the Pauline emphasis on social justice that emerged from his understanding of Jesus is restored to the definition of reconciliation. Particular focus is given to the meaning of two central biblical texts in reconciliation discourse—2 Corinthians 5:16–6:2 and Ephesians 2:11–22. We declare in this chapter that reconciliation is real, radical, and revolutionary.

Chapter 2, "Reconciliation, Risk, and Resistance: The Story of Rizpah," reaches deep into the Hebrew scriptures and introduces us to the story of Rizpah from 2 Samuel. It is a riveting tale of the abuse of power, powerlessness, and exclusion. It tells how religious symbols are used for political ends and how reconciliation is used in a callous and shamelessly political maneuver to exclude, justify, and distort. Rizpah not only refuses to be a victim, she refuses to confuse the word of the king with the Word of God. She becomes the true face of reconciliation. She knows genuine reconciliation is not to found in the shadow of the throne, molded by power and intrigue, but by the side of the cross, called forth by love. Rizpah seeks justice and brings true reconciliation with God and with the people. Her courageous stand forced the king to do what is right. Rizpah teaches us much about reconciliation.

In chapter 3, we consider the central theme of the book, "Jesus the Radical Reconciler: Two Takes, One Perspective." At the time of Jesus' birth there were at least twelve other persons named Jesus who played a role in the national and religious life of Israel during the period of Greco-Roman domination. All of them, however, were scions of wealthy, influential, priestly families who in one way or another formed part of the governing elites. This thirteenth Jesus was radically different in every way. He lived among the poor and exploited in the "Galilee of the Gentiles." He challenged and confronted the elites with power and authority. Jesus of Nazareth was an occupied, oppressed, and colonized subject of the Roman Empire who created a paradigm for radical reconciliation through his words, relationships, and actions for social justice. His life was a consistent witness to reconciliation from his birth to death. Through his resurrection the radical reconciler of yesterday lives on today bringing liberation to people in contexts of exclusion and division in the twenty-first century based on religion, race, culture, economics, gender, and the like as he did in the midst of first-century realities. It is in the name of Jesus that we are called to be agents of reconciliation.

Chapter 4, "'Just Another Jew in the Ditch': Incarnated Reconciliation," continues the engagement with Jesus of Nazareth. Taking Howard Thurman's fascinating observation as a point of departure, this chapter revisits Luke 4:16–18 to discover the radicality with which Jesus confronted his world and the powers that ruled it. But in order to do this, the chapter reaches back into the original context of the Isaiah 61 text to which Jesus anchors his ministry. Understanding this context, the chapter then focuses on the story of Zacchaeus in Luke 19:1–9 and grapples with the meaning of this story and draws lessons for the realization of radical reconciliation in our own contexts today.

Multiracial churches in the United States are rapidly increasing in number. This phenomenon is most noticeable among the megachurch movement. Chapter 5, "Reconciliation in Diverse Congregations: Restoring the Beloved Community," poses the question: Do racially diverse congregations automatically experience reconciliation, or could they simply become demographically diverse but not racially reconciled? This question is answered by examining the process of reconciliation in first-century biblical congregations. The first-century biblical model of congregations was one where an oppressed minority community welcomed privileged dominant culture persons into the local church. This chapter explores what this biblical model suggests for congregations today.

Chapter 6, "Between Reitz, a Rock, and a Hard Place: Reconciliation after the Reitz Event," tells the story of the racial crime perpetrated on a university campus by four white students against five workers. It is an event that, as few others, caused tremendous upheaval in South African society and continues to raise fundamental questions about South African society and its reconciliation project. It questions our assumptions about nation-building and the meaning of reconciliation, confronts anew issues such as forgiveness, remorse, power, and powerlessness. It grapples with the question of generational responsibility and the response of the "post-apartheid" generation and tests the validity and worth of political reconciliation within the context of the political pietism that, in Allan's view, has governed South Africans' understanding of reconciliation.

Chapter 7, "When Prophets Are Silenced, Injustice Prevails," suggests that reconcilers must take on the mantle of social justice prophecy. Prophets in society are often silenced through persecution, imprisonment, and death. Yet when we stop listening to prophets, society and individuals do not fare well, because authenticity is lost in reconciliation efforts. Using the African American prophetic tradition and the story of the Hebrew prophet Amos, the importance and power of truth telling is explored. Prophets hold accountable both individuals and organizations in embodying values of social justice. Prophets ask questions and demand answers that lead to integrity. In order for justice and reconciliation to prevail, the hard words of prophets must be heard and implemented.

The theme of prophetic truth telling continues in chapter 8, "Subversive Piety: The Reradicalization of Desmond Tutu." Archbishop Desmond Tutu is perhaps the religious personality the world most easily identifies with reconciliation. That is undoubtedly because of South Africa's dramatic negotiated settlement and the country's choice for reconciliation rather than Nuremberg-style judicial and political revenge and the archbishop's role as chair of the Truth and Reconciliation Commission (TRC). But Desmond Tutu comes to mind also because of the archbishop's personal faith and his embrace of it in his public life. During the TRC process, Desmond Tutu became forgiveness personified and cemented his reputation as a truly pious Christian. This chapter asks whether much of this veneration has not something to do with a process of domestication, shaping Tutu into a mold of political pietism he does not truly represent. His piety, this chapter argues, is genuine, but it is a subversive piety that has called the apartheid regime to account, seemed to have been submerged in a nonthreatening spirituality, but has now reemerged in the last few years. It calls for much more than the popular media image demands and South Africans seem to need.

This book calls attention to the need for a reconciliation that is more than conflict resolution and political accommodation: a reconciliation that resists the temptation to domesticate the radical Jesus, pandering to our need for comfortable reconciliation under the guise of a kind of political pietism and Christian quietism that deny the victims of affliction the comfort of justice.

Part I

Reconciliation
Redefined

Chapter 1

Reconciliation in the Empire
Real, Radical, Revolutionary
Curtiss Paul DeYoung

In 1993 the nation of South Africa was preparing for a transition process that would end apartheid and lead to the election of Nelson Mandela as president. A team of leaders was planning the establishment of a truth commission to address the crimes of the apartheid era. My coauthor Allan Boesak reflects, "Our discussions were interrupted by a request from then President F.W. de Klerk. The National Party was not happy with the term 'truth commission.' It felt strongly that South Africa would be better served if the commission was to be a 'truth *and* reconciliation commission.'" As a theologian and pastor, Boesak welcomed this suggestion but warned of the implications. "The issue was not reconciliation; it was, rather, our understanding and interpretation of it. . . . From experience in the church as well as politics we knew how the Bible was used in Afrikaner politics, and how the radical message of the Bible was made servant to ideology, domesticated for purposes of subjection and control. . . . Mr. De Klerk and his party did not intend to allow reconciliation to confront the country with the demands of the gospel, but to blunt the progress of radical change and transformation."[1]

The politicians all agreed, even those who would soon lead the nation, that adding "reconciliation" was prudent. Boesak writes, "They all consciously or unconsciously accepted F.W. de Klerk's subliminal text: adding the word 'reconciliation' would smooth a process fraught with contradictions, risks and danger, loaded as it was with unspeakable things from the past. The religious twist would help tame it, domesticate it, make it more pliable and palatable for the broader public."[2] Boesak recognized their flawed analysis. "The Scriptures will not be ideologized, manipulated or managed to suit our political endeavors, processes or desires. The demands of the Scriptures will always lay a greater claim than these processes are willing to concede."[3] The word that was presumed to make the process impotent provided the Truth and Reconciliation Commission (TRC) with enough theological power to disclose the truth of apartheid's crimes, demand justice, prompt forgiveness, and hasten the process of healing. As Boesak notes, TRC chair Archbishop Desmond Tutu had to follow his biblical instincts. "The radical nature of the Christian faith and the very reality of biblically motivated reconciliation would often push the TRC into deeper waters than it wanted, or had planned, or could be allowed to go."[4]

This story illustrates the way that reconciliation is often understood today as assimilation, appeasement, a passive peace, a unity without cost, and maintaining power with only cosmetic changes. For this reason, some theologians like Willie Jennings avoid using the term. "I have purposefully stayed away from the theological language of reconciliation because of its terrible misuse in Western Christianity and its tormented deployment in so many theological systems and projects." Jennings believes that "all theological discussions of reconciliation (are) ideological tools for facilitating the negotiations of power; or socially exhausted idealist claims masquerading as serious theological accounts. In truth, it is not at all clear that most Christians are ready to imagine reconciliation."[5]

Preaching professor Richard Lischer goes so far as to question whether preachers should refrain from speaking the word of reconciliation. In his book, *The End of Words: The Language of Reconciliation in a Culture of Violence*, he declares, "After Auschwitz, Hiroshima, Vietnam, Cambodia, Rwanda, all the words seem hollow. What does one *say* after a televised beheading? The proclamation of God's justice or God's love meets a wall of resistance first in the throat of the proclaimer, then in the ears of the hearer. . . . When the message of Jesus Christ can be Nazified or made the tool of racism, anti-Semitism, apartheid, or capitalism, it is time for preachers to shut up and take stock of themselves."[6] Lischer's words are startling and sobering.

As Allan Boesak said, the issue is not reconciliation. The problem is our understanding and interpretation of it. Reconciliation is a powerful and radical (to the roots) process. Theologian John W. de Gruchy notes that as Dietrich Bonhoeffer reflected on what would happen to Christian faith after

Nazism, Bonhoeffer wrote that in the church's "traditional words and acts (like) reconciliation . . . there may be something quite new and revolutionary."[7] De Gruchy sees here the origins of Bonhoeffer's "call to the Church to proceed by engaging in acts of justice and prayer, for out of such action the great words of Christian faith would be set free, both shocking people and overcoming them by its power."[8]

Can we reclaim and rediscover the power of reconciliation? Are we ready to imagine reconciliation?

Prevailing notions of reconciliation are often limited and use misguided assumptions. Inadequate and insufficient definitions of reconciliation restrict and block the full process required for authentic biblical reconciliation. In this book we contend that efforts at reconciliation often do not go deep enough or far enough. In this chapter we will reexamine what the apostle Paul meant when he called for reconciliation. We will take into account the understandings of biblical scholars. Yet we add another lens for interpretation, the context in which Paul lived and his letters were written, that of the Roman Empire—a colonial context.

The Pauline emphasis on reconciliation emerged from his understanding of the life, message, death on a cross, and resurrection of a Roman colonial subject named Jesus, from the town of Nazareth in the occupied territory of Galilee. Paul's interpretation of this life and these events was also influenced by his own status as a colonized and oppressed member of an ethnic and religious minority. Two familiar and traditional biblical texts in reconciliation discourse—2 Corinthians 5:16–6:2 and Ephesians 2:14–16—will anchor the understandings that emerge in this chapter.[9] Today these texts are mostly used to promote reconciliation between persons and cultural groups. Yet in the context of the Roman Empire, we contend, they spoke strongly to oppressive societal realities. Here I will reexamine these scriptural passages, which were penned in the midst of nonviolent resistance to the power of the Roman Empire. We seek to set free the word *reconciliation* to shock and overcome us by its power!

New Testament Reconciliation Defined

The word *reconciliation* appears only occasionally in the New Testament and, with a few exceptions, always in the Pauline literature. The word translates several related Greek words: the verbs *katallassō* and *apokatallassō* and the noun *katallagē*. These words were utilized by Greek writers to discuss interpersonal relationships. In particular, they were used in peace treaties between nations and groups. So, in common Greek usage, there were very often political dimensions to the meaning of reconciliation. When Jewish scholars translated the Hebrew scriptures into Greek, they used these words to translate the Hebrew words related to atonement—that is, to God being reconciled with humanity. In this usage of *katallassō*, they did not retain the political dimension found in the Greek understanding of reconciliation. On the other hand, when Greek writers used the words, they never implied a spiritual connotation to reconciliation. In Paul's use of *katallassō* and related terms, we find both the spiritual and political meanings. His readership, both Greeks and Jews, would have understood reconciliation in this way as they discussed his letters in their gatherings.[10]

Katallassō means literally, "to change, or exchange; to effect a change."[11] As John de Gruchy draws out the implication, when we are "reconciled," we exchange places "with 'the other,' and (are) in solidarity with rather than against 'the other.'" Reconciliation is a process that causes us to overcome "alienation through identification and in solidarity with 'the other,' thus making peace and restoring relationships."[12] Biblical scholar James Earl Massey writes, "The image in the word shows something having been set aside or put down [*kata*]: an attitude, a grievance, a position, a deed, a distance, a result, in order to induce or bring about a change for the better. A new disposition is exhibited, a new stance is assumed, a new framework is established granting a rich togetherness where enmity and distance previously were the order."[13] Reconciliation can be understood as exchanging places with "the other," overcoming alienation through identification, solidarity, restoring relationships, positive change, new frameworks, and a rich togetherness that is both spiritual and political.

The Colonial Context

Our attempt to comprehend Paul's usage of *reconciliation* requires us to understand his context. Remarkably, one of the most important aspects of Paul's context has received little attention until recently. The life of the apostle Paul was shaped by the daily reality of the military presence and political domination of the Roman Empire. As an ethnic Jew, Paul's sense of history was defined, in part, by his people's experience of subjugation to a series of empires: Egypt, Assyria, Babylon, Persia, Greece, and Rome. As a student of Judaism, his religious instincts were influenced by the very origins of the people of Israel as a "reaction against oppressive imperial regimes."[14] The core understanding of faith for Jews was the often recounted and recited liberation from the Egyptian empire. "We were Pharaoh's slaves in Egypt, but the LORD brought us out of Egypt with a mighty hand" (Dt 6:21). Inevitably, then, Paul (and Jesus) understood Judaism as involving a reaction against empire and domination.

Empires enforce and maintain domination on subject peoples through military might, economic oppression, and ideological belief systems, no matter what era in history they emerge. The influence of an empire is pervasive as it "inextricably interweaves *religion* (what binds people together) with *politics* (what people do together) and *economics* (how people produce and exchange goods and services together)."[15] This was true for the Roman Empire and the empires of history. It is also true of empires today.

The Roman Empire believed it had a divine mission to rule and civilize the world. Among those ruled by Rome were Judeans, who were regarded by members of the Roman elite as "'the conquered' . . . a people 'born of servitude.'"[16] Jews experienced significant bias and stereotypes. They also suffered the brutally violent oppression of Rome. The Roman Empire used crucifixion to terrorize subject peoples. Nowhere was this more evident than in their domination of Jews. Crucifixion was a constant symbol of Roman rule, as thousands of Judeans were executed on crosses. Biblical scholar Richard A. Horsley notes,

> Many of the victims were never buried but simply left on the crosses as carrion for wild beasts and birds of prey. As with other forms of terrorism, crucifixions were displayed in prominent places for their "demonstration effect" on the rest of the population. . . . Seeing their relatives, friends, and other fellow villagers suffering such agonizing death would presumably intimidate the surviving populace into acquiescence in the reestablished Roman imperial order.[17]

The crucifixion of Jesus was just such a public spectacle of cruelty meant to terrorize his followers and any potential sympathizers. Jesus was crucified as a rebel leader resisting the Roman domination of first-century Judeans. This political function of crucifixion must be kept in mind when we read what Paul wrote in Galatians 3:1, "It was before your eyes that Jesus Christ was publicly exhibited as crucified!"

The apostle Paul was a subject of the Roman Empire. In Acts, the author quoted Paul saying he was a Roman citizen (22:25). Paul never made this claim in his writings, however. While Roman citizenship offered limited benefits for a colonized subject, Paul was still an oppressed Jew. (Similarly, an African American may be a citizen of the United States but will still experience racial discrimination.) Rather Paul's identity was rooted in his Jewishness—"circumcised on the eighth day, a member of the people of Israel, of the tribe of Benjamin, a Hebrew born of Hebrews; as to the law, a Pharisee" (Phil 3:5). But he was an oppressed Jew, a member of an ethnic and religious minority, and a colonized person. He likely felt terrorized at times by the government. His whole life was lived within the physical and psychic boundaries of the Roman Empire.

Colonized subjects and oppressed persons throughout history experience an assault on their human dignity and sense of identity. Allan Boesak notes that under apartheid, blacks experienced a "'colonializing' of our humanity." Blacks in South Africa were classified as "nonwhite," as nonpersons. "'Nonwhite' is a negation. 'Nonwhite' points to a nonentity."[18] Postcolonialist theorists and writers in the 1950s and 1960s expounded on the effects of colonialism. Aimé Césaire wrote that "colonization = 'thingification.'" He observed that colonialism resulted in "societies drained of their essence, cultures trampled underfoot, institutions undermined, lands confiscated, religions smashed, magnificent artistic creations destroyed, extraordinary possibilities wiped out."[19] Frantz Fanon noted that "colonized people (were) people in whose soul an inferiority complex has been created by the death and burial of its local cultural originality."[20] Albert Memmi stated, "I was Tunisian, therefore colonized. I discovered that few aspects of my life and my personality were untouched by this fact. Not only my own thoughts, my passions and my conduct, but also the conduct of others towards me was affected. . . . The most serious blow suffered by the colonized is being removed from history and from the community."[21]

The postcolonialists noticed that oppressed people would often develop a split personality—acting and thinking one way with their own people and another way in the presence of the colonizer. Fanon remarked, "The black man has two dimensions. One with his fellows, the other with the white man. A Negro behaves differently with a white man and with another Negro. That this self-division is a direct result of colonialist sub-jugation is beyond question"[22] W. E. B. DuBois called this a "double con-sciousness."[23]

Over time the self-definition of oppressed people begins to mirror more and more of the colonizer's perspective. They understand themselves through the contextual lens of the colonizer taking on a "derivative identity."[24] Paulo Freire called this "an attitude of adhesion to the oppressor."[25] Colonized people feel pressured to assimilate—to assume the posture and perspective of their oppressors. Memmi wrote, "The point is that whether Negro, Jew or colonized, one must resemble the white man, the non-Jew, the colonizer."[26] Fanon concluded that "his reality as a man [had] been challenged." He ex-plained, "I begin to suffer from not being a white man to the degree that the white man imposes discrimination on me, makes me a colonized native, robs me of all worth, all individuality, tells me that I am a parasite on the world, that I must bring myself as quickly as possible into step with the white world ...Then I will quite simply try to make myself white: that is, I will compel the white man to acknowledge that I am human."[27] Eventually the identity of colonized people can be so diminished that they internalize the viewpoint of the oppressor and see themselves, others, and even their oppressor through the lens of colonization.

Reconciliation Considered from Paul's Colonial Context

The apostle Paul was a Jew, and thus a member of a people subjected to the colonizing rule of the Roman Empire. His letters were sent to people living under the brutal repression of Rome. It is likely that the recipients of Paul's letters were experiencing the effects of colonization as just described. Paul himself was influenced by the Roman colonial context. Paul's social location as a colonized person shaped his perspective on life and on what he meant when he used the word *reconciliation*. Let us read these two texts with an eye for the colonial context:

> From now on, therefore, we regard no one from a human point of view; even though we once knew Christ from a human point of view, we know him no longer in that way. So if anyone is in Christ, there is a new creation: everything old has passed away; see, everything

has become new! All this is from God, who reconciled us to himself through Christ, and has given us the ministry of reconciliation; that is, in Christ God was reconciling the world to himself, not counting their trespasses against them, and entrusting the message of reconciliation to us. So we are ambassadors for Christ, since God is making his appeal through us; we entreat you on behalf of Christ, be reconciled to God. . . . For he says, "At an acceptable time I have listened to you, and on a day of salvation I have helped you." See, now is the acceptable time; see, now is the day of salvation! (2 Cor 5:16–20, 6:2)

For (Jesus Christ) is our peace; in his flesh he has made both groups (Jews and Gentiles) into one and has broken down the dividing wall, that is, the hostility between us . . . that he might create in himself one new humanity in place of the two, thus making peace, and might reconcile both groups to God in one body through the cross, thus putting to death that hostility through it. (Eph 2:14, 15b–16)[28]

When we read these texts through a postcolonial lens, we see that reconciliation is real, that is, experiential; reconciliation is radical, that is, focused on social justice; reconciliation is revolutionary, that is, oriented to structural change.

Reconciliation Is Real

In 2 Corinthians 5, Paul alluded to a life-changing encounter with a resurrected Jesus that occurred on the road to Damascus (Acts 9:3–16).[29] Paul encountered *the crucified one*—now alive! Biblical scholar Corneliu Constantineanu notes, "The experience on the Damascus road introduced a radically new element into Paul's symbolic universe: Jesus of Nazareth, crucified in Jerusalem, appears to Paul as alive, confronting Paul with a reality he could not deny—Jesus was raised by God."[30] An act of brutal finality by Rome's state-sponsored terrorism was reversed by a more powerful and completely just God. Biblical scholars John Crossan and Jonathan Reed write, "On the one hand, (Paul's) theology would not be the same if Christ had simply died in his bed and been raised thereafter by God. . . . It was not simply death and resurrection. It was execution by *Rome* and therefore resurrection against *Rome*."[31] The cross, for first-century followers of Jesus, became both "the signature in history of the forces that killed Jesus"[32] and the symbol of hope for freedom from the forces of domination. Paul's declaration of reconciliation through the cross and resurrection of Jesus was a bold claim that liberation was available from the effects of colonialism and the deconstruction of systems of oppression was possible. The Empire does not have the final word!

What does this really mean? Reconciliation produces a "decolonized humanity."[33] A damaged, enslaved, and colonized identity is restored to its original design as a human identity created in the image of God. The logic of Paul's proclamation is that because death by Rome was reversed through resurrection by God, the death of one's identity could be reversed and returned to full humanity. All identities—ethnic, gender, religious, and the like—were reframed in one's self-definition. One's colonial identity was switched to an identity in Jesus Christ. The language used for Caesar— "Son of God," "Lord," "Redeemer," "Savior," "Liberator," "God"—Paul used for Jesus Christ, in order to announce a new identity. Crossan and Reed write, "In a world where identity was often shaped by one's relationship to Rome, by being, as it were, 'in Rome,' insisting on a self-definition exclusively by being 'in Christ' was subversive at best and treasonous at worst."[34] This is what it meant to reclaim identity. Paul wrote, "we regard no one from a human point of view"—that is, as colonizer or colonized. Or we could rephrase Paul's words to say, we regard no one from a dominant, Roman Empire point of view; we regard no one from the colonizer's point of view. Paul was witnessing to his own transformation and to the promise of internal healing from the effects of colonialism, racism, sexism, classism, and all forms of bigotry. This reconciliation through the cross of Jesus was real!

Paul's dramatic change took place while traveling to Damascus to silence Jews who were followers of Jesus through a campaign of arrest and violence. Pauline scholar Neil Elliott suggests that Paul was persecuting Jewish followers of Jesus because they "had begun to proclaim publicly that a man crucified by Rome was in fact God's chosen king, who would soon return to rule the peoples. That would inevitably have sounded subversive in Roman ears. And Paul could reasonably expect that such a message would bring repercussions against vulnerable Judean communities throughout the empire." Elliott reminds us that crucifixion "was an instrument for terrorizing subject peoples by publicly torturing to death individuals who Rome considered politically troublesome. Taking the side of the crucified was irreducibly an act of defiance."[35] Elliott concludes that Paul persecuted a small group of fellow Jews (who followed Jesus) as a way of protecting the larger oppressed Jewish community from further repression from Rome.

Is it possible that Paul persecuted his own people because he had internalized the dominant Roman view of Jews? The postcolonialists would suggest that we consider this as an option. Certainly Elliott's proposal that before his call, Paul was silencing political activists among his own people to accommodate the power of the Roman Empire suggests the effects of colonization on him. Paul wrote of his transformation, "For I am the least of the apostles, unfit to be called an apostle, because I persecuted the church of God. But by the grace of God I am what I am, and his grace towards me has not been in vain" (1 Cor 15:9–10a). Reconciliation is real and available to restore the battered and bruised identities of people who experience oppression.

Reconciliation Is Radical

Reconciliation is real, life changing, and healing. 2 Corinthians 5 has an experiential feel to it. But Paul's manifesto on reconciliation does not end with chapter five. He continued, "For (God) says, 'At an acceptable time I have listened to you and on a day of salvation I have helped you.' See, now is *the acceptable time*; see, now is *the day of salvation!*" (2 Cor 6:2, my emphasis). Paul linked reconciliation with social justice. In order to claim that reconciliation is the work of social justice, Paul quoted Isaiah 49:8, a reference to Israel's liberation from Egypt—the core understanding of Judaism. This may be an intentional echo of Jesus' quote from Isaiah to launch his ministry from Nazareth. "'The Spirit of the Lord is upon me, because he has anointed me to bring good news to the poor. He has sent me to proclaim release to the captives and recovery of sight to the blind, to let the oppressed go free, to proclaim *the year of the Lord's favor*'" (Lk 4:18–19, my emphasis).

Reconciliation is radical in that it reaches to the very roots of injustice. Paul understood that injustice creates the need for reconciliation. Therefore reconciliation is about social justice. As John de Gruchy confirms in his book, *Reconciliation: Restoring Justice*, "Reconciliation is properly understood as a process in which we become engaged at the heart of the struggle for justice and peace in the world. . . . to say that God was reconciling the world in Christ is another way of saying that God was busy restoring God's reign of justice."[36]

What biblical scholar Tat-siong Benny Liew says particularly of the Corinthian letters is also true more generally when Paul makes "statements about racial/ethnic 'oneness' within the church, he immediately links them with similar statements about the differences between slaves and free persons."[37] This is true in Galatians 3:28, where Paul also adds gender: "There is no longer Jew or Greek, there is no longer slave or free, there is no longer male and female; for all of you are one in Christ Jesus." We will return to the connection between reconciliation and social justice throughout the book. For now, it is important for us to make the point that social justice is central to any biblical understanding of reconciliation. Social justice and reconciliation are two sides of the same coin.

Reconciliation Is Revolutionary

Reconciliation is a real experience that is radical, going to the roots of injustice. Reconciliation is also revolutionary. Theologian Gustavo Gutiérrez writes that revolution means "to abolish the present status quo and attempt to replace it with a qualitatively different one."[38] Ephesians 2 says that Jesus created "in himself one new humanity in place of the two, thus making peace, and might reconcile both groups to God in one body through the cross" (2:15b–16a). The passage seems to be saying that in place of two categories of humanity—powerful Romans and oppressed Jews (along with other colonized people)—a qualitatively different understanding of humanity was implemented. Ephesians 2 calls for a revolution of human identity. It signals to us that apartheid, Jim Crow, patriarchy, class status, and other systemic forms of classifying humanity for domination are being replaced by a new structure of "one new humanity" through Jesus' death on a cross and resurrection.

In order for this to happen, the reconciliation process must be embraced by both the colonized and the colonizers. Earlier we discussed how reconciliation transforms the colonized person through healing identity and replacing a forced colonial loyalty with a consciousness of being "in Christ." Paul's call to reconciliation was issued not only to his fellow Jews and others oppressed by Rome. It also included those who were among the colonizers, the oppressors, the occupiers, and the rulers. Biblical scholar Ched Myers notes that "despite his unequivocal antipathy toward the empire, Paul refused to exclude Roman citizens from the circle of YHWH's grace."[39] The effects of colonization are not limited to those oppressed by the system. Empires also injure those in control and those benefiting from oppression.

We return to the postcolonialists for their take on what needs to happen in the life of the colonizer. Albert Memmi wrote that in order for the persons in power to embrace reconciliation, they must accept that their roles have been as "nonlegitimate privileged person[s]."[40] Then the colonizer must reject this nonlegitimate identity of superiority and the privileges that go with that position. Sacrifice by people of privilege and power results in dramatic changes for members of the dominant group even when done intentionally. Unjust systems appear normal to those in power, and any change will produce feelings of loss. True reconciliation, through the cross of Jesus, will affect the lives of the privileged. The colonizer has to completely leave the confines of power and privilege and join with those who are colonized. Of the colonizer Memmi declared, "let him adopt the colonized people and be adopted by them; let him become a turncoat."[41]

Paulo Freire warned that even when people "cease to be exploiters or indifferent spectators or simply the heirs of exploitation and move to the side of the exploited, they almost always bring with them the marks of their origin: their prejudices and their deformations, which include a lack of confidence in the people's ability to think, to want, and to know." Even with sincere motives, "because of their background they believe that they must be the executors of the transformation."[42] During South African apartheid, Steve Biko noted that there were whites participating in the struggle who said they had "black souls wrapped in white skins." Yet they felt like they "always knew what was good for the blacks and told them so."[43] There was no trust and no transfer of power. Reconciliation for the powerful and privileged means trusting those who have lived under oppression and even following their lead in becoming one new humanity.

In a book I wrote about reconciliation fifteen years ago, I stated that "reconciliation occurs between equals."[44] That simple statement was the most cited sentence from the book. We all seem to know that reconciliation is a call for just and full equality between persons that requires a change in personal, economic, and power relationships. Our biblical definition earlier spoke of exchanging places with the other as the process of getting to this equality. The person of power must change places with the person without power. Tat-siong Benny Liew offers a helpful reading of 1 Corinthians 9:19–23 where Paul claimed that he became a Jew with Jews and a Gentile with Gentiles. Liew states, "If Paul can turn Gentile and infiltrate the Corinthian world, the Corinthians can also slide down the racial/ethnic scales and become stigmatized Jews."[45] Reconciliation requires more than leaving places of power for periodic visits to communities of oppressed people. Reconciliation requires more than inviting persons from the margins to visit for conversations in places of comfort. It means ongoing relationships with many persons from marginalized communities. It means engaging in such relationships for the duration of our lives—"so powerful is the lure of privilege and so long is the shadow of power."[46] It is a call for an exchange of places with "the other."

Albert Memmi was not hopeful regarding his colonizers. He warned that the colonizer "lacks the necessary imagination for a revolution of that kind. While he happens to dream of a tomorrow, a brand-new social state in which the colonized cease to be colonized, he certainly does not conceive, on the other hand, of a deep transformation of his own situation and of his own personality. In that new, more harmonious state, he will go on being what he is, with his language intact and his cultural traditions dominating." Domination and privilege must end for the process of reconciliation to be complete. Memmi continued his analysis: the colonizer "invokes the end of colonization, but refuses to conceive that this revolution can result in the overthrow of his situation and himself. For it is too much to ask one's imagination to visualize one's own end, even if it be in order to be reborn another; especially if, like the colonizer, one can hardly evaluate such a rebirth."[47]

The apostle Paul differed from Albert Memmi at this point. He believed that through the death on a cross and resurrection of Jesus *even* a colonizing Roman with power and privilege could be transformed by God's reconciling grace. *Even* for the Roman, the signature of the empire's terror—crucifixion—could become the symbol of liberation from the captivity of power. Too often we offer God's reconciling grace only to those victimized by power. Paul and the first-century followers of Jesus were able to look through the distortions of domination and colonization to the humanity of Romans and to offer them the process of reconciliation through the crucified Christ.

Ephesians 2 suggests more than just the transformation of individuals. It speaks of the creation of a new structure. Thirty-five years ago, my coauthor made this same assessment: "Reconciliation requires a new image of humanity which is why reconciliation without liberation is impossible. But the new image of humanity requires new structures in society—new wine in wineskins!"[48] Paulo Freire wrote, "The man or woman who emerges is a new person, viable only as the oppressor-oppressed contradiction is superseded by the humanization of all people."[49] This can only happen in communities built on principles of social justice. Paul and the first-century disciples of Jesus created communities that "prefigure and embody the reconciliation and healing of the world."[50] The "one new humanity" envisioned in Ephesians was emerging in new faith communities. Richard Horsley summarizes what was happening:

> Perhaps the most remarkable evidence that the empire had not had the last word was that Jesus' followers expanded their movement among other subjected peoples of the empire. They did this with astounding confidence and drive. From indications in the early chapters of Acts and in Paul's letters it is evident that Peter, Paul, and other "apostles" were convinced that history was running not through Rome but through Israel. Jesus' death and resurrection in fact had become the turning point in history. . . . Other peoples as well as Israelites had now become the heirs of the promised blessings. It was now possible therefore for the multiethnic and multicultural communities of these heirs of the promises to form more egalitarian social relations that cut across the fundamental social hierarchies of the imperial order, between Greeks and barbarians (including Jews), between free and slaves, and between male and female. . . . Paul was, in effect, building an international anti-imperial movement of an alternative society based in local communities.[51]

Conclusion

The first-century church was established as a new revolutionary structure for colonized and colonizers to rediscover their true identity in Christ and to experience a reconciliation that was personally and socially real, radical, and revolutionary. These faith communities created space and place for people to live into the full realization of what it meant to be one new humanity. We will examine more fully these communities in chapter five and suggest what this means in the twenty-first century.

We live in the midst of domination systems today. Living in the midst of empire, we need reconciliation that is real, radical, and revolutionary. Unfortunately the values of the empire now also reign in our religious institutions and congregational communities. Much of what goes under the guise of reconciliation in the United States features a white male-centered identity, assumes that women and persons of color need to assimilate, accommodate, or at the very least submit to the needs of whites and males. Reconciliation is often assumed to mean white institutions *adding* or *including* persons of color but never transforming the central identity from white (and male) to a truly inclusive human identity.

In the pages that follow we address the challenges of liberating faith communities that have been colonized by empire value systems and the ongoing struggle for reconciliation in a world still under the spell and domination of empires.

Chapter 2

Reconciliation, Risk, and Resistance
The Story of Rizpah
Allan Aubrey Boesak

A Deliberate Intrusion

Second Samuel 21–24 is an odd add-on to the David narratives of the two books of Samuel. It is a common view of scholars, states Hebrew Bible scholar Walter Brueggemann, that 1 Kings 1–2 directly continues the narrative of 2 Samuel 20.[1] This means that 2 Samuel 21–24 is an "intrusion" into that single continuing story, "a miscellaneous appendix, consisting of materials that are old and have originated at various times but now have been grouped here. . . . [I]t is commonly thought that this arrangement is not accidental."[2] These materials have been placed here for a reason. That is a first, crucially important point to keep in mind. The second, just as important in my view, is that not just the story, but Rizpah herself is an intrusion, a disturbance, an uncomfortable presence deliberately brought into the cycle of triumphant David-stories. As such, and on second thought, this intrusion is not merely an add-on to the narratives pivotal to David's kingship.

It was first told, not as embellishment, nor as correction, but in resistance to the official narrative favored by the king, recorded by his scribes, and loved by the people. Somewhere in the circle of ancient Israel's scribes, there lived a determination to tell the alternative story that lived in the memory of those outside the circles of might and privilege. It's a story that ends the second Samuel book where the first book begins: a story of how the powerless gird on strength and how one shall prevail, but not by might

(1 Sm 2:1–10). And if that first truth was uttered by a woman, this truth, too, shall be uttered by a woman, representative of the powerless, the downtrodden, the voiceless, albeit not in song but in song personified, come to life. I do believe this indeed is not accidental. This is how the prophetic tradition lives, survives, and overcomes.

Strangely though, Rizpah and her story are not very well known at all. Not many find time to reflect upon this woman; most, perhaps apart from a reference or two, tend to ignore her. Even books on women in the Bible, many of them written by feminist theologians, easily skip her. In the very authoritative women's commentary on the Bible written especially by women, intended as correction of the Eurocentric, male, patriarchal interpretations and understandings of the Bible, *The Women's Bible Commentary,* the name of Rizpah is not mentioned in its treatment of 2 Samuel.[3] But she is, I think, the subject and the heart of one of the most radical and inspiring stories in the Bible.

Most commentators who do reflect on this story read the story from King David's point of view, and almost always their point of departure is acceptance of David's "innocence" in this matter.[4] After all, this is Davidic material, naturally taking David as the highly favored center of the story. The books of Samuel are part of that Davidic material, written from the viewpoint of, and to the advantage of, the powerful, ruling elites, and specifically to favor the king. Hence, the very flattering ending of 2 Samuel 20 (which most consider the end of the David narratives, picked up again in 1 Kings[5]), in which Sheba, son of Bichri, who had "lifted up his hand against King David" (20:21), was beheaded and his head thrown over the city wall as evidence for and appeasement of Joab, who then withdraws his army and "returned to Jerusalem to the king" (20:22). The Rizpah narrative, coming after such an obvious triumphant closing scene, is indeed a "jolt to our expectations" as Walter Brueggemann correctly notes.[6] I suggest, though, that this "jolt" is not so much because of David's shocking behavior—after all, we have met such behavior before in 2 Samuel 11 already!—but because of the extraordinary actions of Rizpah, daughter of Aiah. She, not David, is the central figure in this intriguing narrative. *She* claims the commanding heights of the story, and through this story—an intrusion in the ordering of the second Samuel book—Rizpah, her courageous act of solidarity, her outrageous love, her embrace of risk for the sake of justice and humanity, and her determined challenge to the powers, becomes an intrusion in our political and social orderings, in our longing for the untroubled waters of unafflicted politics and comfortable and comforting reconciliation.

King David, the Gibeonites, and the Sons of Saul

So here's how the story goes as recorded in 2 Samuel 21:1–14. Saul was on the throne and apparently he had, so we must deduce from what we read here, a nonaggression pact with the Gibeonites who, purely by the grace of the king of Israel, lived in the territory of Israel, amongst them. For some reason—we do not know why, for the story remains vague on this point—Saul unilaterally breaks this pact. Whether there was actual bloodshed we do not know but there is reference to it in the term "bloodguilt" and in the word "destroy" used by the Gibeonites (2 Sm 21:1, 5). What Saul had exactly done is never clear from the narrative. Some think there was some sort of political oppression of the Gibeonites rather than military action.[7] Years later, after the unification of the kingdoms of Israel and Judah, David is on the throne and has to deal with what is held up as a terrible legacy. Saul had committed bloodguilt, the bloodguilt causes famine. It is a national disaster. David "expiates" the bloodguilt, ending the famine. He does this by killing seven heirs of Saul and "thus makes life possible where Saul had brought death."[8]

The famine is a punishment from God for the sins of Saul. David, pious king that he is, "inquired of the LORD" (2 Sm 21:1), which means he consults the prophets of the court, the priests and theologians on this matter. Twice David asks the Gibeonites a crucial question: "What shall I do for you?" and again, "How shall I make expiation?" (2 Sm 21:3). In using the word "expiation" David brings in an important theological dimension: that of reconciliation, for expiation literally means to make good for what has been done wrong.[9] Our word "restitution" is the closest we come to the word David uses. How can I turn this evil into good? What is it that I can do that can set the relationship right between us, that would make you feel that justice had been done to you? The answer is fairly simple: "The shedding of blood will bring about reconciliation between the Gibeonites and Israel."[10]

David is eager to do the right thing, "so that you may bless the heritage of the LORD" (2 Sm 21:3). The "blessing" for the people of Israel, the breaking of the drought, is apparently expected to come from the Gibeonites. The Gibeonites seem reluctant to make a decision but do raise the unresolved matter regarding Saul's actions and the fact that his heirs are still living as a problem that might hinder the reconciliation David desires (2 Sm 21:4). David determines to comply. Seven young men are hung on crosses on the hills outside the city. All of this is done because David "inquired from the Lord," had heard God's voice through the oracle, the priests and prophets had assured him, and so what is being done is because God wills it so. Everybody is pleased, including God. Every purpose, national and holy, is thus served.

There are a number of important things about this gruesome event. It is a ritual killing. It is done in expiation. It is a blood sacrifice to appease both the Gibeonites and God. But it also is a punishment for the sins of Saul, and so it has a political aspect to it: a king that makes right what another king had done wrong in order to make peace. It is a public execution. David means to set an example for all to see. A public impalement is like a crucifixion, exactly what the Romans would excel at with such great effect much later.[11] It is meant to strike fear into the hearts of those who might have the same kind of ideas. It is intimidation by terror. It is calling for unquestioning obedience by instilling terror and fear of death. And this is precisely David's purpose here.

Casting a Colder but Clearer Eye

We made the point earlier that our story does not belong where it is in 2 Samuel 21, and most scholars hold that it tells of an incident that might have taken place earlier.[12] It is possible that it belongs closer to 2 Samuel 15, the story of the uprising organized by Absalom, David's son, against his father. It would explain the insulting behavior of Shimei, a member of Saul's family, toward David (2 Sm 16:5–14).

Perhaps the story belongs there or, more likely, had originated in circles more critical of the king and the ruling elites. In either case it means that we must cast a clearer eye than the romantic view of David as pious, faithful king a more traditional reading demands.[13] Then it means that the oracle, the "word from the Lord," that links the famine to the alleged misdeeds of Saul is not a "word from the Lord" at all but instead "serves primarily to give David warrant for his violence against the house of Saul," as Brueggemann argues, in my view correctly.[14] David's acts are not inspired by a desire to reconcile with the Gibeonites or by obedience to Yahweh.

It is true that the seven young men could not have been much of a threat to David. Two of them were sons of a concubine, and five were grandsons. In the fierce and brutal battles for the throne after Saul's death (2 Sm 1–5), their names are not even mentioned. But for David and the court, goes the counter argument that follows from the traditional, uncritical reading, the issue of national security is paramount here.[15]

In that view, the important thing is that peace with the Gibeonites must be kept and the famine ended. Clearly the fact that David inquires of the Lord and his consultation with the men in the palace who advise the king in such matters tells us that David's concern is not just for himself. It is a national concern. Then anything and everything is justified.

But a serious twofold problem arises. One, there is no evidence of the wrong Saul had done that would have caused the "bloodguilt" that now puts David in this unenviable position.[16] Two, the Gibeonites, who lived among Israel purely by the grace of Israel's king, were in no position to make demands. Joshua 9 tells the story of how they, with deviousness and cunning, came to live among Israel and how precarious their position was.[17]

Indeed, David might be arguing that the matter is not personal: national security overrides all. The individual is subsumed in the nation; the nation's interests must take preference. Hard decisions have to be made: *uneasy lies the head that wears the crown.* Hence, the king's "courage" is noted without irony: "David did not shirk the heart-wrenching task of selecting seven grandsons of Saul."[18] When national security, or trade, stability, or diplomatic relations are at stake, governments respond with what is called "political realism." In the process the betrayal of justice is mere "collateral damage." This is how David's mind works, I think. This is how *power* works. So they are "impaled before the Lord": all seven sons of the line of Saul except poor, crippled, nonthreatening Mephibosheth, the son of his friend Jonathan, who says of David, "My lord the king is like an angel of God" (2 Sm 19:27) and, prostrate before the king, refers to himself as a "dead dog" (2 Sm 9:8). The Gibeonites perform the executions, but only with the king's consent: "I will hand them over" (2 Sm 21:6). The narrator wants us to know precisely where the responsibility lies. "The king took the two sons of Rizpah . . . and the five sons of Merab . . . and he gave them into the hands of the Gibeonites" (2 Sm 21:8, 9). Blood has flowed. Everyone is appeased.

The bodies are not taken off the crosses and given a decent burial. That's part of the punishment, the terror and intimidation, meant also as a deterrent for whatever thoughts or deeds might be conceived as a threat to the throne. Against the Deuteronomic law, the bodies are kept hanging on the crosses.[19] The bodies are not to be decently buried and mourned over by the family but are instead left to be eaten by the carrion birds and by the beasts of the field, bit by bit by bit, so that all who pass by can see: this is what happens when you rise up against the king, or when you displease the palace, when you question the powerful, or when you bring the security of the state in danger. Looking at those bodies on the trees, this is what the people see: a ritual killing, done "before the Lord," required by the Lord. They also see a political killing, a public execution with a lesson for all. The absence of a decent burial heaps shame upon shame. There shall be no closure for these families. No comfort. There shall be no end to the shame and the pain. In the conventional reading, nonetheless, it is not the young men, or their mothers, who are the victims here, but David: of Saul's sins; of a possible threat; of the heavy burden of power and governing responsibility; and of his obedience to a God whose wrath has to be appeased in order for blessings to come. After all, it fell upon David to make that "heart-wrenching decision."

But we remind ourselves that our story, told at this place, is not "random, without any organizing principle or purpose."[20] To the contrary, it is told deliberately against the grain, in calculated protest against the official narrative emanating from the palace and backed by the power of the privileged elite. It is told in resistance to the manipulation of God and the abuse of the powerlessness of the people. It is a story of solidarity, risk, and defiance, and central to it all is a woman.

Rizpah, the Daughter of Aiah

Then enters Rizpah, the daughter of Aiah, and with her presence the whole tone of the story changes. Even more; for the first time the point of the story becomes clear. Up to now, the focus of the story had been on the palace and on the men in the palace, their deliberations and decisions, and their power over life and death. But now the focus shifts from the palace and the throne to the hill and the crosses, and the bodies on the crosses. Below those, on the rock, in sharp and tight focus, appears Rizpah. She spreads sackcloth "for herself" because she is alone and because she is in mourning. She is determined to stay on that rock for as long as is necessary. She will not go away. Amazingly, the story tells us, she remains there "from the beginning of harvest until rain fell on them from the heavens. She did not allow the birds of the air to come on the bodies by day, or the wild animals by night" (2 Sm 21:10). All this time, every day, every night—she does not rest for a single moment.

Even though some commentators write fairly dispassionately about this crucifixion, reflecting the cold-bloodedness of the act itself, Cheryl Exum is right: "The tale is strange and disturbing in many ways. It verges on a world of elemental terror . . . a place where human actions are undertaken in response both to perceived supernatural demands and a sense of primal obligation of the living to the dead."[21]

On the hill, Rizpah sees this elemental terror for what it is. She is running from cross to cross, from body to body, looking everywhere: to the heavens for the carrion birds and along the ground for the predators. Her resistance is so fierce and so relentless that not a single beast and not a single bird can touch, maim, or damage those bodies on the crosses. And know this, Rizpah looks up and she does not see crosses, she sees *bodies* on crosses. Unlike David, she is not objectifying the young men. She does not see sacrifices for the sake of peace; she sees cold-blooded murder. For her it is not just a political spectacle or even a national disgrace. It is a human tragedy. It is not only indignity and shame heaped upon the men on the crosses; it is an assault upon the dignity and worthiness of God. She is driven by compassion, and by righteousness, and by justice, and by the fact that she knows she is right, despite her powerlessness. As she fights against the beasts of the field, she fights at the same time against the beasts in the palace—those men who rule, who have decided they have power, like God, over the lives and the deaths of these young men. They define reconciliation and they decide what God wants: restitution to secure peace, dead bodies to secure survival, a blood sacrifice to secure a future. But it is not peace they secure; they secure power.

Rizpah, by her act of love and solidarity, releases us, reading this story, from the paralyzing power of the king and the mortifying grip of expedient sacrifice into the freedom of sacrificial resistance. She completely claims our attention: away from the centers of power to the margins of suffering and righteousness. She does not remain in the coolness of the palace, in the shadow of the throne, but under those crosses she exposes herself to the burning sun. That's where her commitment lies. That's where her solidarity comes to life. She understands: however much the name of Yahweh is mentioned here, not everyone who calls "Lord, Lord!" knows the Lord. To know the Lord is to do justice, and justice is not what is happening here. Rizpah recognizes this as a political game with deadly consequences. She knows about political games, this woman. Not for nothing was she once the wife of a king, saw from within the games power-hungry men play, felt in her body the sharp thrusts of their avaricious appetites.

We meet her for the first time in 2 Samuel 3 when Israel and Judah were still separate nations. Saul dies, and as Saul's widow she becomes a plaything in the politics of succession. A key plaything true, but a plaything nonetheless. Ishboseth, son of Saul, claims the throne. Abner, general in Saul's army, also has succession designs, and in the cauldron of the political battle that follows, he raises his claim by sleeping with Rizpah. Like the wives of David who are forced to sleep with Absalom on the roof of the palace for all to see in his claim on David's throne, she has no say in the matter. The one who sleeps with the wife of the king is one step closer to the throne. There is no love, there is no affection, and they hold her hostage until Abner wins the battle and owns the throne of Saul. Then they move on. David first makes a deal with Abner; then Abner is killed by two assassins, removed as a threat, and when the game is finally over, Rizpah is discarded like a used rag.

We don't hear from her for all this time until chapter 21, and here she is, the victim of chapter 3, whose refusal to be a victim is seen in the dignity of her outrage and in her persistent resistance to the power of the throne. She refuses victimhood and stands up in resistance instead. She knows that victimhood saps one's courage and drains one's sense of justice and dignity. She knows that victimhood focused solely on oneself, and on oneself alone, is both inhibiting and debilitating, so that one forgets about others and the need for justice. One forgets that true solidarity calls all of us across all the boundaries of self-defense, self-preservation, and self-justification, and that it is far more important, in fact life-giving, to stand on the side of those to whom injustice is being done than to sit in the shadow where self-pity is cloaked in victimhood.

So she rises above all of that personal, painful history, even as she rises above the brutal, merciless realities of power. A most remarkable woman—this Rizpah. She challenges the king, the generals, and all of the men in the palace, and everybody who thinks that the way to appease God and secure the nation is through the sacrifice of the innocent: *that* sacrifice is one sacrifice too many. She will not have it, because God will not have it. A victim of abuse she might have been, but she becomes the champion of justice. In her resistance she gives all—her body, her energy, and her love; her dignity and courage; protecting, preserving, uplifting, redeeming.

She does not believe, clearly, the king and his priests. You might say that this is the word of God, she says, but to me this word of God fits just too neatly into the word of the king; the will of God just covers too snugly the will of the king. She does not believe that, and her resistance is her testimony. This God you claim for this deed of murder, she says, is not the God I know. It is not the God of Sarah, or of Hannah, or of Hagar, the slave woman, the mother of Ishmael, as dismal in the household of Sarai as Rizpah herself felt in the household of David.[22] Whose heart, she asks, is being wrenched here?

In her actions Rizpah is searching for the God betrayed by power, determined to find that God. And in what she does she represents Yahweh truly, unlike the powerful in the palace who made that claim into a falsehood. She unmasks the ideology that parades as religious devotion; she challenges the idolatry that claims the right to determine life and death; she exposes the heresy that proffers political expedience and the abuse of power as the will of God; she rejects the belief that the spilling of blood secures reconciliation. She strips of their power those precious myths that beguile the people and purport to be sanctioned by God—those myths emanating from the palace: "peace," and "national security," "survival," David as God's "chosen" (who could do no wrong), and most of all, "the will of God." For if the nation's security is secured by injustice and oppression, if one's chosenness is to be upheld by the rejection of one's flesh and blood, then nothing can be farther from the truth; and if the land is defiled by innocent blood, it loses it sacredness. Rizpah does not only question the assumptions of male, patriarchal dominance and ideologies of the palace, she shakes the very foundations of David's kingship.

The Heart of the Matter

The vigil on the rock amongst those crosses is a testimony emblazoned in courage, faith, and endless solidarity. As we probe this story's meaning for reconciliation, nothing should be taken for granted here. First of all, Rizpah is a woman, a wife of secondary rank now widowed, with no authority of her own. Authority rests with the royal house of David. She is the widow of a dead king whose sons have become a threat to the living king. Why does she take those risks? Who is she doing it for? What makes her think that she can take on David who on this point has turned into this Goliath of evil? David has "compassion" for Mephibosheth, son of Jonathan, because of his "oath" to Jonathan (2 Sm 21:7), but can find no such compassion for the seven sons and grandsons of Saul, despite his oath to Saul. Why would David find compassion in his heart for her?

Secondly, Rizpah does this all alone. Right through the story it's just her. There is no man who recognizes that outside, on the hill at night, it is not a safe place for a woman on her own. Not a single one. There is not a single woman who comes to hold her hand in sisterly solidarity. Not in all that time. No doubt, she probably had lots of sympathy. There might have been those who wondered how the king could do this. But nobody has the courage to speak up, to be seen with her, to join her in her struggle for truth and justice. Nobody leaves the comfort of their home to join her on that lonely rock. Sympathy is not solidarity. Crying "shame" is not solidarity. Complaining behind the safety of four walls and a locked door is not solidarity. Rizpah shows what solidarity means: with her body and with the risks she takes on behalf of those who have died, in exposure of injustice; and for those who are living, in testimony to righteousness and hope.

Third, and this is probably the most remarkable thing if certainly not the last, Rizpah fights for all those seven young men on the crosses. *All of them.* Yet only two of them are hers. The other five belong to Merab. But Merab is nowhere to be found. Maybe Merab has good reasons why she's not there, with Rizpah, protesting the death of her children. Perhaps Merab is thinking of the risks for herself or her family—what is left of it. She cannot possibly fight the king. Maybe Merab thinks she does not have the strength for this or that perhaps this is a hopeless case. After all, her children are dead. Unlike Rizpah, she is perhaps wary of looking foolish in the eyes of the city. Because this is without doubt: up on that hill, Rizpah *did* look absolutely foolish. The whole city probably thought she was crazy. But, Rizpah thinks, I'd rather be crazy with love than drunk with power.

Rizpah says, only two children on those crosses are mine, but I don't care; *every* child on a cross is my child. As long as there is one single child on the cross of pain, and indignity, of suffering, and futurelessness, I will stand up and I will fight for that child—a crucified child is my child. That is what solidarity means: *every child on a cross is my child.* That is the deepest truth that lies behind the African proverb: "It takes a village to raise a child." Every child in that village becomes *my* child. Her hurts and pains, her fears and joys, her hopes and aspirations, her very life—they become mine. Every single one of the 1,463 Palestinian children killed by the Israeli Defense Force since September 2000, and every one of the six children dying every day in drought-stricken Somalia as I write, is a child hanging on a cross—and they are *all our* children.

Fourth, she is in mourning, this woman, but she mourns for the dead, her children, as well as for the living, her people. She rises above her private sorrow and, like the prophet she is, sees the plight of her people. Her children might be dead but Israel is going astray; she knows this is the wrong path to take. This is not where security lies; this is not the way to peace. Security for both the king and the people cannot lie in the shedding of the innocent blood of young men who have done no harm, except in being who they were: the embodiment of David's fear. Rizpah understands what that means. And so she cries for her own children, but she cries for all of the children of Israel.

There might perhaps be a final thing that flows from the point we have just made. The young men are dead. In that sense it is entirely a hopeless case. But her protest is about more than against death, it is *for* life: she cannot save her children on the cross, but she can save the soul of her people because she knows what is at stake here. To those who walk by, looking pityingly at her, reminding her that she can't bring them to life again, Rizpah responds, "It does not matter. My sons are dead. I know that. What is in danger of dying, however, is the soul of Israel." Solidarity means understanding that what is at stake is not just the lives or deaths of those who are crucified day by day. At stake is the dying of our soul. And for Rizpah that is the heart of the matter. But her vigil on the rock makes it clear: our soul does not have to die. Instead, the solidarity of risk makes of it a habitation of love and life and reconciliation.

And at last, the story says, at last, she shamed the king into doing what is right. Right through the story Rizpah says not a single word. She has no need of, or any use for, oracles and ritualized political sophistry. Like any true prophet, she knows when the time for pious words is over. But how marvelously eloquent and convincing are her deeds! She does not speak, so her courage speaks for her, and now the king can no longer ignore her. He knows it is not the priests or the prophets and theologians of the court on the king's payroll through whom God had spoken in that false oracle. In the acts of this amazing woman he hears the very voice of God. *Now,* for the first time in this story, he recognizes it.

"David went and took the bones of Saul and the bones of his son Jonathan from the people of Jabesh-gilead, who had stolen them from the public square in Beth-shan" (2 Sm 21:12). He brings the bones of Saul and Jonathan home, takes the bodies off the crosses and gives them all a decent burial. It is indeed the decent thing to do. So finally they come to rest: Jonathan and Saul and the seven young men. There is no sign in the story that David understands this, but the interpretation is entirely possible: in his shame at what he had done is the essence of repentance, his repentance is the acknowledgement of the truth, and the acknowledgement of truth is the beginning of restitution and restoration, and in restoration is the acknowledgement of the righteousness of Rizpah. Sometimes reconciliation begins with just acknowledging the shame and doing the decent thing. By the grace of God the rest will follow.

Rizpah, Resistance, Risk, and Reconciliation

What do Rizpah, and this amazing story, teach us about reconciliation? Several things, I would suggest.

- First, Rizpah shows us what reconciliation is *not*, and that is as important as to know what reconciliation *is*. Reconciliation is never cheap, but it cannot be bought with innocent blood. Costly reconciliation does not lie in the costs we pile on the bent shoulders of the powerless, those who already "labor and are heavy-laden," whose burdens refuse them rest for their souls, but in the radical risks we take on behalf of others; in the yoke *we* are willing to bear in costly discipleship. Pointing far ahead into the future, Rizpah knows that the cross is not a symbol of expiation, much less of satisfaction. It is, rather, a symbol of the abuse of power, of execution and ultimate violence, and that that is not the character of the God she worships. The cross is not "the great symbol of the vicarious benefits of violence, slick with the blood of its non-violent victim."[23] The cross is rather God's ultimate solidarity with the victims of power, those hanging on the crosses of extermination, racism, sexism, marginalization, and powerlessness. Doing violence on behalf of God is not what "satisfies" God. An instrument of terror that silences love cannot be the symbol of love. With Jesus, the cross is the ultimate assault upon God, upon God's desire to let God's will be done on earth as it is in heaven, and upon the One who seeks to bring God's true justice and reconciliation into the world. That is why the resurrection is such a victory—it nullifies not only death, but also the power of violence.

- Second, that those in positions of power and privilege cannot define reconciliation nor affect it on behalf of others over whom they have power. Reconciliation, like forgiveness, cannot be declared from the thrones of the powerful. It flows from the wounds of the crucified, and for forgiveness to be meaningful, it has to be seen to flow from woundedness. Rizpah shifts the focus away from the powerful, their duplicity and manipulation of faith and of God, to the victims of that power, and holds up their plight and suffering as holy before God.

- Third, she makes clear who the real victims are: not David, but the sons of Saul. She does not allow the oppressor to play the victim either through arrogance or pious wringing of hands about the "heart-wrenching" decisions the powerful must make while the pain is laid on the powerless. She does not allow the king, now that "satisfaction" has been pronounced, to "move on," as if the "satisfaction" ends the suffering. Neither does she allow the people to clothe themselves with the pseudo innocence of neutrality and not knowing. Her solidarity keeps the crosses visible and unmissable. But there is something more. She does not once claim victim status for herself, but through her selfless, sacrificial love, she reveals it in others. Through it all she is silent. She never once calls attention to herself despite the right her history gives her, but she rises above the temptation of victimhood to stand in solidarity with others. Her righteous anger is not out of pity for herself but because of the injustice done to others and the danger it poses to the soul of her people.

- Fourth, she shows what a single person can do, even against mighty forces, if she is willing to take the risk of faith and courage. The genius of evil is not that perpetrators of evil are otherwise such "normal" persons: a loving father, a pious churchgoer, a conscientious official, or—like Hitler—an ardent lover of dogs. Nor does it lie in piling up one terrifying, sense-numbing atrocity upon the other as we have seen in the horrific scenes from the Gaza war. The genius of evil lies in making us believe, in the face of one overwhelming, unthinkable injustice, that we are helpless, that evil is unstoppable and irreversible, that there is nothing we can do. Rizpah magnificently dispels that myth.

- Finally, Rizpah teaches us that reconciliation is not possible without a sense of shame, of knowing that wrongs have been done, that injustice should be overturned. David would otherwise not have any reason to do what he had in 2 Samuel 21:12–14. Guilt is a private, inner emotion, but shame is public. David's acts of power were shamelessly public; the young men were impaled "before the Lord," in public. Rizpah, accordingly, took the risk of resistance in public, day and night, exposing the king for his ruthless duplicity and the people for their silence and complicity, and she forced David to recant.

But it does not end there. Forgiveness and healing follow. "[David] brought from up there the bones of Saul and the bones of his son Jonathan; and they gathered the bones of those who were impaled" and they buried them (2 Sm 21:13). And "after that," verse 14 goes on, "God heeded supplications for the land." We have to ask the following questions: After what? After David's shameful political games? After the undignified political expediency they called expiation, restitution, reconciliation? After blood has been spilled, after the crosses have been displayed and the bodies on them left for birds and animals to devour? After all that? No. After Rizpah and her acts of resistance, of faith and justice, of fearless solidarity. Then, and only then, did Yahweh heed the supplications for the land. Only when Rizpah did what she did, did Yahweh hear and break the drought, and the rains came down. And only then, when "rain fell (on the bodies and the scorched earth) from the heavens" (2 Sm 21:10), did Rizpah leave her lonely rock and reclaim her life. And it does not even end there. After *that*, the story tells us, the Lord heeded supplications, "for the land."

Who thought she was doing it for her children; just for the seven of them? God knew what she was doing. And so this woman, in her love, in her faithfulness and her solidarity, in her courage in taking the risks, in making herself vulnerable, in her willingness to make herself look foolish, in her utter audacity in taking on the men of power in every single palace in the world, in doing that, she saved the whole land. The whole people were blessed because she remained faithful. They were *all* blessed. Not just those who suffered, but also those who stood idly by, looking the other way, and also those who caused the pain. Radical reconciliation does that.

Part II

Jesus Christ
Reclaimed

Chapter 3

Jesus the Radical Reconciler
Two Takes, One Perspective
Curtiss Paul DeYoung and Allan Aubrey Boesak

Take One: The Same Yesterday, Today, and Forever
(*Curtiss Paul DeYoung*)

Bethlehem is known internationally as the birthplace of Jesus of Nazareth. The Gospels of Matthew and Luke both narrate this event. Today in
Bethlehem much of the commerce is focused on this claim to prominence.
One can visit the Church of the Nativity, which claims to be built on the
site of Jesus' birth. Near the nativity church and throughout the town,
beautiful olive wood carvings of nativity scenes are available from many
vendors. Meanwhile another reality is evident. Present-day Bethlehem is
under occupation. The city is encircled by modern "security" walls and accessed through checkpoints controlled by the Israeli Defense Force. Nearby
are towns populated by Israeli settlers—the evidence of a colonial settler
enterprise. Followers of Jesus in twenty-first century Bethlehem live under
occupation. The tranquil olive wood nativity scenes sold by local entrepre-
neurs betray rather than portray what is the present reality.

These nativity scenes also betray rather than portray the reality in Bethlehem at the time of the birth of Jesus. Residents in Bethlehem in the first
century lived under the colonial occupation of Rome. Their circumstances
were not tranquil. Jews in Palestine were oppressed. The olive wood nativity scenes do not display this reality. The Gospel writers though did not
hide this reality when narrating the birth of Jesus. Luke's story began, "In
those days a decree went out from Emperor Augustus" (2:1). Matthew's

43

story began, "In the time of King Herod" (2:1). Luke identified the colonial context of Jewish oppression under the Roman Empire. Matthew
identified the daily reality of occupation by citing the name of King Herod,
Rome's appointed overseer of Palestine. While Matthew and Luke told the
story differently, they both shared the perspective that the birth of Jesus
foreshadowed a confrontation with the empire.

The Gospel writers placed Jesus' birth stories in the midst of real-life
colonization and occupation. In Luke, Emperor Augustus decreed a census
in order to organize taxation of his subject peoples. In Matthew, Herod ordered a mass murder of children to enforce and secure his rule as occupier.
Biblical scholar Richard A. Horsley writes, "Christmas celebrates the birth
of a peasant child as the true 'Savior' of a people who had been conquered
and laid under tribute (the census) by Caesar, whom the whole world had
already acclaimed as the 'Savior' who had brought 'Peace and Security'
to the world. It also commemorates the Roman client king's dispatch of
counterinsurgency forces to massacre the innocents in order to check the
deliverance movement before it got started."[1]

Yet in the midst of brutal colonization and occupation, the birth of Jesus
signaled the emergence of a vision of reconciliation. The Gospels of Matthew
and Luke welcomed the advent of Jesus as a light to the nations. Their story
was one of global proportions connecting poor Palestinian shepherds and
rich Magi from Asia with people on the continent of Africa who received
Jesus and his parents as Palestinian refugees under threat from the Roman
Empire's Governor Herod. The story featured strong women and strong men
(Mary and Elizabeth, Zachariah and Joseph). These Gospels announced the
birth of a reconciliation event that would address social inequalities, ethnic
separation, gender hierarchies, economic disparities, and the like.

Jesus of Nazareth was an exemplar of radical reconciliation. Jesus embodied reconciliation even while under very oppressive conditions. The
apostle Paul's later call for one new humanity (Eph 2) mirrored what Jesus
lived. Jesus was the incarnation of reconciliation! The author of Hebrews
wrote, "Jesus Christ is the same yesterday and today and forever" (13:8).
This notion that Jesus is the same yesterday, today, and forever is central to
our reclaiming of Jesus as a radical reconciler. Jesus has as much to say to
contexts of exclusion and division in the twenty-first century as he did in
the midst of first century realities. But first we must understand the Jesus
of yesterday, so that we can know the Jesus of today.

Jesus was raised in the village of Nazareth in the occupied region of Galilee in Palestine (ancient Israel). The Roman Empire invaded and occupied Palestine in 63 BCE with the army burning villages, enslaving people, and killing the elderly and the sick. Rome considered Judeans "as good for nothing but slavery."[2] Some years later, but prior to the birth of Jesus, the town of Sepphoris was burned, and the inhabitants were enslaved. Sepphoris was located very close to Nazareth. Jesus grew up in a region experiencing the trauma of Roman imperial power. House demolitions and killings of local civilians reenforced Roman rule on the occupied Jewish subjects.[3] In his book *Jesus and the Disinherited*, Howard Thurman summed up the spiritual effect on Palestine's Jewish residents, "The gruesome details of loss of status were etched, line by line, in the sensitive soul of Israel, dramatized ever by an increasing desecration of the Holy Land. . . . Taxes of all kinds increased, and out of these funds, extracted from the vitals of the people, temples in honor of Emperor Augustus were built within the boundaries of the holy soil. It was a sad and desolate time for the people."[4]

Jesus' upbringing in Galilee was shaped by the realities of colonization and occupation. Therefore, he learned to read the "Torah as an instrument for spelling out the justice of the reign of God" as well as learning to also "read his colonial context, which was dominated by Roman overlords."[5] It is no surprise that the message that welled up and spilled out of Jesus' soul was a call for God's reign on earth, the kingdom of God. Teaching and preaching the kingdom of God would have been considered "potent political language" in first-century Palestine and understood as calling for "the restoration of an Israel free from outside domination."[6] In pictorial language biblical scholar John Dominic Crossan adds that the kingdom of God "was what this world would look like if and when God sat on Caesar's throne." Crossan continues, "The Kingdom of God is inextricably and simultaneously 100 percent political and 100 percent religious. 'Kingdom' is a political term, 'God' is a religious term, and Jesus would be executed for that 'of' in a world where, for Rome, God already sat on Caesar's throne because Caesar was God."[7]

Jesus' inaugural sermon declared good news for the poor and oppressed (Lk 4:18–19). His parables often contained powerful rhetoric directed at the context of colonization and occupation by shining "the harsh light of the prophetic tradition on the fundamental injustice of the Roman economy in Palestine—juxtaposing sharecroppers and day laborers with cruel landowners and indifferent landlords."[8] The teaching and preaching of Jesus challenged the status quo of "religious and political power in his society" calling for "a fundamental transvaluation of values, an exalting of the humble and a critique of the mighty."[9]

Not only did Jesus preach a message of radical reconciliation and social justice in the context of Roman oppression, he actively lived out radical reconciliation among marginalized victims of Roman imperialism, patriarchy, and bigotry. "In a country where the Roman fist was the highest authority," Allan Boesak declares, "Jesus enthroned the human value of the oppressed."[10] Jesus developed real relationships with people living at the margins of society in Galilee and Judea—people with disabilities, Samaritans, militant activists, women, tax collectors, lepers, physically ill individuals, widows, homeless folks, and poor and working class people. He included these folks in the intimacy of table fellowship, eating meals quite publicly with people considered outcasts from the fringes of society —a lived proclamation of reconciliation. Jesus brought together the full range of society among his followers. There was even political diversity. He included zealots who were intent on the violent overthrow of Roman imperialism and tax collectors who were collaborating with the Roman power structure.

Biblical scholar Andries van Aarde contends that Jesus' connection to folks at the margins was partially a result of his own marginal status as a fatherless man. Questions of illegitimacy were raised regarding the identity of his birth father. Van Aarde states, "It remains a dilemma that Jesus' father is altogether absent in the Gospel accounts of Jesus' public ministry while other members of his family are specified. This is even more remarkable when one takes the central role of a father in first-century Mediterranean culture into consideration." To make matters worse, in Mark 6:3, Jesus was referred to as the "son of Mary." Van Aarde notes that this "expression is an indication that Jesus is without identity, an illegitimate person without a father who could have given him credibility."[11]

Van Aarde presents a somewhat controversial view that Jesus' status was that of fatherless—without a male ancestor and without claim of lineage and identity. Yet, the lack of a biological father in a highly patriarchal society could explain Jesus' amazing number of women followers. Jesus had marginal status because of no father, while women could only gain identity through their father or husband. Perhaps Jesus' most radical actions were the ways he engaged with women as true friends and equals. In a culture and society that segregated women and men, he was at ease in the presence of women. Women were among those who followed Jesus as disciples: Mary Magdalene, Mary the mother of James and Joseph, the mother of the sons of Zebedee, Salome, Susanna, Joanna (the wife of Herod's steward), and many unnamed others. Women provided financial resources for Jesus and his traveling entourage (Mk 15:40–41; Lk 8:2–3). It seems that Jesus' home base for ministry in Galilee was at the home of Mary and Martha of Bethany (Lk 10:38–42; Jn 11).

Women were central to the important events in the life of Jesus. Women played some of the most significant roles in the life and ministry of Jesus. A woman in Samaria was the first person to learn that Jesus was the Messiah (Jn 4:25–26). Martha of Bethany proclaimed that Jesus was the Messiah (Jn 11:27). Women stayed with Jesus through the crucifixion (Mt 26:56; Mk 15:40–41; Jn 19:25). Women discovered the empty tomb (Mt 28:1; Mk 16:1–2; Lk 24:1–12; Jn 20:1). Women were the first people to see Jesus resurrected (Mt 28:8–10; Mk 16:9; Jn 20:11–18).

While life in the oppressive conditions of Galilee may have negatively affected Jesus, his upbringing in the multicultural, multilingual "Galilee of the nations" (or "Galilee of the Gentiles") provided a context where he could be shaped with strong reconciliation instincts (Is 9:1; Mt 4:15). Jews in Galilee were interspersed among a wide range of people including Assyrians, Babylonians, Egyptians, Macedonians, Persians, Syrians, indigenous Canaanites, and Romans.[12] The ethnic diversity of people living in the region of Galilee represented the composition of the Roman Empire. One could assume that Jesus became comfortable with a wide range of culturally diverse people and acquired some proficiency in multiple languages.

The ministry of Jesus reflected the influence of his Galilean roots. The Gospel of Mark has Jesus ministering in both Jewish and Gentile regions of Galilee. Biblical scholar Brian Blount writes that Mark created a "virtual Jesus Gentile mission."[13] Readers of Mark's Gospel who knew the places of first-century Galilee would recognize when Jesus was ministering to Jews or to Gentiles by virtue of the noted locations. As we read the Gospel of Mark, we learn that Jesus reached out to many Gentiles including a man who called himself "Legion" (5:1–20), the daughter of a Greek woman from Syrian Phoenicia (7:24–30), and a man living in the Gentile city of Decapolis (7:31–35). Mark's telling of Jesus traversing back and forth between

Jewish and Gentile communities created a reconciliation dynamic that culminated in two feeding stories. In chapter six he wrote of the feeding of five thousand Jews (6:35–44) and in chapter eight the feeding of four thousand Gentiles (8:1–9).

The Jesus of yesterday preached about radical reconciliation coming in the reign of God. His grassroots relationships served as a picture of what this reconciliation should look like. Jesus also prophetically engaged the structures in society. Richard Horsley notes, "For generations both before and after the ministry of Jesus, the Galilean and Judean people mounted repeated protests and revolts against the Romans and their client rulers, the Herodian kings and Jerusalem high priests."[14] It seems that Jesus participated in this activist tradition. Biblical scholars Marcus J. Borg and John Dominic Crossan argue in their book *The Last Week* that the Palm Sunday procession was a protest march.[15] Jesus led a "peasant procession" entering Jerusalem from the east. At the same time, Pontius Pilate and his Roman soldiers entered Jerusalem from the west in an "imperial procession."[16] Borg and Crossan state, "Jesus' procession deliberately countered what was happening on the other side of the city. Pilate's procession embodied the power, glory, and violence of the empire that ruled the world. Jesus' procession embodied an alternative vision, the kingdom of God."[17] What we call Palm Sunday was a nonviolent protest against empire and occupation. Following the protest march, Jesus entered the temple and cleared the money changers as "a protest against a temple regime that some saw as collaborating with Rome."[18]

Jesus' protests against imperial domination, messages calling for the reign of God, and life lived with people at the margins led to his arrest by the temple police. He was then handed over to the imperial authorities. Roman Governor Pilate gave the orders for the execution of Jesus of Nazareth as an enemy of the empire. A life of radical reconciliation led to crucifixion. Richard A. Horsley puts Jesus' crucifixion in context:

> In the course of repeated military expeditions to put down repeated insurgencies and revolts over a period of two centuries, one of their governors in Judea crucified a certain Jesus of Nazareth as an insurgent leader, "the king of the Judeans." But Jesus' followers, including the apostle Paul, insisted on loyalty to Jesus Christ, instead of Caesar, as their "Lord" and "Savior." So not only did the Judeans

and Galileans, who were deeply rooted in Israelite traditions, resist domination by Rome for generations, but the mission of Jesus, one of those Galileans, and that of Paul, one of those Judeans, was in opposition to the Roman Empire.[19]

Jesus of Nazareth was a subject of Rome: colonized, occupied, and crucified. Yet, the life of Jesus of Nazareth ends in a moment of symbolic reconciliation as his Roman cross was carried by an African, Simon of Cyrene, and at the crucifixion a Roman guard spoke words of faith. A powerless African and a soldier of the Roman Empire both participated in the final act of the life of Jesus of Nazareth. Yet the crucifixion as reconciliation became the first act in what the apostle Paul called the new humanity —the powerless and the powerful equal at the cross. As the story began, so it ended, with full inclusion and radical reconciliation.

We must ask the question, "What does this first-century life of Jesus of Nazareth mean to us today?" Sometime after yesterday and before today, his life story was co-opted, reconfigured, and reissued. The story of a colonized and occupied Jesus was replaced with a meek and mild savior who did not disrupt the status quo or with the image of a colonial Christ who sided with the powerful and blessed imperial realities. The colonized first-century Christian communities preaching liberation and practicing reconciliation were replaced by Christians who were quiet and politically pious or who became colonizers, slaveholders, crusaders, terrorists, dictators, and the like.

As time went on, colonization was racialized, and so was the image Jesus. A white European colonial image of Jesus was constructed, owned, and manipulated by empires for domination. The memory of an occupied, colonized, oppressed Jesus of Nazareth quietly disappeared. A white image of Christ was God's stamp of approval on colonization and white racism. This image demonstrated to the masses that white people were superior to people of color by virtue of the whiteness of Jesus. Nearly every published Bible contained white images of Jesus. Vincent Harding declares,

> We first met this (white) Christ on slave ships. We heard his name sung in praise while we died in our thousands, chained in stinking holds beneath the decks, locked in with terror and disease and sad memories of our families and homes. When we leaped from the

decks to be seized by sharks we saw his name carved in the ship's solid sides. When our women were raped in the cabins, they must have noted the great and holy books on the shelves. Our introduction to this Christ was not propitious and the horrors continued on America's soil.[20]

Similar stories were heard around the globe. The white imperial image of Jesus served as a powerful tool for undergirding European colonialism, enslavement of Africans, genocide of indigenous peoples, and white racial superiority.[21]

Yet the biblical witness cannot be silenced. Throughout the centuries, there were always individuals and communities inspired by Jesus to work for social justice and reconciliation. Howard Thurman wrote, "The basic fact is that Christianity as it was born in the mind of this Jewish teacher and thinker appears as a technique of survival for the oppressed. That it became, through the intervening years, a religion of the powerful and the dominant, used sometimes as an instrument of oppression, must not tempt us into believing that it was thus in the mind and life of Jesus."[22] In the twentieth century the biblical Jesus of yesterday was once again rediscovered, and the meaning of Jesus for today was reclaimed. Theologies emerged that were indigenous to Latin America, African America, Asia, Africa, Native America, Australia, and the islands of the oceans. Oppressed people read again the stories of a colonized and oppressed Jesus—and found hope. People facing the imperial realities of today found healing.

Jesus was also de-racialized. Biblical scholars examined genealogies of Jesus of Nazareth in Matthew and Luke and discovered he was an Afro-Asiatic Jew.[23] The singular image of Jesus Christ as white was challenged by a Jesus who was African and Asian. Jesus was multiracial and multicultural. Jesus was mestizo, Creole, Coloured, interracial. This newly rediscovered biblical perspective reminds us that throughout most of the history of the United States, Jesus would have been classified as black due to his African ancestry. Jesus was reclaimed from a white racial image of Christ that favored the dominant class and restored to a Jesus of full inclusion and radical reconciliation.

Jesus of Nazareth, the Jesus of yesterday, creates a paradigm for radical reconciliation today through his words, relationships, and actions and offers hope for the future. We the followers of Jesus must embody this paradigm for radical reconciliation speaking words of liberation and healing, embracing relationships that are fully inclusive, and acting for social justice.

Take Two: What's in a Name?
(Allan Aubrey Boesak)

In his fascinating study of the historical Jesus, South African New Testament scholar Andries van Aarde reminds us that the Jewish historian Josephus mentions twelve other persons called "Jesus," who "played a part in the history of Israel during the period of Greco-Roman geopolitical domination." In a footnote, van Aarde mentions them all.[24] So, in biblical times, the name Jesus was fairly common. What is it then that makes Jesus of Nazareth stand out amongst them all? The Jesus of the New Testament is the one "who is called the Christ," who Christians worship as the Son of God, but that, I believe, is not the deepest reason why Jesus drew as much attention as he drew crowds in the surroundings of Galilee. The Roman rulers could care less whether Jesus called himself the Son of God: their own emperors called themselves gods! What bothered them was the possibility that he might be the "king of the Jews,"[25] and that he might, as king and messiah, stir up revolt. The Jewish ruling elite were offended by the title "Son of God" but not nearly as offended as when Jesus proclaimed himself the Messiah, the Spirit-anointed One of God who came to proclaim good news to the poor.[26]

Amongst those Josephus mentions, only one was a "robber," in all probability a "social bandit," an important factor in ancient Jewish society, often providing leadership for Judean peasants in their struggle for justice.[27] All the rest came from priestly families, which means they were all from a wealthy, privileged background, men of high social standing with powerful political connections. Jesus of Nazareth was none of that. And here is the first distinctive difference between Jesus of Nazareth son of Mary and Joseph, and the others also called Jesus. This Jesus was not like the others. He was not of the privileged, priestly classes, not of the elite, wealthy families with their profitable relationships with the Roman occupier in exchange for rich rewards in the collaboration with the Romans in the oppression of their own people. That fact alone made for a decisive difference between Jesus of Nazareth and the others who shared his name.

Right from the beginning, Jesus of Nazareth, son of Mary and Joseph, looked at the world through different eyes. Jesus was born as a child with contested parentage and as a result lived with the "stigma" of fatherlessness.[28] He was born in a stable, laid down in a manger, amongst the animals and the dung. At an early age, his life was threatened according to Matthew's Gospel, and he became a refugee. As a fatherless child, the question of illegitimacy hounded him all his life.[29] He lived among the peasants, pagans, and bandits of "Galilee of the Gentiles," where people "lived in darkness," the interracial, multilingual impoverished community looked down upon by Judeans.[30] He lived his life in service to the poor and oppressed, the sick, excluded, and the downtrodden, and it was through their eyes that this Jesus saw the world and its workings.

The great distinction was not in the church's worshipping of Jesus as the Son of God. That came later, after those who saw and heard him and believed in him discovered that in his life and deeds he so much resembled and reflected the God they knew—the God of the exodus, of liberation and compassionate justice, the God who took sides with the oppressed, the wronged and the destitute—that they believed that to see Jesus in action, was to see God in action (Jn 14:9–11).

When they contrasted him to the overlords of the dominating powers in their lives who ruled by all manner of terror—the ruling elites in Jerusalem, the priests and the Jewish political leadership, the Roman soldiers who made their lives hell, the tax collectors, whether collecting for the empire or for the temple in Jerusalem, who robbed and exploited them; the governor (*hegemon*) in Jerusalem, representative of Caesar, the one who called himself "Lord" and "God," and was, as such, feared, honored and obeyed by all in the empire—they decided to deny Caesar that right, honor, and title, and called Jesus "Lord."[31] Central to Roman domination was Roman imperial theology, and central to *that* was the cult of emperor worship.[32] And when they had to choose between loyalty to and fear of Caesar and obedience to God, they chose obedience to God, even though it cost them their lives.

Andries van Aarde writes, "When believers in the first and second centuries referred to Jesus *as* God's Christ, *as* God's equal, *as* Child of Humanity, *as* God's image which manifests God, *as* Child of God who comes forth from God or who is legitimated by God or who was with God, or who emanated from God's 'fullness', they used recognized cultural metaphors to speak about God."[33] That may well be so, but I think there was something more than just cultural metaphors at work here. These Christians were groping for something they were struggling to put into words, something that came to them in the traditions derived from the early generations of the Jesus community. They were trying to express how someone who was born as a human being, poor, despised, stigmatized and oppressed, humiliated and abused as those first followers were, could be so extraordinary, his presence so life changing, his words so life giving, his life and death so transformational, that it was impossible to forget him. He became a permanent transformational presence in their lives. But those who knew him as he walked and worked among them, knew that with his coming something drastic was changing in the scheme of things in the world, something Jesus called the reign of God.

While European Christians in later centuries described Jesus in the distant and distancing language of the Creeds, for black people, writes James Cone, Jesus is as he is in the spirituals:

> He's the King of kings, and Lord of lords,
> Jesus Christ, the first and the last,
> No man works like him.[34]

Or as Kelley Delaine Brown says, "God is as Jesus does."[35] Jesus is the preserver of the weak in time of trouble and as the sustaining Spirit of freedom in wretched places, and because Jesus is with black people in their wretchedness, as well as in their struggles for liberation, Jesus is black. But, Cone asserts, "the 'blackness of Christ' therefore, is not simply a statement about skin color, but rather, the transcendent affirmation that God has not ever, no not ever, left the oppressed alone in struggle. He was with them in Pharaoh's Egypt, is with them in America, Africa and Latin America, and will come in the end of time to consummate fully their human freedom."[36] Cone's concept of a "Black Christ" may be contested today,[37] but the truth of his understanding of who Jesus is (the One who is with the oppressed in their struggles), remains incontrovertible. Since liberation theology's insistence that Jesus is God's incarnate option for the poor and the oppressed, recent, postcolonial studies have thrown new light on the historical Jesus, the significance of his historical context, the Roman Empire, and the meaning of his life and work.[38]

This has been a significant development. Building upon the work of liberation theology, these studies have revealed how thoroughly the New

Testament, and as a consequence Jesus, has been domesticated, de-politi-cized, and one may add, de-revolutionized. Richard Horsley speaks of the "construction of a de-politicized Jesus" in traditional Western New Testament studies, and Nicholas Wolterstorff speaks of the "dejusticizing" of the New Testament.[39] The result of this new work is the emergence of a Jesus more properly understood within the realities of the context within which he lived and worked, namely, that of the Roman Empire, an oppressive, totalitarian, and extremely pervasive force, its systems of domination and exploitation devastatingly at work. This is a Jesus much closer to the radical Black Messiah of black liberation theology.[40]

So whether Jesus is called a "Mediterranean Jewish Peasant" (Crossan), a "social revolutionary" (Horsley), or a (revolutionary) "prophet and teacher," subversive "pedagogue of the oppressed (Herzog),"[41] or as van Aarde sees him, a stigmatized Galilean whose fatherlessness made him a "revolutionary and healer, teacher and helper,"[42] the consensus that seems to be emerging is that Jesus of Nazareth was no ordinary prophet, but a revolutionary outsider who thoroughly disturbed the powers that be in Jerusalem and who was seen as a threat to the existing systems of domination. He was radical in his words and in his doings.

And that is how his followers experienced him. In a very short time after his crucifixion, at least some of Jesus' followers were referring to him as "Jesus Christ" (i.e. *Christos,* being the Greek translation for *Messhiach* in Hebrew), the anointed king who has come to save his people. From what we read in the Gospels, Jesus and his movement fairly early on attracted the attention of the Jerusalem priestly rulers and the Roman governor, who had determined to destroy him. He certainly had become a threat to these ruling elites, but how significant was that threat? Was he really not just a social revolutionary, but indeed a "political revolutionary," as Obery M. Hendricks insists?[43] But what does that mean? It means, says Hendricks,

> That if Jesus had had his way, The Roman Empire and the ruling elites among his own people either would no longer have held their positions of power, or if they did, would have had to conduct themselves very, very differently. It means that an important goal of his ministry was to radically change the distribution of authority and power, goods and resources, so all people—particularly the little people, or 'the least of these', as Jesus called them—might have lives

free of political oppression, enforced hunger and poverty, and undue insecurity. It means that Jesus sought not only to heal people's pain but also to inspire and empower people to remove the unjust social and political structures that too often were the cause of their pain. It means that Jesus had a clear and unambiguous vision of the healthy world God intended and that he addressed any issue—social, economic, or political—that violated that vision.[44]

But Horsley offers us one more persuasive point. Andries van Aarde mentions twelve other persons called Jesus. Horsley knows of yet another one who, like Jesus, prophesied doom against Jerusalem in the mid-first century, Yeshua ben Hananiah. Arrested by the high-priestly aristocracy, he, too, was turned over to the Roman governor for execution. So, on the surface, this Jesus, son of Hananiah, seemed very much like Jesus, son of Joseph. But the Roman governor, convinced that this prophet was simply crazy, ordered him beaten and then released him. In the case of Yeshua ben Yoseph, however, the Roman governor ordered him beaten and then had him executed by crucifixion, "the torturous death reserved for provincial rebels, as well as slaves."[45]

The fact that the Roman authorities had Jesus crucified in this way shows that they regarded him as a serious threat to the imperial order.[46] "However it may have happened historically," Horsley says, "the execution of Yeshua ben Yoseph as a rebel may well have resulted from a similar concern about the threat he posed to the Roman imperial order."[47] Yeshua ben Hananiah may also have been called "prophet," but he was not nearly as radical a prophet as Yeshua ben Yoseph. Even then, powers that be and those suffering under those powers understood that there is something in a name after all.

It all begins with the giving of the name that would distinguish him from all others, the Spirit-filled One of God who came to bring justice for the poor and the oppressed, who incarnated Yahweh's "arm of justice" in the world and intervened to bring injustice to an end and to announce the acceptable year of the Lord. It is in *that* name that the Gentiles will hope.

This is the Jesus in whose name Christians are called to be agents of reconciliation. It's a name that makes a difference in the world and in the lives of all who encounter him.

Chapter 4

"Just Another Jew in the Ditch"
Incarnated Reconciliation
Allan Aubrey Boesak

The Spirit-Anointed One

The prophet Isaiah's vision of a time when justice shall restore the community of ancient Israel is rooted in Yahweh's burning desire for justice; Yahweh's outrage at the continued oppression of God's people; at the betrayal of the cause of Yahweh, which is to "seek justice, rescue the oppressed, defend the orphan, (and) plead for the widow" (Is 1:17). Yahweh was "angered" at the injustice that reigned in Israel and took its toll amongst the poor and vulnerable, and "appalled" that "there was no one to intervene" (Is 59:15–16). In the gospel of Luke (4:16–18), Jesus pronounces himself as the one who was to intervene, who was to become Yahweh's incarnated justice, Yahweh's "own arm" brought him victory and whose own righteousness shall uphold him (Is 59:16). Jesus cites the oppression of his people as the focus of his own intervention.

Liberation theologian Miguel de la Torre is absolutely correct when he writes that "those wishing to ground their understanding of reconciliation within the Christian tradition are forced to deal with the figure of Jesus Christ."[1] The question, however, is, "Which Jesus?" It cannot be the Jesus of whom Vincent Harding speaks, as we have seen, the one captured Africans first met when we saw his name carved in the sides of the slave ship that carried Africans from their homelands into slavery. Neither can it be the Christ of the church doctrines who evolved into the blond, blue-eyed Christ of Western culture so alien to the enslaved, oppressed, exploited peoples who were baptized in his name. Nor can it be the Jesus only known as the one who offered unconditional forgiveness to all. For us, as for the Gospel, this Jesus first and foremost has to be the Jesus who stood in the synagogue in Nazareth, according to the Gospel of Luke, and proclaimed himself the Spirit-anointed One of God.

Jesus could speak of himself thus and become Yahweh's incarnated justice not because he claimed lofty places and privileged power when he came to live among us, but precisely because he "emptied himself, taking the form of a slave . . . [humbling] himself, became obedient to the point of death" (Phil 2:7, 8). These words from Paul have far too often been mystified into doctrinal, pietistic metaphysics, fatally removed from the understanding and life of ordinary Christians and a world in desperate need of justice and reconciliation. More than sixty years ago, Howard Thurman understood those words, grasped God's intentions, and perceived Jesus' historical reality better than the makers of doctrine when he wrote that God took on flesh as one of the lowly and oppressed in Judea, as vulnerable to the vicious vagaries and pressures of power as any of the poor who had no hope except in God: "If a Roman soldier pushed Jesus into a ditch, he could not appeal to Caesar; he would be just another Jew in the ditch."[2]

For that reason Jesus of Nazareth captured the hearts and minds of the oppressed people of his time and of oppressed people of all times and places ever since. For that reason too, Luke 4:16–18 has always been a central text in liberation theology. Jesus is Yahweh's incarnated justice and, in so being, becomes Yahweh's incarnated reconciliation. This is what we are called to when we are called to be "agents of reconciliation."

In this chapter we return to that text, reaching back to Isaiah in an effort to understand the context of those words there, the better to understand what Jesus was doing when he cited that text as the public proclamation of God's intentions with him in the world and the better to understand the story of Zacchaeus and how he, in following Jesus, in his turn, becomes the incarnation of radical reconciliation.

It is remarkable how consistent, and consistently radical, was Isaiah's concern for justice. This concern dominates the first chapters of his book as it leads up to his calling as prophet so that Isaiah's calling is embedded in Yahweh's concern for the poor and oppressed and Yahweh's anger at the injustices done to them, culminating in Yahweh's desire for justice in Isaiah 61, the text Jesus understands as *his* calling and ministry. In Isaiah 42, we hear for the first time of God's servant who will bring the justice Israel's ruling elites refuse to do:

> Here is my servant, whom I uphold,
>   I have put my spirit upon him;
> he will bring justice to the nations . . .
>   he will faithfully bring forth justice:
> he will not grow faint or be crushed
>   until he has brought justice in the earth. (Is 42:1, 3–4)

This is the passage Matthew, in his own interpretation of the significance of events he has narrated concerning the work of Jesus in the world, applies to Jesus. "And in his name the Gentiles will hope," Matthew adds, emphasizing in his own way, as Luke will in his, the inclusiveness of God's embrace (Mt 12:17–21).

Isaiah 56, that wonderful passage in praise of God's inclusive, reconciling love—"For my house shall be called a house of prayer for *all* peoples" (56:7)—is set within the framework of verse 1: "Maintain justice, and do what is right," and that framework is the context first for the embrace of the stranger and the eunuch, and secondly for the denunciation of Israel's rulers in verses 9–12. Justice means inclusion, and radically so.[3] In Isaiah 58 we find the well-known passage in which Yahweh's demand for justice is linked to the fast:

> Is this not the fast that I choose:
>   to loose the bonds of injustice,
>   to undo the thongs of the yoke,
> to let the oppressed go free,
>   and to break every yoke? (Is 58:6)

Isaiah 59 is one, long, moving litany of the sins of social injustice superbly summed up in the words "The way of peace they do not know" (59:8). Justice is nowhere to be found and salvation (from injustice) is "far from" the oppressed—an expression Isaiah uses several times—but the prophet is certain that Yahweh's "hand is not too short to help," nor is Yahweh's ear "too dull to hear." The oppressed find in Yahweh a helper and an avenger. In Isaiah 59, Yahweh sees the injustice and is angered by it. Yahweh also is "appalled" to see "that there was no one to intervene" (59:15b–16). Then follow the words of Isaiah 61:1–2, which Jesus, in Luke 4, makes his self-proclamation.

"Today This Scripture Is Fulfilled"

In Luke's version of the Isaiah 61 passage, Nicholas Wolterstorff observes, Luke adapted the passage from Isaiah to which Jesus' words refer by dropping a line and adding a line from another related passage, Isaiah 58:6, "to let the oppressed go free."[4] The "good news" is for "the poor" who do not appear in the Isaiah text. So Luke includes both the poor, the captives and the oppressed, and, importantly, the "year of the Lord's favor" is for all, not just for Israel. In Luke's mind (as he has seen in Jesus' life), Isaiah 58 with its radical demands for justice and Isaiah 61 with its all-embracing inclusiveness are linked. And here begins the radicalization of the Isaiah text.

The radical Isaiah context we have discussed above is what Jesus calls to mind as he makes his announcement about his work and his intentions. "The import is unmistakable," Wolterstorff writes, "Jesus identified himself in the synagogue as God's anointed one, the Messiah, whose vocation it is to proclaim to the poor, the blind, the captives, and the oppressed the good news of the inauguration of the 'year of the Lord's favor,' when justice-in-shalom will reign."[5] Jesus is the fulfilment of God's longing for "someone to intervene" by bringing justice into the earth. The radicality of Jesus' words and intentions have not gone unnoticed: the fact that the word for "poor" denotes a class identity; that the "prisoners" are those unjustly imprisoned, including the many political prisoners Rome kept in hell holes and those reduced to debt because of economic exploitation; that the "oppressed" cannot but refer to the people of Judea and Galilee oppressed by the crushing weight of the Roman Empire. These words are Jesus' pronouncement of his divine appointment to bring economic, political, and social justice to his people. "One can scarcely make a more radical political statement than this," writes Obery M. Hendricks. "These sentiments were so politically radical that under Roman law they fully constituted treason against the state—the very crime for which Jesus was executed."[6]

But Jesus takes his radical interpretation one step further. When Jesus had finished reading, writes Luke, he "rolled up the scroll, gave it back to the attendant and sat down" (4:20). Jesus did not comment on the passage, except to say that "today this scripture has been fulfilled in your hearing" (Lk 4:21). The congregants responded with approval and amazement. But then Jesus goes on to state, using stories about the prophets Elijah and Elisha, that God's favor, that is, God's reconciling love and justice, is not restricted to Israel, but includes all humankind: they were "filled with rage." "They got up, drove him out of the town, and led him to the brow of the hill . . . so that they might hurl him off the cliff" (Lk 4:28–29). When Jesus told them the "year of the Lord's favor" was upon them, they were jubilant. But when he made clear that that included everyone, even those they regarded as enemies and outside the circle of God's mercy, *everyone,* rich and poor alike, they were "outraged." This is a radicalization of justice and reconciliation with huge consequences for the practice of reconciliation in our situations.

Nicholas Wolterstorff draws our attention to another, in my view, highly important matter, as we continue to learn just how radical Jesus of Nazareth was. It is an insight crucial to our understanding of justice, of rights and wrongs, and of the bringing of justice to the wronged. "Metaphors common in present-day discourse" he writes, "are those of *the margin* and *the outside.*"[7] Some people are in the center, some on the circumference, and some are on the outside. Biblical writers, however, worked instead with the image of "up and down." Some are at the top of the social hierarchy, some are at the bottom. They are the bottom not because of their own fault; they are there because they are downtrodden.[8] Those at the top "trample the head of the poor into the dust of the earth" (Am 2:7).

"When center and circumference are one's basic metaphors," Wolterstorff argues,

> the undoing of injustice will be described as *including* the outsiders. When *up* and *down* are one's basic metaphors, the undoing of injustice will be described as *lifting up* those at the bottom. The poor do not have to be included in the social order; they have always been there, usually indispensable to its functioning. They have to be lifted up.[9]

This is true for all biblical writers, says Wolterstorff. But the New Testament writers use the up and down metaphor in a way the "Old Testament writers at most hint at: The rectification of injustice requires not only the *lifting up* of the low ones but the *casting down* of the high ones. The coming of justice requires social inversion."[10]

This is crystal clear in the Magnificat, implicit in the lowly shepherd's "good news of great joy" to all people and picked up in Luke's report of the Sermon on the Mount: "Blessed are you who are poor . . . woe to you who are rich." And not only does Jesus say, "Blessed are you who are hungry now," he adds, "Woe to you who are full now" (Lk 6:20–25). Wolterstorff notes,

> The import of this is unmistakable. For the coming of justice it is not sufficient to raise the ones at the bottom, *leaving everything else the same.* Something must also happen to those at the top: they must be cast down. Justice for the downtrodden requires casting down the ones who tread them down. The coming of justice is a painful experience.[11]

This is the radicality Jesus displays throughout the Gospels, and this is the radical reconciliation Christians are called to establish. Today, as in Jesus' day, it still scandalizes and causes outrage, and raises the bar for genuine reconciliation above mere political accommodation and negotiated neighborliness. Jesus, like Isaiah, places the poor and vulnerable in the center of God's concern. But Isaiah does one more thing. Isaiah 61:8 underscores the sinful irony of inversion in our own justice systems:

> For I the LORD love justice,
>   I hate robbery and wrongdoing.

In our justice systems, "robbery" and "wrongdoing" are typically and almost automatically ascribed to the poor, the "lower, criminal classes" who are "responsible" for the crime in society. But in Isaiah 61:8 Yahweh speaks of *the robbery of the poor by the rich and privileged.* The "wrongdoers" and criminals are not the poor but the powerful who deprive the poor of the right to justice and a fulfilled, dignified life.

Without justice, a reconciled, restored community is not possible. And it is for this reason that the story of Zacchaeus the tax collector is such a wonderful illustration of radical reconciliation.

Zacchaeus the Tax Collector

In a previous collaboration with Curtiss DeYoung, I have used the story of Zacchaeus to illustrate a major shortcoming in South Africa's reconciliation process.[12] This story is crucial because South Africa's reconciliation process was not just a matter of pure political accommodation. By adding the word "reconciliation" to the word "truth," our government did an extremely important thing. It chose not simply for a "Truth Commission," run by judges, lawyers, and politicians, but for a "Truth *and* Reconciliation Commission (TRC)." Then, in an even more extraordinary move, they appointed a Christian priest, Archbishop Desmond Tutu, to lead the commission. Many Christians subsequently played a prominent role in the commission's work.[13]

The archbishop then turned the whole process into a decidedly Christian event, opening with Christian prayers, praying not to a universal "God of justice" but specifically "in the name of Jesus," invoking the "Holy Spirit of God" to guide the proceedings. In this name also he called for forgiveness, telling the victims of apartheid crimes that we must forgive because God forgives us and because we ask God's forgiveness every day when we pray the Lord's Prayer.[14] By doing that, the TRC not only Christianized the process, it has set the standards for reconciliation for the victims of apartheid crimes, most of them black Christians who take their faith very seriously indeed, very high. It makes little sense, therefore, to argue that the South African reconciliation process is a purely secular, political process, or that the demand for social justice, restitution, and restoration of human dignity is something we ordinary human beings cannot easily achieve, or that this demand would have made a negotiated settlement impossible, as some have indeed done.[15] Why is the biblical demand for forgiveness, because it is a demand set for the victims, welcomed and praised, if not to say demanded, but the biblical demands for justice, because they are set for the beneficiaries of apartheid, are "setting the standard too high?" If one says "forgiveness," one must also say "justice."[16] If one expects forgiveness from the victim, why can we not expect justice from the perpetrators and beneficiaries? Once the name of Jesus (for forgiveness) is invoked, one cannot then ignore Jesus when one thinks what Jesus is asking (in terms of justice) is "too difficult."

It is for that reason that the story of Zacchaeus is so important. And it is for that reason I believe the TRC should have taken the Gospel as seriously in the proceedings and its consequences as they did at the formal opening of each session. Once they opened the doors to invite Jesus and the Holy Spirit, they should also have called Zacchaeus to testify, so to speak, to hear from him what reconciliation meant for him. That would have given the TRC, and the whole country, a totally different understanding, and expectation of reconciliation.

The story of Zacchaeus (Lk 19:1–9) is well known, and it is not necessary to repeat it here. Important, though, are the following facts to help us in our understanding.[17]

Jericho, in Jesus' time, was a very important city. In its surroundings, Herod the Great, king of the Jews, appointed by the Roman emperor, had built a great winter palace with large, ornamental gardens, near the famous palm and balsam groves that yielded lucrative revenues, not just for the rich who lived there, but also, through taxes, for the Romans as well. Zacchaeus' job and money made him one of the rich, privileged class. In all probability Zacchaeus lived in this fashionable district of Jericho.

Herod the Great was renowned for all the great buildings he had built, not only in his own territory, but also in other territories as well, as far afield as Athens, Greece. In his own realm he had rebuilt Samaria, as well as what was known as Strato's Tower on the Mediterranean coast, equipped it with a splendid harbor and called the city Caesarea, named after the Caesar in Rome. During his rule, other settlements were founded throughout the land. In Jerusalem he built a new palace for himself as well as rebuilding a fortress for the Roman troops stationed in the city near the northeastern wall. The greatest of all his building enterprises, though, was the rebuilding of the temple of Solomon.

We say that "Herod built" all these grand and expensive buildings. But in reality it was built not from his own money but with forced labor and with the taxes he raised from the poor. On top of the usual taxes, these building projects, which conferred much glory and fame on Herod, brought even more misery for the people. The more buildings he built, the more taxes he needed, and the harsher became the methods by which these were extracted.

Taxes were a very heavy burden upon the people of Jesus' time. They were often the cause of great tensions, social upheaval, and political unrest.

The people had to pay taxes to Rome and separate taxes to the governors of their provinces. In Jesus' time Judea was governed by Valerius Gratus (from AD 15–26) and then Pontius Pilate (from AD 26–36). On top of these taxes there were the large amounts the Jewish people had to pay in temple taxes, and these were paid to the priestly hierarchy in Jerusalem. Then there were tithes and offerings the people had to make whenever they visited the temple—these were required to support the priests. There were twelve different classes of tithes and offerings required from the people. Such taxes could go up to 40 percent of a peasant's income.

Tax collectors worked under contract on behalf of the Romans, and their work included the collection of various types of direct and indirect taxes and tributes. Often they would have subcontractors. Tax collectors were closely related to, and supported and protected by, the Roman authorities. The system was notoriously open to abuse and corruption; malpractice and extortion were rife. Sometimes, but very rarely, extreme cases of the grossest excesses were reported and sometimes dealt with, but generally tax collectors were left to do what they wanted, as long as the authorities received their share of what was collected.

In this way, tax collectors rightly acquired a sordid reputation. The people hated and despised them, and saw them as instruments of oppression and collaborators of the oppressive, occupying regime. Jesus referred to them as typical of a selfish and extortionate nature (Mt 5:46). Mostly the main contractors were Roman citizens from elsewhere with native subcontractors, but often contracts were given to locals. It was helpful, for they knew the local conditions and the local people, and how to avoid being deceived by them, making sure that tax collection was done as efficiently as possible. Zacchaeus seems to have been such a native contractor, and he more than likely had collectors under him. For the strict Jew, the attitude of hatred was aggravated by the religious consideration that tax collectors were "unclean" because of their continual contact with Gentiles, and their need to work on the Sabbath. That is why the rabbis taught that observant Jews should not eat with such people and why they spoke of "tax collectors and sinners" in one breath.[18]

In Jesus' time, the elite, although comprising only 2 percent of the population, controlled most of the wealth (up to 65 percent), its produce, and its cultivators—the peasantry—whose labor created the produce. This was done by means of imposed taxes, tributes, and rents. The Roman tribute consisted of the *tributum soli* (land tax), and the *tributum capitas* (poll tax). To this annual tribute—which obviously came from the peasantry—was added a second level of tribute and taxes levied by Herod Antipas to furnish his lavish lifestyle and pay for his extravagant building projects.[19] Zacchaeus, as collector, was crucial to the smooth working of this system of exploitation and domination.

Because the people had no choice, they had to pay whatever was charged by such corrupt collectors. They were vulnerable precisely because they were poor and powerless. Whatever his agents collected, Zacchaeus would get his percentage, on top of what the Romans paid him. As a result, he became extremely rich. Meanwhile the poor became increasingly impoverished. This is one of the reasons why Jesus was so radical about wealth and poverty. Great wealth and great oppression and exploitation always go together.

It is understandable that the people hated the tax collectors. They were the symbol of their oppression they met every day. They were the face of the oppressor in Rome or of the governor in Jerusalem. If they were Jews, and they worked for Rome, the betrayal was enormous.

In the Gospels, Zacchaeus has, in many ways, come to epitomize the image of the "tax collector and sinner." No wonder he could not find a place among the crowds who waited for Jesus that day. It was not just because he was a man of small stature. The people knew him. He knew he would not be welcomed by them. Why would anyone give up their place in the crowd, and their chance to see Jesus, for someone like him? Amongst the crowd, the hostility would have been palpable and perhaps physical. That tree was the safest spot for him. It is also a symbol of his complete isolation. Amongst the poor and oppressed, those extorted by men like Zacchaeus every day of their lives, but expectant and hopeful that day, Zacchaeus would not have been made to feel welcome.

The Day Salvation Comes

Zacchaeus went anyway, apparently willing to face whatever might happen. That is remarkable enough. But it becomes even more so. Jesus stopped underneath that tree and looked up. Zacchaeus knew that his day of salvation had come. But what did that salvation mean?

Zacchaeus understood that he was alienated from God *and* from his neighbors. Through his life of exploitation and self-enrichment, he had robbed the poor not only of their money, but also of their dignity. He had broken the bonds of solidarity and had exploited their fear of the Roman occupier by his extortion. He knew they had no choice but to come through those gates where he lay in wait. He knew that even if he charged them double, there was no appeal possible, nothing they could do to stop him. He could do what he wanted: they were helpless and their helplessness was his power. Zacchaeus knew he needed to be reconciled with God and with the people. That is why it was so important that he was willing to face the people that day—those he had robbed and exploited.

So, without waiting for Jesus to tell him what to do, he came forward and offered: "Look half of my possessions, Lord, I will give to the poor" (Lk 19:8). He gives half of his wealth, not on a percentage basis, over a period of time; nor does he pledge that he will do so come next harvest time but here and now. Then he added, "And if I have defrauded anyone of anything, I will pay back four times as much" (Lk 19:8), presumably out of the other half. That is not "generosity," and certainly it is not charity; it is Zacchaeus' desire to do justice. Some argue that Zacchaeus did that because, as a very rich man, he would not miss it. But even if one were rich, giving away half of one's wealth and repaying people four times what one has robbed of them, still amounts to a great deal of money. There was a whole city that needed to be compensated for what Zacchaeus had done over many years. One has to wonder what Zacchaeus had left after these extraordinary acts.

But it is more than just the money. It is also the spirit in which Zacchaeus made his offer that makes it different, and radical. I mean this: in reality Zacchaeus was offering to give up his status as one of the richest men in Jericho in order to do restitution, to make right what he has done wrong, in order to restore his relationship with his neighbors. Notice also that he does not say that he will order his subcontractors to make a contribution, since they all had benefited from their corruption: he takes responsibility himself for the wrongs he had done and for the justice he must do to undo those wrongs.

Immediately here Zacchaeus teaches us some extremely valuable lessons, which Christians will do well to learn and embrace if we want to make our reconciliation genuine, workable, and sustainable. He teaches us what true radical reconciliation is. I have discovered ten such lessons.

First, reconciliation cannot be shallow: it is not covering up the evil or simply papering over the cracks. Zacchaeus *acknowledges* what he has done wrong: I stole, I exploited, I cheated, I betrayed. Zacchaeus did not try to make excuses for himself, blaming "the system" against which he was help-less. He did not try and defend himself by arguing that he simply had to make a living, that this was merely his job, or that he had a family to look after. He knew that he unjustly benefited from oppression and suffering. That is self-justification, and he knows that self-justification always stands in the way of true reconciliation: it mocks the wronged, nullifies repen-tance, and trivializes forgiveness.

Second, he knows reconciliation is not possible without remorse. But for him, remorse is not a lot of words, wringing his hands and saying "sorry" just to get it over and done with as quickly as possible. Remorse means knowing that I have done wrong; that through my actions *someone* was wronged, acknowledging that my victim has a right to righteous anger. My victim also has a right to restitution—it has nothing to do with my magnanimity, it is all about justice. It is acknowledging my victim's pain as a result of what I have done, and making it right with acts of justice: that is what saying "I'm sorry" means. Understanding fully that forgiveness is not his right nor his reward, but an invaluable gift, Zacchaeus does not demand nor expect it. He does justice in fragile hope and faith, not in the certitude of power. He who wielded such power over others now renders himself powerless and vulnerable before the ones he had wronged: God and the poor.

Third, Zacchaeus knows that reconciliation is not cheap, not just in a spiritual sense but literally. "Half my possessions, Lord, I give to the poor," and "I will pay back four times all that I have stolen" (Lk 19:8). Zacchaeus' theft from the poor was not spiritual; it was real and tangible. His wealth was undeserved as the impoverishment of the poor was undeserved, and he knows that. That is restitution. Without restitution, reconciliation is not possible. Zacchaeus does not just give away "half" of his possessions—he repays "four times as much." That is absolutely unheard of.

But in my view, that is only part of what makes his restitution so radi-cal, and it becomes clear in our *fourth* lesson. Zacchaeus did that because he understood that there can be no reconciliation without equality. All along, his wealth and his connections to Rome and the powerful Jerusalem elite with their hierarchical, exclusionary systems of patronage had placed him above his people. He had participated in, and benefited from, a political, economic, and social system that created and maintained profound inequalities in his society. Roman imperial society was unthinkable without the hierarchies built on class, power, and privilege, and the arrogance and entitlement that went with it. Jesus repeatedly condemned domination in all its forms, and he stood up against it not as a minor reformer, writes Walter Wink, but as an "egalitarian prophet who repudiates the very premises on which domination is based: the right of some to lord it over others by means of power."[20]

That is why Jesus told his followers, "Let it not be so among you!" Paul understood that very well. When he asked the church in Corinth to collect money for the poor Christians in Jerusalem, he was explicit: they must do it not out of arrogance, false generosity, or for charity, but for the sake of equality (2 Cor 8:13ff). And here Paul bases his call for equality on what we might call "the manna principle." "The one who had much did not have too much, and the one who had little did not have too little" (2 Cor 8:15; see also Ex 16: 17–18). Zacchaeus gives away his wealth. He is no longer a member of the exclusive club of the very rich, but he is now able to join Jesus' inclusive community of equals.

But *fifthly*, Zacchaeus teaches us that reconciliation is not just about restoring our broken relationship with God. It is also about restoring our broken relationships with the community, with the other. In the story the people did not consider that broken relationship restored when Zacchaeus was talking to Jesus alone, and Jesus announced his acceptance of Zacchaeus by going to his house. They grumbled, still distancing themselves from him. But the Gospel story reads that "Zacchaeus stood there" and made his intentions clear; that he was not trying to get away with cheap grace (Lk 19:8). He was willing to show his remorse and conversion by doing justice.

Zacchaeus knew, and this is the *sixth* lesson he teaches us, that he had sinned against God *and* against his neighbors and that he had to make public recompense. A cozy chat with Jesus in the privacy of his home would not do. Zacchaeus does not try to hide behind the "this is between me and my God" cop-out. His remorse is no echo of David's, so completely wrapped up in his personal relationship with God that he gives no thought to the wrong against Bathsheba and Uriah and the pain he caused them: "Against you, you alone, have I sinned" (Ps 51:4). Or perhaps David believed that as king he might sin against God but never against an underling. That belief is but one consequence of the seduction of power: it gives equal room to piety and callousness. Zacchaeus does not think that way any longer. His sins of extortion and robbery were public sins against the poor and vulnerable, and therefore against God.

The rich rewards from his life of extortion for him and his family were public rewards: favor with the Romans, connections with the elite and enjoyment of the patronage system, social and political privilege, opulence and comfort, and a worry-free life. The suffering of his victims was a public suffering. His remorse had to be public as well, and so should be the restoration of his broken relationship with his community. This requires a sense of shame at the wrong done to others, and he recognized it as *wrong*. Reconciliation is not possible without that sense of shame. However, and this Zacchaeus knew as well, the sense of shame turns into an internal pit of paralyzing self-abuse and self-pity if it is not turned into redemptive deeds of justice and restitution. Hence, Zacchaeus' public announcement of restitution and restoration.

Seventh, we learn that when reconciliation means uncovering the sin, showing remorse, making restitution, and restoring relationships with deeds of compassionate justice, then, and only then, is reconciliation complete, right, sustainable, and radical, because it becomes transformational. Then reconciliation has integrity, because it restores human integrity. That is its salvific power. Political reconciliation's concern is that we must come to a point where we do not kill each other.[21] And indeed we do well if we do not kill one another, if we tolerate each other as political adversaries, no longer treating each other as deadly enemies who have to be eliminated. That is no small thing. But biblical, radical reconciliation wants to bring us to the point where we learn to live, not just *with* the other—because we have no choice—but *for* the other—because that *is* our choice—where the peace among us is not just the absence of violence but the active presence of justice. When reconciliation is all of these, it is salvation: being saved from the lust for power, the lure of greed, the arrogance of self-aggrandizement, and the hard-heartedness of self-gratification. Zacchaeus was also saved, liberated, from that other thing that eats away at our soul and makes reconciliation so hard, namely, the need for the justification of the past. Jesus did not count his past trespasses against him, and by going to his house and eating with him, Jesus is asking the community to do the same.

Some would say "God saved his soul," and that is right, because his soul was addicted to all those things: the wealth, the status, the power, and the arrogance that comes with it. These things were his whole life, but they no longer held Zacchaeus captive. "Today," Jesus says, "salvation has come to this house" (Lk 19:9). Salvation came to Zacchaeus *on that day*. Jesus made no promises about Zacchaeus being repaid in the afterlife, because that would have meant that all those people he had robbed, cheated, and exploited would have had to wait for their reward "in heaven." Jesus does not play at reconciliation. Here there is no eschatological procrastination. Zacchaeus made things right *here and now*, and he received salvation *on that day*. The building of trust with the community, the political accomodationists will argue, no doubt takes longer, and that is true. But the true foundation for that trust is the salvation that comes as soon as one embraces it.

Eighth, when genuine reconciliation takes place, it brings more than just individual salvation. It brings salvation for Zacchaeus *and his house*. There is wholeness to his restoration. Zacchaeus and his whole house had benefited from his life of exploitation. His whole house had been cursed by the people who saw their opulent lifestyles built upon the impoverishment of the peasants. But through genuine reconciliation, that whole generation was restored to wholeness and community with others and with God. For the children of Zacchaeus, the strongest memory will no longer be the broken relationships with the community or the sins of their father (as the crowd even on that day grumbled about). Nor will it be the history of exploitation their father had been part of and had benefited from. Since he had given those benefits away and restored others through restitution, they too, are restored to full humanity and acceptance. Instead, their strongest memory will be of that day when "salvation came to that house." They are released from the generational curse of guilt and shame that comes with exploitative, systemic relationships.

Ninth, by doing this, Zacchaeus switched sides. I do not think that after such a public display of shame and such a public conversion it was possible for him to go back and continue to do what he did all his life: tax collecting, robbing, cheating, exploiting, living the life of the idle rich so vividly described by Isaiah. His confrontation with Jesus was also a confrontation with his own life and with the choices he had made. From that moment on, nothing could be the same for him again. Importantly also, this conversion meant that Zacchaeus could no longer work for the Romans: his political allegiances changed now that his spiritual allegiance has changed.

His choice for Jesus was a choice for justice, and his choice for justice was a choice for the poor. Zacchaeus could now only stand where God stands: with the wronged and the destitute and against the wealthy, the powerful, and the privileged.[22] Instead of sharing the privileges of the wealthy, he would now share the pain of the oppressed. He became, like Jesus, just another Jew in the ditch. By choice. For the first time perhaps, Zacchaeus has a real sense of belonging.

Tenth, and finally, all this time Zacchaeus was known as "the tax collector," a man who had estranged himself from his own people, a traitor who had sold his soul to Rome for money. He ingratiated himself with the Romans, the occupying force of colonialist oppression, but found no place amongst his own people. He lived in an opulent house, amongst the privileged and powerful of Jericho, but when he wanted to see Jesus, he had to climb in a tree, for fear of being shunned by his own people. Beholden to Rome, selling out to the powerful, despised by those same powerful occupiers precisely because he served them in the oppression of his own, kow-towing to the ruling elites in Jerusalem who in all probability looked down on him because rich as he was, he could never be one of them; but at the same time, he trampled on the poor and got fat and rich from their oppression. What kind of man was he really? Where did he belong? How did he see himself, if he dared to look beyond his ill-gotten wealth? Did he have an identity of his own?

I see Zacchaeus, and I imagine him to be like so many we had known throughout our long struggle: those who sold out to apartheid for money, position, and the pitiful privileges apartheid afforded its minions in the black communities. They sided with the oppressor, robbed their own people, exchanged information on activists for money, and saw from within dark-windowed police vehicles how the security police came in the dead of night and took away those whom they had fingered and put on "the list," knowing of the imprisonment, the torture, the pain, the killing that would follow. They would sit there, listening to their white bosses' disdainful talk of black people, and they would try to outdo the white boss in the derisive laughter, desperately trying to forget that they were laughing at themselves, joking away their dignity. And when they got their reward, what did they feel? Were they angrier at themselves than at those who made them who they were? And as we have seen and heard to our absolute and numbing horror, when they had to grin and say, "yes, Boss, thank you Boss" to prove their trustworthiness, they took their anger out on their own people—more powerless than they.[23]

Was Zacchaeus like that, I wonder? Comforting himself with his money while losing his soul? Apparently Zacchaeus was exactly like that, writes Herman Waetjen: "The tax collectors . . . who work as retainers for the rich and the powerful by preying upon the poor and the weak, are trapped in a vertical relationship of symbolic dependency. They are dispossessors, but they are also dispossessed; oppressors, but they are also oppressed. Exploited by those above them, despised by those below them, they are reduced to a life of inhumanness by their daily practice of extortion and its resulting experiences of contempt and self-hatred."[24]

But on that day, as Zacchaeus discovered the meaning of true reconciliation, Jesus, in offering him salvation, also offered him a new identity, his *true* identity. From now on, he would not be called Zacchaeus, "the tax collector." He would be called Zacchaeus, "the son of Abraham" (Lk 19:9). The rabbis had declared him "unclean," unfit to be a son of Abraham. Jesus cleanses and renames him. He is restored, made whole. The people had written him off, but Jesus said he was only lost. Now he was found and claimed by God.

Jesus responds to Zacchaeus' acts of justice with an act of justice of his own. Zacchaeus was shunned by his people. They would not eat with him, because sharing a meal with someone was identifying with them, affirming them as part of oneself, as part of the community. They could not bring themselves to do that with this unclean sinner. Now Jesus, knowing that Zacchaeus would not dare invite him, invites himself. In so doing, Jesus overrules the prejudices created by law and custom, takes away the stigma that has clung to Zacchaeus and his family. In breaking bread with him Jesus affirms his humanity, his inclusion. Calling him a "son of Abraham" was huge but not enough for Jesus. Jesus seals that with the intimate act of breaking bread with this despised, hated tool of Rome. Jesus teaches the people that radical reconciliation means the solidarity of unconditional love; it means inclusion, affirmation, consecration.

One last point: The name Zacchaeus actually means "the innocent one." How the people must have laughed and joked with that name. But it was a bitter joke—for the people as well as for Zacchaeus. That crook, that traitor, that exploiter of our fear and helplessness, that manipulator of our powerlessness; that robber of our dignity and our rest; *him—the innocent one?* Now the jokes are over. The laughter has stopped, because Jesus stopped it. Zacchaeus has a new name; he is a new creation; he is a son of Abraham. He has been rescued from lost-ness, given a new identity, a renewed existence within the community that now makes it possible for him to live with and for others. That is what radical reconciliation does.

Part III

Beloved Communities Restored

Chapter 5

Reconciliation in Diverse Congregations
Restoring the Beloved Community

Curtiss Paul DeYoung

A headline on the cover of *Time Magazine* at the beginning of the decade read, "How Megachurches are Helping Bridge America's Racial Divide."[1] Among congregations with an attendance of over one thousand people in the United States, currently 25 percent are considered multiracial.[2] A definition developed by sociologists studying congregations and race is that a multiracial congregation is one where no single racial or cultural group is more than 80 percent of the membership. In other words, at least 20 percent of the members are not part of the dominant group. Only 7.5 percent of congregations in the United States meet this minimal definition of a diverse congregation, while 25 percent of megachurches qualify.[3] Many of these multiracial megachurches originated as predominately or exclusively white congregations. The January 2010 *Time Magazine* article featured the story of how the very white Willow Creek Community Church with nearly 25,000 members in a Chicago suburb transitioned to be at least 20 percent persons of color—joining the ranks of congregations defined as multiracial. The article also noted that the biggest congregation in the United States at nearly 45,000 members was the Lakewood Church in Houston, Texas. While this congregation has always had white senior pastors—the late John Osteen and his son Joel Osteen—it is a faith community where whites are now in the minority.

In 2003 I was an author along with three sociologists—Michael Emerson, George Yancey, and Karen Chai Kim—of *United by Faith: The Multiracial Congregation as an Answer to the Problem of Race*. When we wrote the book, we did not foresee that evangelical megachurches would be at the vanguard of a growing movement of multiracial congregations in the United States. Our goal was to write a book that would become foundational for the discussion about, and the development of, multiracial and multicultural congregations in the United States. We made a strong biblical case combined with a wide array of sociological insights arguing that "Christian congregations, when possible, should be multiracial."[4] The book has served as a foundational volume for many writing on the subject and for numerous pastors and seminary students developing diverse congregations. The fact that large congregations in the suburbs originally populated by whites would become increasingly more diverse in their membership was an unexpected development.

Many of these congregations, like Willow Creek Community Church, found compelling the arguments in *United by Faith* that the Bible called for churches, when possible, to be multiracial.[5] In the United States, where racism and racial segregation have been such dominant features of the country's history, it seems reasonable to celebrate any growth of racial diversity in local congregations. One could argue that all forward progress toward greater diversity is a positive response to the haunting critique of the late Martin Luther King Jr. that the eleven o'clock hour on Sunday morning is the most segregated hour of the week.[6] Yet the rapid growth of diversity in evangelical megachurches caused me to consider a question that must be asked of all multiracial and multicultural congregations: Do racially diverse congregations automatically experience reconciliation, or could they simply become demographically diverse but not reconciled? Sociologist Richard N. Pitt observes that diverse congregations are often "more multicultural in makeup than multicultural in behavior."[7]

Sociologist Korie Edwards has provided a helpful critique in her book *The Elusive Dream: The Power of Race in Interracial Churches.* She writes, "I visited interracial churches of various racial compositions to gain initial insight into what made these organizations capable of encouraging people of different races to voluntarily worship together. . . . Nearly all of the churches, regardless of their specific racial compositions, reminded me of the predominantly white churches I had visited. . . . The diversity did not seem to affect the core culture and practices of the religious organizations."[8] So congregations can be diverse culturally and racially without departing from the dominant white cultural values and practices of mainstream United States that inform their congregational life. This occurs because, as Edwards' research indicates, "Interracial churches tend to cater to the predilections of whites. The worship styles and practices mainly suit the desires of whites. Most interracial churches are also led by whites." She continues, "Where an African American heads the church, proficiency in and support of white religious culture is vital."[9] Korie Edwards concludes that many multicultural and multiracial congregations are guided by a sensibility that reflects the white dominant culture of the United States. Is this problematic? In order to answer this question we need to consider how first-century congregations in the New Testament implemented reconciliation in the formation of diverse congregations.

Reconciliation in First-Century Biblical Congregations

In *United by Faith* we noted that most first-century congregations described in the New Testament were multicultural—a diverse mix of Jews and folks from other cultural backgrounds (Gentiles). We outlined strategies used by first-century followers of Jesus to develop congregations that mirrored his radically inclusive reconciliation ministry and call for "a house of prayer for all the nations" (Mk 11:17). Paul often wrote that he and his co-workers went first to the Jews and then to the Gentiles when creating multicultural worshipping congregations. We concluded our section on congregations in the first century by declaring, "Together these congregations produced a movement for social unity across the great divide of culture, tradition, class, and race. Ultimately, the unity of the first-century church was the result of the miracle of reconciliation—a conversion from their ethnocentrism to the intention, practice, and vision of Jesus."[10]

Yet when one remembers that these congregations were formed in the context of the Roman Empire, it becomes clear that there was more occurring than a conversion from ethnocentricism. These congregations were a mix of colonized persons and those who were colonizers (or beneficiaries of colonization). When Jews saw Roman soldiers and citizens in their midst, they remembered their oppression. When Jews sat next to Gentiles who benefited from Roman rule, they were painfully aware of their low social status. Every time these assemblies spoke of Jesus crucified, they were reminded of the Roman state-sponsored terrorism used to kill Jesus and intimidate Jewish people. Given the brutality and bigotry experienced by

Jews as subjects of the Roman Empire, it is difficult to believe that Romans (and others benefiting from their position in the empire) would be invited into Jewish faith communities. But this is what happened.

In the midst of Roman colonial realities, the church in Antioch was developed by Jews, members of an oppressed ethnic minority, who welcomed dominant culture Greeks (and likely Romans as well) into their fellowship under the leadership of Jews (Acts 11:19–26, 13:1). Paul and his co-workers used a similar strategy to establish congregations by going first into Jewish communities oppressed and colonized by the Roman Empire. After establishing faith communities among the marginalized, they invited in those from contexts of privilege and power. The strategy of Paul and his associates was to first develop a community of Jews who were ethnic minority oppressed subjects of the empire and had embraced faith in Jesus Christ. Once a core community was established, they invited Romans and Greeks from the dominant culture to join. The primary biblical model of congregations was one where members of an oppressed minority community welcomed people from the privileged dominant culture into the local church.[11]

These early followers of a crucified and resurrected Jesus went first into oppressed Jewish communities preaching the healing word of reconciliation. The embryonic congregations they established were healing laboratories for oppressed and colonized Jews. Communities of healing were created in the midst of an oppressive society to counter the harmful effects of colonialism. This ministry of reconciliation healed bruised and crushed psyches where oppression had been internalized and identities had been demeaned and diminished. The reality of dehumanization was reversed through a process of reconciliation or, as Paulo Freire called it, humanization.[12] Reconciliation through a crucified and resurrected Jesus Christ restored damaged, enslaved, and colonized identities to their original design as human identities created in the image of God.

What makes the first-century church truly amazing is what happened next. After establishing a healing process for fellow members of the oppressed Jewish community, these early Jewish followers of Jesus then invited in persons of power and privilege to be reconciled. Biblical scholar Ched Myers writes, "Given the fact that Jews were a hard-pressed minority culture within the Roman empire, this was a remarkable strategy of inclusion. As an educated Jew trained in Torah, Paul was empathetic with his people's struggle to retain their identity and group cohesion, particularly given the fragmentation resulting from the Mediterranean diaspora." The first-century church was "a minority community (trying) to forge liberation both for itself *and* for the oppressor majority."[13] Paulo Freire wrote, "The great humanistic and historical task of the oppressed (is) to liberate themselves and their oppressors as well. The oppressors, who oppress, exploit, and rape by virtue of their power, cannot find in this power the strength to liberate either the oppressed or themselves."[14] Jews who were oppressed ministered to Romans, who were members of the oppressing group, hoping for liberation and reconciliation.

As Romans and Greeks embraced the reconciliation process, they replaced their loyalty to the empire with an "in Christ" consciousness. Caesar was no longer their Savior. Jesus was their Redeemer. Myers notes, "Gentile Christians (had) to defect from their own entitlements and loyalties."[15] They rejected the privileges that go with power and position and joined with those who were colonized. As our biblical definition of reconciliation (from chapter 1) implies, persons with much power and privilege *exchanged places* with persons of little privilege and power. Theologian Willie Jennings emphasizes this exchange of places as an embrace or intimacy across and via culture. He reminds us that after Peter's encounter with the Roman soldier Cornelius, Peter was invited by the Roman to stay for several days at his home (Acts 10:48). Jennings declares, "If a centurion and his household could be drawn into a new circle of belonging, then its implications for challenging the claims of the Roman state were revolutionary."[16] This was a clear demonstration of the healing power of reconciliation. A Roman soldier invited a Jew to stay in his home—a Jew whom he was under orders to keep oppressed. And Peter accepted the invitation. Cornelius was a changed person. When he returned to his work as a soldier, he could no longer allow for the mistreatment of Jews. In fact, the more he communed with people who were oppressed, the more he was internally required by the Spirit of God to challenge the claims of the Roman state, even the very legitimacy of the Roman Empire.

The next step came when Romans and Greeks entered the homes of Jews as guests and as equals—which is what happened when small Jewish home-based congregations invited Gentiles into their fellowship. In chapter 1, we discussed Albert Memmi's notion that in order for a colonizer to depart from oppressor status he or she must be adopted by the colonized.

In essence this is what was happening as Romans and Greeks entered the homes of Jews for worship and fellowship as sisters and brothers. As Romans and Greeks reconciled (exchanged places) with Jews who were oppressed, privileged perspectives and positions were discarded and replaced with true familial bonds. Jennings warns that, "If the struggle toward cultural intimacy was not faced by the church as inherent to the gospel itself . . . then over time the only other option was the emergence of a Christian segregationalist mentality."[17] Sadly, much of history post the first-century church proves this true. This remains the reality in the United States, where the church is the most segregated institution in society.

Biblical scholar Tat-siong Benny Liew furthers our understanding of what reconciliation meant to privileged folks in first-century Pauline congregations. Regarding the church in Corinth he writes, "According to most Corinthians scholars, the population of Corinth was mostly made up of Greeks and perhaps some Romans. The Corinthians might not have originated from noble or aristocratic families, but in terms of race/ethnicity, they still belonged to the people who succeeded each other in colonizing the Jews of Paul's time."[18] This demographic reality created an unusual social context for the few Jews in the Corinthian congregation and for the Jewish founder, the apostle Paul. Liew notes, "The one who founded, fathered, and now hopes to counsel the mainly Gentile Corinthian church happens to be a Jewish 'no-body' (that is, one who is insignificant, invisible, and hence disembodied because his racial/ethnic or bodily inscriptions have been have been made stereotypical by the dominant culture)."[19] Liew's further analysis offers insight, "Because of Paul's ministry, his Corinthian converts experienced a status inversion in joining a religious minority" and they experienced the social affect of submission to a leader with a "diasporic Jewish body within the imperial ideology of the Roman Empire."[20]

Throughout Acts and the letters of Paul, it is evident that a status inversion occurred in the first-century church as a result of the centrality of reconciliation between Gentiles and Jews. When Romans and Greeks joined congregations, they became identified with a socially stigmatized people. They were adopted by marginalized people—becoming family with Jews who were oppressed by Rome. They were worshipping with people stereotyped as "unworthy"[21] as well as expressing faith in Jesus of Nazareth who was crucified as an enemy of the state. This had life-altering repercussions for their lifestyle and social status in the Roman Empire.

The fact that the leaders in the first generation of the Christian church were Jews was perhaps even more disruptive for the social status of Gentile Christians. Empire privileges ceased to be acknowledged in the church. In society Jews were socially beneath Greeks and Romans. In the church Jews were in leadership. This was a reversal of social expectations, a status inversion. I believe the purpose of the reversal was healing and redemptive. A marginalized community in the Roman Empire, like Jews, had to understand the ways of the dominant group in order to survive. People of privilege had no felt need to understand minority or oppressed groups. For Gentiles to fully reconcile with Jews, they had to learn firsthand the effects of marginalization from those who understood it best. We see this in Paul's commitment to mentoring Gentiles in preparation for leadership. Paul mentored Titus, Luke, Epaphras, and many other Greeks for leadership. They were mentored side by side with Jews, thereby gaining the same training under the same circumstances as others oppressed by Rome. In other words, Gentiles were mentored for leadership as though they were Jews. The second generation of leaders did include Gentiles who had been mentored by Jewish leaders.

In Palestine the first-century church was under Roman occupation. So the mother church of Christianity in Jerusalem had very limited meaningful contact with persons outside of the Jewish community. Therefore, Jews in Jerusalem had few opportunities to reconcile with Gentiles. It is interesting to note that the Jerusalem congregation, which was comprised of Jews, also practiced a similar reconciliation model. The Jerusalem church was founded and led by Galilean Jews who were lower status in society. They welcomed Jews of higher status from Jerusalem and the Diaspora into membership and under the leadership of Galilean Jews (Acts 2: 5–6). The Galilean Jews were followers of Jesus during his three years of active ministry of reconciliation. After Jesus' crucifixion and resurrection, they established a congregation in Jerusalem. On the day of Pentecost many Jews who had relocated to Jerusalem from throughout the Roman Empire entered the church (Acts 2:5, 9–11, 41). Sometime later, members of the Jewish priesthood joined the Galilean-led Jerusalem church (Acts 6:7). The Jerusalem church was organized so that Galilean Jews who were marginalized were in positions of leadership over Jews of higher status. In addition to a reconciliation process between colonizers and the colonized (with its ethnic dimensions), the early church also applied a reconciliation process to class status.

The reconciliation that was unleashed through Jesus' ministry, crucifixion, and resurrection also addressed gender realities. New Testament scholar Richard B. Hays notes, "The roster of significant female characters in Luke-Acts is far longer than that of any other New Testament writing. This is not because Luke was consciously a feminist; the term is an anachronism when applied to a first-century writer. Rather, it is because the Spirit's eschatological power of reversal was at work in the tradition that Luke knew, raising women to a status they had not formerly enjoyed."[22] The early church placed women into positions of leadership challenging sexism and further pressing the meaning of reconciliation. Many of these women leaders were doubly oppressed as colonized subjects and as women. Church historian Mimi Haddad writes, "Paul exalted the leadership of women . . . throughout his epistles. He commends female deacons (Roman 16:1), prophets (1 Corinthians 11:4–5; 14:31; Acts 2:17–18; 21; 9), house church leaders (Acts 16:13–15, 40; Romans 16:3–5), a female apostle (Romans 16:7), teachers of the gospel (Acts 18:26), evangelists (Philippians 4:3; Romans 16:3), and those did the very heaviest of gospel labor (Romans 16:12)."[23] Women were in leadership in the same ways as men. For first-century men, this was a status inversion. Hays writes, "Women in these communities enjoyed a greater measure of freedom and dignity than they could have experienced in Greco-Roman society outside the Christian fellowship." They benefited from "the relatively egalitarian social structure of the Pauline communities."[24]

Relationships between women and men, colonized and colonizer, and marginalized and privileged were being reconciled through the Spirit's power of reversal. Yet the healing process of reconciliation was often challenging and disruptive. As Gentiles entered Jewish faith communities, circumcision and table fellowship had to be negotiated. Questions related to cultural perspectives and practices had to be answered. What was required of Romans and Greeks to be fully adopted into the community? As more and more Gentiles came into local congregations becoming a majority in many places (as in Corinth), how much culture did Jewish Christians need to retain in communal life to ensure they were not assimilated into the dominant culture?[25] As congregations reconciled people from various socioeconomic realities, class issues were addressed in church life (1 Cor 11:17–22; Jas 2:1–9). Congregations needed to courageously apply a reconciliation process in a highly sexist society where religious institutions also perpetuated patriarchy.

Reconciliation reversed the hierarchies of society implementing the words of Jesus, "The last will be first, and the first will be last" (Mt 20:16). Persons and communities marginalized in society found themselves at the center of life in these congregations. The revolutionary "one new humanity" Paul theologized about in Ephesians 2 was emerging in new faith communities that engaged "the double task of *deconstructing* the 'divided house' and *reconstructing* it on a foundation of race, class, and gender equality."[26] First-century followers of Jesus were "building an international anti-imperial movement of an alternative society based in local communities."[27] First-century congregations established new revolutionary reconciliation structures for colonized and colonizers, women and men, marginalized and privileged, to rediscover their true identity in Christ and live into the full realization of what it meant to be one new humanity.

Reconciliation in Twenty-First Century Congregations

First-century congregations embraced a reconciliation that was revolutionary. The status quo was replaced by a qualitatively different reality. So are the portrayals of first-century congregations in Acts and Paul's letters a case of being descriptive or proscriptive? I contend it is both! Twenty centuries later what do first-century congregations teach the twenty-first century church about reconciliation? The church in the United States has been constructed on a very different model than the first-century church. Throughout its history, the church in the United States has produced segregated congregations (and denominations) defined by race and ethnicity.[28] Rather than transforming society through a process of reconciliation, congregations have overwhelmingly conformed to a racialized, patriarchal, and class-based society. As theologian Brian Bantum writes, "We are born into a world of race even while we are baptized into Christ."[29] For most of U.S. history the world of race has trumped our baptism in Christ. Theologian Soong-Chan Rah goes so far as to speak of "the white captivity of the church." He writes that "white culture has dominated, shaped and captured Christianity in the United States. . . . The formation of a theology based upon a Western, white cultural captivity yields a theology focused on furthering and affirming the existing power paradigm."[30] White cultural captivity is counter to and opposite of the focus of the first-century church, which was deconstructing the existing power paradigm of the Roman Empire, liberating both the marginalized and the privileged, and reconciling them into a new community. The first-century church might not recognize much of what we call church in the twenty-first century.

The church in the United States has too often been formed using models emerging from contexts of privilege. Rather than perspectives shaped by those at the margins of society, the church reflects a white, male, middle-class, able-bodied, heterosexual, exclusive viewpoint. Too many congregations are fashioned on a model of privilege, exclusion, and prosperity. Given the divide imposed by a racialized church, we also find African American congregations, ethnic immigrant congregations (immigrants and refugees from Asia, Latin America, Africa, etc.), and a small number of Native American congregations. In many cases these congregations exhibit the first phase of the reconciliation process described above—they are communities of healing for people who are oppressed and marginalized. Unfortunately few whites have ventured into these faith communities.

With the onset of multiracial and multicultural congregations, it would seem that they would naturally adhere to the first-century biblical model of reconciling marginalized persons with those more privileged. Yet even multicultural congregations committed to reconciliation often find their vision and ministry shaped by a dominant culture perspective. Korie Edwards reminds us, "Interracial churches are not immune to white privilege and the normativity of white culture and beliefs. . . . I propose that interracial churches work, that is remain racially integrated, to the extent that they are *first* comfortable places for whites to attend."[31] This is the complete opposite of first-century church expectations, which were focused on making their congregations *first* comfortable places for members of ethnic minority and oppressed communities. Today white congregations invite persons of color into privilege rather than asking whites to discard racial privileges and join with persons of color. Reconciliation in multicultural congregations is often defined by external realities such as suburban locations, white origins, and society's racialization rather than by biblical witness.

Biblical congregations invited colonizers and privileged persons to join churches comprised of folks from oppressed communities who were engaging in a process of healing and reconciliation. This part of the biblical model of congregations seems to have been missed in most of the writings and practices of the present day multicultural congregation movement. White congregations and white leaders invite people of color to join in a process that often is more about assimilation than reconciliation. Or congregations of color and leaders of color adapt to white models in order to attract whites, thereby losing the core of their healing and reconciliation DNA. Today's models of multiracial and multicultural congregations are too often created in the womb of privilege. The church must get serious about implementing more than an incomplete process of reconciliation.[32]

Implementing a Process of Reconciliation

So what does reconciliation in congregations look like in the twenty-first century? Despite Korie Edwards' critiques of multiracial congregations she says, "I can imagine interracial churches where whiteness does not dictate congregational life. . . . Interracial churches that understand the broader implications of race for congregation members and for the churches' culture and that intentionally structure their congregations to counter whiteness are more apt to develop and sustain egalitarian interracial religious organizations."[33] How do we implement a process of reconciliation modeled on first-century biblical congregations where whiteness does not dictate congregational life?

Congregations must be places of healing for persons marginalized in society. This was central to the relational ministry of Jesus and the culture of first-century churches, and is nonnegotiable. People feel marginalized in society today because of race, gender, class, sexual orientation, ability, age, religion, lifestyle choices, life circumstances, and the like. Do they experience local congregations as an oasis of healing? For multiracial and multicultural congregations, this means that persons of color will experience a community where they can recover from society's racism and rediscover the fullness of their identity. Many African American, ethnic immigrant, and Native American congregations are places of healing. Before engaging in reconciliation with whites, people of color must be secure in their own cultural and racial identity.[34]

People with privilege and power need congregations where they can exchange places (reconcile) with people who have been marginalized. They must experience the healing possibilities of real relationships and status inversion. Richard Pitt asks, "If there is this growing desire by white congregants to be in diverse religious communities, to experience 'authentic' multiracial worship and ministry, why do they only seek those things in predominantly or historically white congregations?"[35] Often whites want to engage in reconciliation on their own terms. They want people of color to come to them in places where they feel comfortable and in control. The temptation is to proceed directly from segregated mono-cultural congregations to multicultural churches without going through a process of reconciliation. This is made easy by just attending diverse Sunday services without actually engaging in deep intimate relationships where you are transformed by the other person's reality. For true reconciliation whites need places where they are challenged to depart from privileges inherent to whiteness in the United States. Whites need to participate in contexts of color, because it is not easy to refuse privilege "while continuing to live with its actual relationships."[36] Whites should experience church as a qualitatively different place than society.

When Gentiles joined a congregation in the first century, they entered a Jewish world. Many whites have never been to a church in a different cultural or racial context. Korie Edwards recounts an anecdote shared by an African American member at a multiracial congregation she was researching. The member reflected, "I remember somebody saying to me, a white person, 'Crosstown is becoming an African-American church.' I said, 'When was the last time you have gone to an African-American church? Because Crosstown is in *no way* an African-American church.'"[37] One of the greatest challenges for multicultural congregations is the gap in cultural understanding and lived experience between whites and persons of color. Persons of color often live and work in a society dominated by whites and white cultural ways, so they know much about whites. Few whites have a deep knowledge of other cultures or have experience that creates an understanding of racism and prejudice. Most do not know the ways of African American, ethnic immigrant, or Native American churches (except for some stereotypes). One of the challenges for white congregations attempting to become diverse is that they do not know how to create healing communities for people of color. Therefore, people of color can experience unintentional slights and racism due to ignorance and white privilege in congregations becoming "reconciled" and multicultural.

As in the case of first-century congregations, status inversion is an important part of reconciliation for privileged people. Soong-Chan Rah states, "If you are a white Christian wanting to be a missionary in this day and age, and you have never had a nonwhite mentor, then you will not be a missionary. You will be colonialist. Instead of taking the gospel message into the world, you will take an Americanized version of the gospel."[38] We could easily paraphrase Rah and say if you are a white person wanting to provide leadership in a multiracial or multicultural congregation, and you have never had a mentor of color, you will be a colonialist reproducing a U.S. white culture version of the church. Whites need to be mentored for leadership by persons of color. Whites trusting the leadership of persons who have been marginalized or oppressed "is the indispensable precondition for revolutionary change."[39] Paul mentored Gentiles side by side with Jews, training them as though they were Jews. Whites desiring to provide leadership in diverse congregations need to be mentored by leaders of color side by side with African Americans, Native Americans, Asians, Latinas/os, Africans, Arabs, etc., as though they were persons of color. Perhaps all seminarians should be required to have an apprenticeship in an African American, ethnic immigrant, or Native American congregation.

Ideally what whites need is for congregations of color to invite them into membership—much the same way first-century colonized Jews invited Romans and Greeks into their fellowship. Can you imagine historic African American congregations taking the lead in reconciliation by becoming the womb for creating and birthing diverse congregations in the twenty-first century? Given our history of racism in the U.S. church, especially against African Americans, I believe that authenticity requires the multiracial church to pursue a process of reconciliation that takes it through the black church experience—and then through the experiences of other marginalized people.[40]

Presently, demographics in our country limit the possibilities of this dream scenario. Although it may not be too far off. Soong-Chan Rah reminds us that "we are looking at a nonwhite majority, multiethnic American Christianity in the immediate future."[41] Church polity and politics also are barriers. As we noted earlier, 92.5 percent of congregations in the United States are not culturally or racially diverse. But for those congregations who desire reconciliation, they must pursue transparent relationships through status inversion. White leaders must have mentors of color. Congregations must strive to be places of healing for persons of color and for whites.

Like first-century faith communities, diverse congregations need to learn how to negotiate power, privilege, culture, and diversity. Power differentials need to be reversed and then transformed into egalitarian structures. White models of church are often imbued with a history of superiority and white cultural dominance. How many church buildings and Bibles have only white images of Jesus Christ?[42] Korie Edwards warns from her study of multiracial congregations that "A threat to whites' structural advantage in the church was followed by losses in white regular attendance."[43] Whites need to stay. Their reconciliation depends on persevering through the process.

Reconciliation is always about more than race. What we have noted above about relationships, status inversion, and mentoring also applies to gender, class, etc. Congregations that become successfully multicultural and multiracial are not fully reconciled unless they are addressing other places of alienation, marginalization, and injustice. Congregations can be racially reconciled but not fully reconciled if they do not include and empower other marginalized persons in their life and leadership as a congregation.

Beloved Communities Restored

Martin Luther King Jr. said, "The end is reconciliation; the end is redemption; the end is the creation of the beloved community."[44] He used the phrase "beloved community" to encase his vision of the actualization of reconciliation. For our purposes, the "beloved community" is a vision of congregations embracing a process of reconciliation to create a space where we can truly relate as humans, sisters and brothers, family, children of God. Twenty-first century congregations can be modeled on the aspirations of first-century congregations and their process of reconciliation. We must restore to the church the vision of a beloved community found in the first-century church. For Brian Bantum, reconciliation leads to a place where persons "can no longer return to their former people for they speak with a new accent, their lives are marked by new rhythms, enemies have become friends, and friends have become enemies. . . . In Christ, we become sutured together into a new people and become surprised by the people we become in the process."[45]

The image of Creoleness discussed by French Caribbean writers Jean Bernabé, Patrick Chamoiseau, and Raphaël Confiant, in their book *In Praise of Creoleness*, suggests how a diversity of individuals that have been sutured together might describe themselves as a congregation. "Neither

Europeans, nor Africans, nor Asians, we proclaim ourselves Creoles. This will be for us an interior attitude—better, a vigilance, or even better, a sort of mental envelope in the middle of which our world will be built in full consciousness of the outer world. These words we are communicating to you here do not stem from theory, nor do they stem from any learned principles. They are, rather, akin to testimony."[46] Bernabé, Chamoiseau, and Confiant then call for a new humanity much like the apostle Paul's theological vision of "one new humanity" reconciled through the crucifixion and resurrection of Jesus. "A new humanity will gradually emerge which will have the same characteristics as our Creole humanity: all the complexity of Creoleness. The son or daughter of a German and a Haitian, born and living in Peking, will be torn between several languages, several histories, caught in the torrential ambiguity of a mosaic identity. To present creative depth, one must perceive that identity in all its complexity. *He or she will be in the situation of a Creole.*"[47] The image is compelling. The reality is daunting. The process is reconciliation. The outcome is a congregation of diverse people in the situation of being reconciled to each other through a crucified and resurrected Jesus Christ.

Chapter 6

Between Reitz, a Rock, and a Hard Place
Reconciliation after the Reitz Event[1]

Allan Aubrey Boesak

"The Kind of Country We Wish to Be"

In February 2008, it came to light that four white students at the University of the Free State in South Africa had decided to demonstrate their rejection of plans by the university to integrate student residences. They chose to do that by putting five workers, cleaners at the students' residence, four women and one man, through a most humiliating experience that they captured on video. In the video Emma Koko, Rebecca Adams, Naomi Phororo, Mittah Ntsaleng and David Malete are seen on their knees while eating a "stew" in which one of the students had apparently urinated. The students stand by laughing and one proclaims, "This is what we think of integration!"

The video was entered into a "cultural competition" held by the white students on campus and, hugely popular, won an award. The white student audience thought the video was hilarious, and the four students, since known as "the Reitz Four," were rewarded for their creativity. All this was kept quiet for some time. Only subsequently did the video see the light of day and did the broader public become aware of both events—the making of the video and the roaring approval of the students who attended the cultural competition. This became known as the "Reitz incident," and as waves of shock and anger reverberated around the country, nothing else in more than a hundred years drew more public attention to the University of the Free State.

The Reitz video exposed the level of racism at the university and subsequently in the white community, but it did more: it threatened to shred the mantle of reconciliation the country was still struggling to wear with some degree of comfort. It exposed the fragility of South Africa's reconciliation as few other "incidents" did, and it gave rise to unprecedented waves of anger and revulsion. The event, its aftermath of justification, defensiveness, and denial drenched the country in shame.

Initially the university, though expressing shock and condemning the students for their actions, strongly gave the impression that it considered the incident a joke in bad taste, blaming the workers for "participating in a student prank" during working hours. In addition, the institution thought it was "wrong to turn its back on the students," because they too were subjected to abusive and degrading gestures from the public.[2] Three years later, at a reportedly moving public "reconciliation event" in February 2011, the university, as well as the students, issued a public apology to the workers, which the workers graciously accepted.[3]

When the students' actions were exposed, they were suspended, the South African Human Rights Commission and the trade union took up the cause of the workers, and the matter was taken to the Equality Court as a criminal case despite efforts by the university to have the matter settled "in ways that dealt both with institutional racism and the desperate need for reconciliation."[4] The court found the students, R. C. Malherbe, Johnny Roberts, Schalk van der Merwe, and Danie Grobler guilty and ordered the students and the university separately to pay a substantial fine in compensation. The matter was finally settled out of court, with undisclosed amounts, though speculation is that it was far less than the R1million each of the five workers had claimed.[5] My concern here, however, is not the legal arrangements and monetary settlements pertaining to the matter, but rather the deeper, long-term issues, their impact on reconciliation, and its meaning for South Africa.

In the event, the courts treated the matter not as an "incident," but as a hate crime, and that in itself was a crucial shift in the debate as well as an important message for the country to understand. It sent another message as well: this was not merely a matter for the university, even though the university's unique responsibility, both before and after the fact, remains clear. This was a matter for the nation. And taking it to the nation was, in my view, a most appropriate way to put the issue within the context of "the desperate need for reconciliation." It is not just the students or the university community that are in need of reconciliation; it is the nation.

Besides, were it not for the nation's intervention, the matter would not have been given the proper attention it deserved.

The university, in its initial reaction, set in place a lamentable context of diminishment that continued to have a serious impact on the public debate and even, more seriously, on the public understanding of what reconciliation in that situation means. One, the university's usage of the word "prank" became a deadly trivialization in the white public mind around which much of the rancor swelled and festered. Two, while the word "incident" was seen as an adequate way to describe what had happened, in the minds of most black people the euphemism belittled those upon whom it was inflicted, decriminalized the crime, while simultaneously conferring a bland kind of innocence upon the white students they did not deserve. Three, while it can be argued that the university did not overtly take the side of the students, it certainly did try to implicate the workers in the act, making them share the responsibility and guilt that should have been the students' alone.

That led to the fourth problem. The university tried to "level the playing field" for the students by expressing its regret that it had "turned its back" on the students, since they were "also subjected to abusive and degrading gestures from the public." Suddenly the initiators and perpetrators of the crime were on the same level as their victims. If this was not a complete inversion of reality, then it certainly was a dislodgement of reality, creating a paradox that was at once a denial and affirmation of the power dynamics at play between the white students and the black workers as well as between the university and the workers. This paradox would plague the process to the very end and, unless it is dealt with, has the potential of scuppering every effort at genuine reconciliation in South Africa. A reconciliation process in which the established power dynamics are not challenged, and shifted, but instead subtly or not so subtly reaffirmed, is doomed to fail. It remains an open question how much of these first fundamental mistakes will continue to take its toll on the process of reconciliation at the university and its own role in the transformation process in the country as a whole.

This university, writes the current Rector (President) Professor Jonathan Jansen, who himself is black, "was easily South Africa's most racially desegregated campus but at the same time its most racially segregated university community."[6] The residences were segregated, with small numbers of white students in largely black residences, and slightly larger numbers of black students in largely white residences. The classes were essentially segregated, with black students in English classes mainly held later in the day and white students in Afrikaans classes held during the early parts of the day. Access to knowledge was "unequal." The Senate (the governing body), was essentially white with "a handful of black colleagues." Social and sporting events were "completely separated by race." So were the student political formations. Any crisis, the rector reports, would become easily racialized. "In other words, and this is critical, *the institutional arrangements* for ordering race and encouraging racialized thinking and, inevitably, racial confrontation were perfectly in place."[7]

In the volatile public debate that followed the racist incident, Jonathan Jansen was trying to contextualize the students' behavior. It is certain that he was not always well heard. It served no one that the debate became so thoroughly politicized—sometimes for all the wrong reasons. Still, it remains remarkably instructive that the angry responses of black people were so easily misunderstood or, worse, that these responses caused so much irritation.

It's not as if South Africans had been naïve about the continued existence of racism in post-apartheid South Africa. Racist crimes abounded, albeit not always treated as seriously as they should have been by courts around the country. But there is a particular issue here. A feature of the well-publicized race crimes in the past ten years or so has been the fact that so many of these were crimes committed by a younger white generation, not older persons nostalgic for apartheid and angry at the loss of power, privilege, and standing once guaranteed by their white skins. And it *is* deeply disturbing when one realizes this: the homeless black man kicked to death by two young white boys while trying to find shelter for the night in the yard of a white church in Cape Town's northern suburbs; the four high school students who attacked and killed a black vagrant in a park in Pretoria (the so-called Waterkloof Four, so named for the wealthy Pretoria suburb where they lived); the 18-year-old Johan Nel who drove miles to a black informal settlement camp to randomly kill defenseless dwellers with a shotgun, including a two-year-old baby.

These crimes were so shocking because somehow the country would understand it better if older, more apartheid-minded persons were involved. But these were democracy's generation, the "Born Frees," we call them,

"Mandela's white children." So what happened after South Africa's peaceful transition from apartheid, President Mandela's sterling example, and his call to build a new nonracial South Africa; after Archbishop Tutu's leadership at the Truth and Reconciliation Commission (TRC) with its emphasis on both Christian forgiveness and *ubuntu,* after the extraordinary magnanimity of black South Africans in choosing forgiveness above revenge; after the hope and idealism embedded in the very term "rainbow nation," which was not just an optimistic Tutuism but the result of a wounded nation's decision to turn the perpetrator of the apartheid crime into a co-survivor of a historic catastrophe? This is a more proper context in which to judge black anger and white justification, an altogether better context to ask the question of the meaning of the Reitz event.

At the University of the Free State, it was not physical murder that took place: an act of sudden anger, a question of young racist thugs seizing an opportunity to act out violent racial fantasies, or a result of deep psychological derangement. There was a cold deliberateness about it that calls for pause. This crime was carefully planned, choreographed, and video-taped; coolly entered for a competition, displayed in public, receiving wide white audience approval while creating wonderful entertainment; then, with injured youthful innocence, defended and justified, justified also by a disturbingly large section of a white community in angry denial. Then they sat back and expected blacks to accept and acquiesce, join in the harmless fun, and when *that* did not happen, they accused blacks of intolerance and racism in reverse; of lacking a sense of humor and festering in unjustified and needless anger; and, worst of all, of the inability to emulate the magnanimity of Mandela. When I vented my own anger at the incident in a media statement, I received an angry, "hurt" letter containing just about all these elements from a white, liberal-thinking Dutch Reformed Church colleague who wanted to know why I "attacked" the Reitz Four but did not address black students' "reverse racism" in their reaction to the events.[8] He, like so many in the white community, did not understand that if in this instance there was indeed racism from black people, it was a racism that racism produced.

Perhaps all this is why Jansen speaks of the Reitz event as determining "what kind of country we want to be."[9] Professor Jansen is not wrong, but perhaps it is not *his* words that make this event a determinant of "what kind of country we want to be." His words come in reaction to the widespread an-

ger and disgust of black people at the Reitz event as well as at his decision
to lift the suspension of the students allowing them to return before the
matter was settled in the courts or at the university. What persuades me to
agree with him, rather, are the words of one of the students: "This is what
we think of integration!" The student was speaking not of the integration
of university residences, not really; his scorn was poured on the nation's
efforts at forgiveness and renewal, nation building, and reconciliation. What
persuades me are the words of one of the workers, with a simple directness
so devastating and eloquent: "We feel like toilets."[10] She was speaking for
all black people.

Exposing "The Great Myth"

The intense public debate, for most of which black South Africans and
white South Africans took sides either for the workers or the students, did
indeed indicate that much was at stake here.

What drives these young people to so much hatred, anger, and fear? In
the case of the Reitz Four, Jonathan Jansen is certain it is the institutionalized racism of the university. In other words, it's not the students themselves—it's the legacy of racial bigotry, the unbroken apartheid mindset, the
untransformed nature of our public institutions, specifically the Free State
University. Hence, this explains Jansen's decision to end the "punishment"
of the students, to lift their suspension and readmit them to the university,
since "the institution was complicit in creating the conditions for racial
thinking and racial attack."[11]

I suggest that there was more behind this than institutional racism. In
2008, in a first real public attempt to grapple with the meaning of the
Reitz event, the university organized a public colloquium under a telling
title, which the title of this chapter reflects: "Between Reitz and a Rock:
What Went Wrong?"[12] It is a title that reveals anxiety, growing maturity,
and honesty. Instead of asking "What next?" the university first asks "What
went wrong?" It reflects an understanding of the immorality of a "let's
move on" hastiness, the refuge of too many white South Africans, and a desire to actually try to determine "what went wrong." It was a hopeful sign.

Certainly Jansen's analysis of the university's responsibility in this matter
must be part of the answer. But veteran journalist and colloquium speaker
Elna Boesak, in a paper bearing the same title, took the matter consider-

ably deeper and further. As a white, Afrikaner woman, she recognizes that the students' attitudes and actions have deep and disturbing roots, and she speaks from experience. The foundations, she writes, the worldview on which the National Party (which embodied the political aspirations and power of the white Afrikaner community) built its mobilization of the Afrikaner masses, "the final consolidation and official implementation of the thought- and action patterns of white supremacy," was what she calls "the Great Myth":

> [A] distorted fabrication concocted from an ideology of social na-
> tionalism and a pseudo theology of racist justification . . . begot-
> ten from sexual congress between settler, slave woman and Khoi—
> sought to fashion a "pure white nation." . . . [They employed] a
> spiritual rhetoric [praising] the victory of God-fearing Civilization
> over and redemption from Heathen Barbarism: the "Other" of col-
> or, culture, religion, history, tradition, experience and perspective; a
> miserable lie that the other—perhaps creatures of God—but cre-
> ated decidedly less human than they, less civilized, less gifted, less
> intelligent, less moral, less trustworthy, less worthy, and therefore less
> deserving.[13]

The "Great Myth" was a powerful ideological tool that served to fash-ion a "white Afrikaner identity."[14] This is the myth "imbibed with mother's milk" from generation to generation, that became the framework of an "artificial identity," fostered deep in the individual and collective psyche of Afrikaans-speaking whites.

> Over three hundred years the fiction, the fable, the narrative, rheto-
> ric and lie has been used to conquer, confuse, poison and paralyze
> the hearts and minds of men, women and children, and to carve,
> with deliberate intent, from the offspring of the Creoles of coloni-
> zation—children of Africa—white racists.[15]

This is the making of the Reitz Four, and it calls for sober reflection. The responsibility for what they have done is theirs, but its roots lie deep, much deeper than merely the institutional responsibility the university ad-mits to. Elections in 1994 brought a chance for redemption, inviting all

South Africans to become vessels of the promise of democracy, dignity, and freedom. It does have to begin, though, with acceptance of the admission reflected in the discussion the university initiated, that not just the university, but South Africa as a whole "is in a hard place."[16]

Apart from her analysis thus far, Elna Boesak sees at least two more reasons for South Africa finding itself "between Reitz and a hard place." Firstly, she argues that South Africans have "overestimated the value of political reconciliation and the stubbornness of a myth built on racism and discrimination. . . . Scrapping of laws and writing a constitution were political decisions that could not undo the damage of decades of brain washing and injustice in the span of fifteen years." Hence our dilemma: "For many white South Africans, reconciliation has become a duty and a curse, not a voluntary choice and God-given calling. It is a political expedience divorced from their faith, emotional welfare and material prosperity."[17]

It is, in the growing climate of racism and ethnic nationalistic mobilization, dangerously optimistic to judge the Reitz event and other racist manifestations as "isolated events, student pranks, or the craziness of extremists." Read it, she writes, as "part of a greater pattern that is emerging." She calls Reitz a "metaphor for the desperate maintenance of objectionable thought- and power expressions," an advertisement "for an agenda that makes it hard for black South Africans to believe that white Afrikaans-speaking South Africans are prepared not just to be *in* Africa, exploiting the continent, but just as ready to be *of* Africa, to share her destiny and to do everything necessary to redress three hundred years of social injustice."[18]

In other words, too little was done to break the suffocating grip of the "Great Myth." It continues to empower those whites who act as if their lives and the future of their children depend upon it, a future that excludes the ideal of nonracial nationhood and continues to disempower those—white and black—who believe that the future lies in the shared promise of a reconciled, restored community. It empowers too, I would suggest, those in the black community, the "racial nativists"[19] who have turned Africanness into a racist, exclusionary concept, and for whom reconciliation beyond political accommodation, conditional upon their enrichment and entitlement, is unthinkable. White racism does not produce their racism, it simply feeds it.

Secondly, she argues that it is not that so much has gone wrong, but rather that so little had gone right since 1994, "despite the deceitful *Invictus-*

phenomenon."[20] While there have indeed been political changes giving hope "that our democracy is beginning to show more structural spine, . . . the transformation of hearts, attitudes and actions without which human society cannot survive did not happen."[21] So Elna Boesak sees both systemic social justice and personal "heart and mind" transformation and personal choices as a way away from the hard place and forward towards genuine reconciliation.

I believe that if the university takes its own view of the grip of racist history on its white students seriously, it should do everything in its power—through critical and self-critical reflection, openness, integrity and honesty, radical transformation of curricula and teaching, as well as the creation of a renewed, transformed nonracial community—to break the "Great Myth" and to help the students to embrace and share in a new promise of freedom.

To Stand Where God Stands

One of the continuingly haunting phrases in the *Belhar Confession* adopted by my church, the Dutch Reformed Mission Church (since 1994 the Uniting Reformed Church in Southern Africa) is found in article 4.2: "That the church, as possession of God, should stand where God stands, namely against injustice and with the wronged; that in following Christ the church must witness against all the powerful and privileged who selfishly seek their own interests and thus control and harm others."[22] The confession itself is a powerfully prophetic document and reflects the church's belief in three key gospel truths: unity, justice, and reconciliation. The confession has proved to be a continuing challenge beyond apartheid and once again now in South Africa's ongoing struggle with justice and reconciliation, not just regarding society, but with regard to the church itself.

The church "should stand where God stands." It is a kind of leitmotif for the liturgical and public worship of the church and in its simplicity calls for equally direct and simple obedience: *against injustice and with the wronged*. There is injustice when someone is being wronged, and the God "who loves justice" (Is 61:8) always takes the side of those who are wronged.[23] It follows that the church, "in following Christ" should therefore stand where God stands and witness against all the powerful and privileged who seek their own interests, seek control over others, and in the process always harm others, that is, those they have made powerless. Where power is at play, the powerless suffer. The justice they deserve is always negated by the interests of the powerful; they are wronged. The wrong not only lies in the injustice being done, but in the *control* the powerful seek to exert, undermining their dignity, their humanity and their rights, bending the powerless to their will. The church must "stand" with the injured and wronged and "follow" Christ in this: meditating upon God's word is acting upon God's word. Thinking of the meaning of reconciliation, caught between Reitz, a rock and a hard place, this is *the first lesson we should draw from this compelling saga: seeing events first of all through the eyes of those who suffer. Reconciliation does not begin with neutrality. It begins with standing where God stands.*

Earlier on, I alluded to some fundamental errors the university, in my view, committed in the initial handling of this matter. All of those, the trivialization and diminishment of the crime of the students, making the workers complicit in their own humiliation, belittling the workers by equating the public exposure of the students with the racist humiliation they inflicted upon the workers, have to do with what I mentioned above: the dynamics of power. In that context I mentioned that unless properly addressed, this might become a problem that would continue to plague the reconciliation process, both at the university and for South Africa as a whole. It seems that it does precisely that.

I am not one of those who sneered at the February 2011 public rec-onciliation event at the university that brought the perpetrators and the victims together in confession and forgiveness. Those are risks one must take if reconciliation has to have any real chance in South Africa. I pray that the process was one of genuine remorse and forgiveness, of restora-tion both for the workers and the students. In conversations afterward with some of those directly involved I have heard enough to understand the deep complexities of such processes; enough to be in awe of the mysteries of the grace of God; and enough to determine to continue to work hard to make our reconciliation real, just, and sustainable.

The university knows it still has much to do, but in my view, it would do well to be alert to the errors that refuse to disappear and become new pitfalls along the way. And again, it has, first of all, to do with power. Caus-ing me acute discomfort was the way in which the university continued to try to make the workers complicit in the crime. That initial statement is repeated by the rector two years after the fact. Jonathan Jansen defended his decision to readmit the students "after they had racially abused five workers *who had agreed to participate* in a video production protesting against the integration of the institution's residences."[24]

It is a startlingly revealing statement, completely devoid of understanding of the power dynamics at play here. These were white students, clearly, according to both Jansen and Elna Boesak, steeped in racist attitudes and history, "brainwashed" into believing in white superiority. But racism is not a matter of attitudes only; it is in essence a matter of power and the abuse of that power to execute and maintain racist oppression. When the students get black, menial workers who scrub their floors and clean their toilets (like the "maids" at home) to appear in a video "protesting against integration," they hardly get them to "participate" as if the workers were doing this willingly. More likely they spoke to them from their historical position of power, and in their powerlessness, the workers heard an order they could not realistically refuse. Were there any real choices here? After all, Jansen himself explains how *everything* at the university was under white control. It was a product of white history, white power, white privilege, white exclusivity, and white supremacy. The place exuded white power: from the physical buildings to the composition of the governing bodies to the administration and the teaching professionals to the attitudes of students toward fellow black students and especially black workers. In the rector's own words, "the *institutional arrangements* for ordering race and for encouraging racial thinking and inevitably, racial confrontation, were perfectly in place."[25]

Instead of dismissing the rector's argument as simply an "excuse" for the horrific behavior of his white students, I think we should take him quite seriously on this point. I suggest that these racialized and racist "institutional arrangements" the rector correctly pinpoints are, in fact, the *power structures* that governed the institution, its history, its thinking, and the behavior of its members. When one analyzes, or even merely observes, these arrangements, one meets stark white power. Secondly, the fact that this was the case after fifteen years of democracy means that the university deliberately, willfully, and successfully had set itself against the processes of transformation our peaceful transition demanded and perhaps naively had taken for granted. It means that this university had, in all the ways Jansen mentions, decided to remain a bastion of apartheid, physically as well as spiritually. The existence of the still racialized realities the rector complains about is a sign of the spirit of resistance at the university, its determination to remain true to its original intentions. That is the one thing those white students have not misunderstood or misinterpreted and that the black workers could not afford to misunderstand.

Thirdly, one should not look at these power structures, realities, and arrangements as *waiting for* some crisis to develop. These were the arrangements and realities black workers had to confront, live with, and knuckle under if they were to survive *every day*. It was in the very air they breathed. The workers were not the crisis waiting to happen—their everyday lives on campus constituted an already existing crisis. It's just that no one seemed to notice. In this context, how does one expect black, powerless workers *not* to be aware of their own precarious position when confronted by the white students? How does one forget that the video shows the workers *on their knees?* My Afrikaner friends on campus tell me that the white students continue to call the female employees by a word they use for their "domestics" at home: "*squeeza*."[26] The very word conjures up disturbing historic images and associations of subservience and domination, of power and powerlessness; a relentless hand squeezing out every drop of submission, draining the overpowered of will and dignity. The black students call them "Mama." The white students call them "squeezas": a frightening conveyer of the dynamics of power in one single word.

Jansen does not deny that the workers were abused; in fact, he deeply sympathizes with them,[27] but his statement reads as if the workers knew that they were being recruited to join the white students in their protest "against integration." What does that say of the black workers? That they actually did have the power to refuse, but did not? That they secretly, like the whites, also longed for the days of apartheid to return, or at least remain undisturbed on the campus, and that they now *decided* to make that longing public? Perhaps the workers were deceived, made to believe that the video was for some other purpose. But even at that, the elements of the video were such that the intentions could not have been misunderstood. They submitted, as generations before them had to do, because the power dynamics would not allow them to do otherwise. There is a reason why the philosophy of Black Consciousness and black power found such a broad and devoted following in the final phases of the struggle.[28]

The denial of the powerlessness of the workers, while at the same time using the white power argument to create understanding for the students, is not sustainable. Conversely, if one were looking for a reason for their submission to this vile act, is decades of subjection, intimidation, and fear not enough? After all, if, according to the argument, it is so hard for the students to overcome their racist upbringing,[29] then how hard is it in hardly transformed South Africa, where the harsh realities of exploitation and shocking inequalities still rule our social and economic dispensation, for minimally educated, unprivileged, powerless black workers, who have yet to see anything of the benefits of struggle and democracy but still bear the burdens of apartheid? At the very least, one should say that the workers were coerced, not suggest that they willingly "participated." *Reitz teaches us a second lesson; that reconciliation is not possible unless the dynamics of power are addressed, and shifted.*

The power dynamic works in another way as well. Professor Jansen *sympathized* with the workers, and I have no doubt his sympathy was genuine; but his *anger* he reserved for the reaction to the crime of the white students. The first thing he tells us about the workers as they sat in his office is that they were "dignified, and respectful, not angry and spiteful."[30] Clearly it is important that the workers not be angry, that they, as Professor Jansen advises his students elsewhere, learn to be "tough," "resilient," accept the fact that one "grows through hardships of various degrees." He believes that anger makes one like "the township *skollie*,[31] the uncouth thug who should never be admitted to a place of higher learning." He points out that "a sign of maturity is to see the abuser as the victim, the one who needs help, rather than to have the abuser determine how you feel about yourself," and quoting Eleanor Roosevelt, Jansen ended: "No one can make you feel inferior without your permission." This discussion with the students ended in triumph: "The smile on the face of the angry student was priceless."[32]

Doubtless there is much wisdom in what Jansen says, and students would do well to take his words to heart. Clearly too, this is a view he himself holds dear and applies to the ways in which he runs his university. Nonetheless, danger is lurking here, not because what he says is untrue, but because it is not all of the truth. Victimhood is much more complicated than Jansen argues, and we owe it to the victim not to reduce the complexities. The abuser is a victim, true, but of a system of the abuser's own making, in a process where others were made victim. This should be foremost in any discussion about victimhood: there are victims, and there are victims because there are real abusers. It is not at all acceptable to seek "understanding" for the victimhood of the abuser, while his real victim remains hurt, damaged, and unrecognized, and the hurt remains unaddressed. It is only when one stands with the wronged, the powerless, the victim, that one sees properly the plight of the abuser. The first step is not to sympathize with the abuser but to point out that he has done wrong and that the wrong should be regretted and addressed.

I cannot imagine saying this to a woman in an abusive relationship: that she should be wise, and strong, and resilient. Before the abuser receives the privilege of sympathy, the victim has the right to acknowledgement that she has been wronged. Before all that, she has the right to solidarity and compassionate justice. Not even two decades into our democratic era, whites claim victim status and seek "justice." "The whole problem with 'white guilt'" (for apartheid), a young white lecturer at a Christian college writes to me in an angry e-mail, "has to be balanced with the losses and suffering of whites since 1994: loss of work, careers, and opportunities through race-driven affirmative action and corrupt tender processes in the name of Black Economic Empowerment as one of the reasons for the 'brain drain,' 'cadre employment,' the rapid growth of white poverty and the disappearance of the ideal of the rainbow nation." Notice how it is the "losses" of whites that constitute the sum total of the "disappearance of the ideal of the rainbow nation," not the unaddressed injustices done to the victims of apartheid and colonialism for over three centuries. De-historized, de-contextualized, and transferred victimhood makes reconciliation impossible, because it becomes the pretext for ongoing, unchallenged, and uncorrected injustices, while shifting the compassionate attention away from the real victim who is simply called upon to endure and suffer.

The argument sounds biblical, but it isn't. It is the political pietism that protects the interests of the powerful. The Bible speaks of God as a loving God, because Yahweh's love is seen in Yahweh's love for justice and Yahweh's outrage at injustice that continues to create victims. It is an outraged God who "observed" the misery of God's people, who "heard" their cry, who "know(s)" their sufferings. Yahweh knows who the victims are. "I have come down to deliver them" (Ex 3:7, 8). It is an outraged God who rails against the injustices inflicted upon the poor and powerless. It is the voice of a God who knows the victims—the poor, the orphan, the widow, the stranger; demeaned, impoverished, voiceless, powerless; and who knows that they were the victims of the rich and powerful who pervert all justice and equity.

It is a paralyzing, unbiblical Christianity that revictimizes the true victim through pious advice to submission, endurance, and quiet acceptance by placing on him the burden of making room for the victimhood of the oppressive abuser while his own pain is not being addressed through justice and compassion. Compassionate justice to the true victim empowers and restores personhood and dignity, and creates room for reconciliation by seeing and sharing the victim's pain and suffering. The abuser will begin to find redemption when he sees himself through the eyes of his victim. The abuser will take this message seriously only when he takes the wounding of his victim seriously, and learns *the third lesson, that reconciliation is not cheap, but a response, through God's grace, to inflicted woundedness.*

It is not that Jonathan Jansen himself does not show anger at the situation. He has sharply worded questions for his own university: "Why did we allow the residence to grant an award for the production of the video? And why are those who granted the award left off the hook? What about all the other incidents of racial confrontation that did not appear in the media? Why was there no intervention to effectively end segregation?"[33] And at angry blacks, "We insist on punishment 'indefinitely'… rather than on the possibilities of 'parole.' We trap ourselves in intimate understandings of our own hurt and will not allow for the possibility of degradation on the other side." But the anger is never on behalf of the humiliated and victimized workers, it is on behalf of the white students who have now become the real victims because of black anger: "We are still deeply angry beneath the skin, an anger that does not and will not allow for reconciliation."[34]

This is hugely problematic, in my view, and it leads us to *a fourth lesson from Reitz. There is a place for rightful anger.* It is not true that being angry about injustice makes one equal to "the township *skollie*" and "the uncouth thug." Not all anger is mindless or hate filled, and not all anger diminishes or destroys. It is impossible for people not to be angry at what happened under apartheid, and it is impossible not to be angry at what happened to the five workers. There is something deeply wrong when we can no longer be outraged by injustice and inhumanity, and it is grossly unfair to act as if that anger is an offense to God or to decent humanity.

"The oppression was bad," said one young woman who testified before the Amnesty Commission of the TRC and found that she was not allowed to show her anger at what was done to her. "[But] what is much worse, what makes me even angrier, is that they are trying to dictate my forgiveness."[35]

Rightful anger must not be belittled, let alone suppressed or even worse, condemned as unchristian or immature. It must be given a respectful hearing and response. Rightful anger denied almost always leads to a "dictated forgiveness." Just as the victim has to hear the words of truth and contrition, I wrote elsewhere, "it is necessary for the perpetrator to hear the words of anger. The perpetrator has to *see* and *hear* the consequences of the wrongful act in order to understand the depth of the wrong that was done so that they can understand the depth of the forgiveness given."[36] It is a torturous logic to offer the perpetrator the comfort and protection of victimhood while denying the victim the freedom of anger and the protection of solidarity, and hence, for both victim and perpetrator, the redemption of remorse, forgiveness, and compassionate justice.

In any oppressive situation, it is always the temptation of the powerful to forbid the powerless their right to rightful anger, since that anger is the affirmation of the very dignity and resilience the powerful consider a threat and seek to destroy. Yahweh's anger at injustice we see throughout the prophets is always on behalf of the poor and powerless because their rightful anger is denied them by the powerful. The workers, the true victims of the Reitz event, have indeed shown resilience, and magnificently so. But it is not the resilience of submission and quiet acceptance; it is the resilience of hope and resistance derived from besieged but uninjured faith and the spirituality of struggle. This is what caused them to triumph over the solidified, multifaceted, institutionalized power that reigned over them for so long. That, and the solidarity of the whole community that encircled them from the moment their plight became known, gave them voice when they felt themselves made voiceless in their powerlessness. In doing this, the community did what the Belhar Confession requires: standing where God stands, and following Christ. Following Jesus in his forgiveness of injustice means following Jesus in his outrage *at* injustice—*that* is following Jesus in his love.

A Way Away from the Hard Place

In reflecting on reconciliation Jonathan Jansen asks a crucial question: "How does one explain the hardening of the moral arteries of many citizens in the new South Africa?"[37] He then takes us through a possible list of answers: the lack of transformation and the failure of basic service delivery; the daily grind just to find money to sustain university studies; the "observed sense of racial inequalities on campus"; the "institutionalization of racial separateness." It could be the "lack of awareness of race and its consequences, not to mention lack of remorse among white students and staff in their daily dealings with black students and staff." Then he raises the bar by asking,

> Or might it be that South Africans never really embraced the reconciliation mandate in the first place, the project of President Nelson Mandela, that the impulse for retribution is much, much stronger than the impulse for reconciliation?[38]

It is a question South Africans must grapple with honestly and constantly even though the catalog lacks awareness of the indispensability of systemic social justice. The evidence suggests, however, that on this point Jansen is not correct. Perhaps his judgment is too much defined by his focus on the University of the Free State and the public reaction to the Reitz event. South Africans have gone to extraordinary lengths to avoid retribution and embrace reconciliation. The very choices made right at the start in our negotiated settlement meant that we have chosen for "survivor's justice" over "victor's justice," a TRC over Nuremberg-style criminal trials, forgiveness and reconciliation over retribution. In light of our violent and devastating history of colonialism, slavery, and apartheid, this is a historic paradigm shift that, astonishingly, "changes the meaning of survivor to include all who survived yesterday's catastrophe, apartheid."[39]

Archbishop Tutu writes movingly about his experiences before the TRC's Amnesty Commission, where people "have been shocked and filled with revulsion to hear of the depths to which we are able to sink in our inhumanity to one another: the capacity for the sadistic enjoyment of suffering"; contrasting this with "another side, more noble and inspiring," where people have been "deeply touched and moved by the resilience of the human spirit (of hope and forgiveness)."[40] But then Tutu expresses a desire that Jansen misses: "The generosity of spirit will be full to overflowing when it meets a like generosity, forgiveness will follow confession and healing will happen."[41]

Black South Africans did embrace reconciliation and rejected retribution. The fact that the country has not gone up in flames despite the ongoing injustices and growing social and economic inequalities, speaks volumes of the remarkable patience of South Africa's people. Despite too, former Human Rights Commission Chair and now Judge Jody Kollapen writes, our "model of reconciliation that confines itself to seeking understanding and forgiveness," focusing "on the fears and vulnerabilities of the minority" (i.e. whites), "but does not engage the legitimate demands and expectations of social justice."[42]

That leaves us with a final question. Is the restoration of community possible after the Reitz event? Is it possible to break the paralyzing hold of past myths and ways of life, to escape the generational curse of systemic injustice? I am convinced it is, if South Africans, as Elna Boesak suggests, genuinely embark on a transformation of the heart, mind, and deed, open their hearts to Tutu's plea for a reciprocal generosity of spirit, and if we all understand that reconciliation without sustained, systemic justice is not possible. We must be determined to avoid the traps of cheap reconciliation driven by political pietism and Christian quietism.

After the reconciliation event on the campus, I had two stunningly moving experiences that give me hope—for that university but also for South Africa. A middle-aged white Afrikaner man, part of the university's administration, Dolf Britz, publicly embraced the guilt of his generation in teaching their children "to hate, to disdain, to look down upon." He stated, "I should have stood in the dock with them, because my generation taught them that to be racist is our given way of life. I humbly ask their forgiveness, and yours. But I also say to them: as from today, let us together break the curse of the past; let us together begin to do what is right." In the stunned silence a young black woman got up and embraced Dolf. Only then did the hundred and fifty or so students break out in applause. Quietly, diligently, Dolf continues to expose to students the folly and fallacies of the "Great Myth," holding up to them the alternative of a promise of shared freedom.

When I asked Moses Masitha, a black student, about the most moving moment of the reconciliation event for him, he said, "When Mama Emma Koko told the white students, 'we forgive you, you are our sons,' I really understood the depth and meaning of their forgiveness. As Africans we understand: if the mothers claim them as their sons, we cannot refuse them as our brothers."

Dolf and Moses teach us *our final lesson from the Reitz event. Genuine, radical reconciliation is perhaps the only way we can walk away from the rock and the hard place: as family; forgiven, healed, restored.*

Part IV

Just Societies Realized

Chapter 7

When Prophets Are Silenced, Injustice Prevails

Curtiss Paul DeYoung

The major story of 2008 was the election of Barack Obama to the presidency of the United States in November of that year. A central theme of Obama's campaign and early days in office was hope, which grabbed the attention of the nation and the world for several reasons. First and foremost was that the United States elected its first African American president. This occurred only forty years after the assassination of civil rights leader Martin Luther King Jr. For people still alive from King's generation, this was experienced as a miracle. Most of them believed they would not live to see the day that a person of African descent would hold the office of president of the United States. This brought hope to African Americans that better days were ahead. Second, the hope for improved race relations was very bright. Obama's votes came from a broad multiracial coalition of supporters. This diversity was particularly true of the many young people who voted for him. This multiracial, multicultural youth vote boded well for a future of racial harmony. For many, "the election of Barack Obama was a powerful moment of reconciliation."[1]

The nation was in the midst of two wars launched as responses to the tragic terrorist attacks on September 11, 2001, and the economy was headed quickly toward recession. So thirdly, the election of Barack Obama brought a fresh wind of hope that these wars could be ended and the economy revived. Finally, the election of Obama brought hope to world leaders that the United States would reengage as a moral leader in global affairs. This sense of hope on the international scene was further enhanced by President Obama's speech to the Muslim world in Cairo, Egypt, in June 2009. Then nine months into his presidency, Barack Obama was awarded the Nobel Peace Prize in October 2009. The press release from the Nobel Committee read, "Only rarely has a person to the same extent as Obama captured the world's attention and given its people hope for a better future."[2] It was the anticipated outcome of a better future based on hope, not any particular accomplishments in peacemaking, which led to the awarding of the Nobel Peace Prize to President Obama.

One person who had given Barack Obama "the audacity to hope" was Rev. Dr. Jeremiah A. Wright Jr., the now retired senior pastor of Trinity United Church of Christ in Chicago, Illinois. Dr. Wright had been Obama's pastor for twenty years. Barack Obama's book *The Audacity to Hope* came from a sermon of the same title preached by Wright.[3] Jeremiah Wright is a fiery preacher of unvarnished and untarnished truth. Wright boldly proclaims the biblical call for social justice directed to those holding power and exercising privilege. He also preached truth to those who attended his church every Sunday. So when Wright's congregational member and spiritual protégé Barack Obama announced his candidacy for president of the United States, some of us were delighted by the possibility that Jeremiah Wright could be in the inner circle of one of the most powerful persons in the world. Persons in power can easily be sidetracked or manipulated by their own needs for power or by those around them with various agendas. They need truth tellers in order to stay on the straight path of God's justice and to persevere through to the end of the process of reconciliation. Truth telling about injustice was central to the prophetic role in the Hebrew scriptures. Wright's counsel would be a strong voice for social justice in a White House administration facing pressing ethical dilemmas of political leadership in society and encountering complex global realities. Unfortunately this envisioned scenario did not happen.

In the midst of Obama's campaign for the presidency, media outlets and the opposition political party showed short video clips taken out of context from Jeremiah Wright's sermons and produced portrayals of Wright as inflammatory, unpatriotic, and unstable. They then linked this portrayal of Wright to Obama's own credibility. The media attacks had the intended effect over time by raising questions about the character and viewpoints of Barack Obama. After a few months, political necessity led Barack Obama to break ties with his pastor and end his membership at the Trinity United Church of Christ. I recall this story not to revisit the pain it caused those involved but to assert there are lessons for us as we seek to claim a role for the prophet—the truth teller—in the process of reconciliation. In their book *The Preacher and the Politician*, historians Clarence E. Walker and Gregory D. Smithers state, "Wright's sermons are part of a long tradition of preaching in the United States that mixes social commentary, scriptural citations, and political activism. Wright's words—be they the often-quoted 'God damn America,' or 'America's chickens are coming home to roost'—are not anti-American, unpatriotic, or even radical sentiments, but are instead words rich in religious and political meaning that draw from a deep well of Christian activism in the American colonies and the United States."[4] The authors note, "Reverend Wright belongs to an American tradition of preaching that dates back to the Puritans . . . when both black and white ministers damned America for its failings."[5] This preaching tradition is often referred to as prophetic preaching, because it is styled after that of the Hebrew prophets.

The prophetic preaching tradition is less evident today in the pulpits of white churches but is still common in the pulpits of many African American congregations. Jeremiah Wright is one of the best examples in recent memory of the Hebrew prophetic tradition in the United States. This was a common sentiment in African American churches long before anyone had heard of Barack Obama and continues to be a strongly held view. Like the prophets from the Hebrew scriptures, Wright speaks truth regarding injustice to those in power. Consistent with the African American prophetic preaching tradition, Walker and Smithers note that "Wright's preaching is political; he speaks to the historic injustices that black people have suffered in a republic that has been characterized by white supremacy."[6] Martin Luther King Jr. was also a preacher in this tradition of speaking truth to power and to his nation. In a 1967 speech he said that "the greatest purveyor of violence in the world today (is) my own government."[7] Had he not been assassinated, King's sermon title for the following Sunday was "Why America May Go to Hell."[8] King's predecessor at Dexter Avenue Baptist Church in Montgomery, Alabama, was Vernon Johns, whose regular prophetic preaching resulted in sermons such as "Segregation after Death," "It's Safe to Murder Negroes in Montgomery," and "When the Rapist Is White."[9]

The focus of the media on the sermons of Jeremiah Wright brought attention to the prophetic preaching tradition. The responses were unsettling. Most people seemed completely unaware of this Christian preaching tradition that used the words of the Hebrew prophets and Jesus to provide a social critique of present day realities. Others found it bewildering or offensive. For some it seemed somehow foreign or inappropriate to Christianity in the United States. The public encounter with the preaching of Wright revealed that the prophetic voice has mostly been lost to public life in the United States. And it is not recognized when it appears. Society refuses to value or even listen to truth telling regarding injustice. When the prophetic voice does emerge, it is quickly marginalized or silenced. Walker and Smithers note, "Implicit in some American's criticism of Wright was the desire to silence this articulate black minister, lest he remind all that black history is a tale of a marginalized and oppressed people."[10]

When Barack Obama broke ties with Jeremiah Wright, he distanced and silenced a prophetic truth telling voice in his life. We do not know how the first term of Obama's presidency could have been different if he still had the counsel of Jeremiah Wright. Nor do we know if Obama invited anyone else to play the role of truth teller in his life as a leader. What we do believe is that nations need prophets in order to remain morally accountable and socially just. The church and other religious institutions need prophets to warn when faith moves toward individualism, self-serving spiritual formulas, prosperity focus, and quietism. Reconciliation advocates need prophets because reconciliation often does not go deep enough or far enough. Prophets challenge reconciliation activists to not stop short of the full process of reconciliation.

Amos of Tekoa

The prophetic preachers of today echo the tradition of the Hebrew prophets. Many are informed and inspired by the message and life of Amos of Tekoa, a Hebrew prophet of social justice speaking the truth to the political powers and religious authorities of his day. He was a shepherd by profession from the small village of Tekoa located about ten miles south of Jerusalem in the Southern Kingdom of Judah. Today Tekoa is in the West Bank of the Occupied Palestinian Territories. Amos was chosen by God to be a prophet with a powerful word and a particular message. The book of Amos begins with the announcement that Amos heard God's call to be a prophet. "The LORD roars from Zion, and utters his voice from Jerusalem; the pastures of the shepherds wither, and the top of Carmel dries up" (Am 1:2). I visited Tekoa a few years ago. At the edge of the village is the Wadi Khareitoun, a mystical and awe-inspiring desert canyon where one can imagine the prophet Amos receiving this powerful word from God.[11]

Amos was called to speak a word from God at the central places of power in a country not his own—the Northern Kingdom of Israel during the reign of King Jeroboam II in the eighth century BCE (Am 1:1). The Northern Kingdom of Israel had its political capital in Samaria and religious center in Bethel. Amos prophesied in both places. The reign of Jeroboam II was a prosperous and peaceful time in the kingdom. Yet there was a large economic gap between rich and poor people. This economic separation translated into a physical segregation between the rich who lived in "large expensive houses" and the poor who lived in "small huddled structures."[12] The poor were exploited economically and legally.

Amos the shepherd became Amos the prophet of social justice announcing God's judgment on Israel and the nations: "They sell the righteous for silver, and the needy for a pair of sandals—they who trample the head of the poor into the dust of the earth, and push the afflicted out of the way . . . but let justice roll down like waters, and righteousness like an ever-flowing stream" (Am 2:6–7, 5:24). Amos heard the cries of poor and oppressed people and gave voice to their laments in places of power. Hebrew Bible scholar Abraham Heschel wrote, "The prophet's ear, however, is attuned to a cry imperceptible to others. . . . Had a poet come to Samaria, the capital of the Northern Kingdom, he would have written songs exalting its magnificent edifices, its beautiful temples and worldly monuments. But when Amos of Tekoa came to Samaria, he spoke not of the magnificence of palaces, but of moral confusion and oppression. Dismay filled the prophet: 'I abhor the pride of Jacob, And hate his palaces,' he cried out in the name of the Lord (Amos 6:8)."[13]

Amos was sent forth from Tekoa by God to announce that nations, societies, kings, communities, religions, and individuals are judged by how they treat the weakest members of society. This God whom Amos spoke truth on behalf of was "not the defender of the political and social system." Rather this God was "the God of the lowly, the victims who were crushed without pity in the economic machinery of the Israel of that age."[14] Amos made it clear that "the entire social system (was) tilted against the poor." The king and the political establishment who were supposed "to be the defender of the poor and guarantor of justice" were themselves actively enabling injustice.[15] The dominant theme of Amos's prophetic word was that social justice is an essential expression of authentic religious faith and should be a central concern for nations.

Amos also critiqued the religious establishment. Theologian Ted Grimsrud writes, "Injustice ran rampant in the midst of thriving religiosity. People flocked to the shrines but totally disregarded God's call for them to show justice to the needy. Amos's message is essentially that religion was making things *worse* for Israel. Their ritualistic faithfulness is masking ethical unfaithfulness."[16] Grimsrud perceptively notes that issues of injustice can be masked through a religion of individualism, legalism, and ritualism. Amos's relentless denouncement of the king and the religious leaders led to a confrontation between Amos and Amaziah, the priest of Bethel and the highest ranking religious official in the Northern Kingdom of Israel. Their conflict offered a glimpse "of the tensions when both an opposition prophet and the officials of a royal sanctuary claimed to speak for the same God."[17]

Demonstrating his loyalties, the priest Amaziah reported to his patron King Jeroboam about Amos's prophetic activities. "Amos has conspired against you in the very center of the house of Israel; the land is not able to bear all his words. For thus Amos has said, 'Jeroboam shall die by the sword, and Israel must go into exile away from his land'" (Am 7:10–11). The prophetic word was perceived as a threat to the kingdom and its religious supporters. This is clear, as Amaziah declared with great drama to the king that Amos had "conspired" at the "very center" of the house of Israel and the land was not able to "bear all his words." Notice how Amaziah referred to Amos as a conspirator rather than as a prophet when speaking to the king. He implied that the prophet was a terrorist, a troublemaker, and unpatriotic. The nonviolent Amos, only armed with a prophetic word about injustice in Israel, was perceived as a serious threat to the king. This reveals the power of truth telling. In direct contrast to Amos is Amaziah as the approved religious leader who was a patriotic uncritical loyal religious leader. Amaziah enjoyed the perks and privileges of his status without any acknowledgement of the truth of Amos's pronouncements. The confrontation at Bethel reveals "the conflict between the power that is created when politics and religion make common cause and he who is the witness of the God of the Bible." When prophets proclaim there is injustice in the land, "the throne and altar combine to silence a person."[18]

And so it happened after consulting with King Jeroboam, Amaziah spoke directly to Amos, "O seer, go, flee away to the land of Judah, earn your bread there, and prophesy there; but never again prophesy at Bethel, for it is the king's sanctuary, and it is a temple of the kingdom" (Am 7:12–13). Amaziah was only concerned with political expediency and not interested in the content of Amos's words. He needed to quickly and permanently silence Amos to ensure the continuation of the political and religious status quo in ancient Israel. Amaziah insulted Amos by claiming that he was in the land as a prophet only for profit. Then Amaziah used his power as the king's appointed and anointed top religious representative and expelled Amos from Israel.

Amos replied to Amaziah, "I am no prophet, nor a prophet's son; but I am a herdsman, and a dresser of sycamore trees, and the LORD took me from following the flock, and the LORD said to me, 'Go, prophesy to my people Israel'" (Am 7:14–15). Amos first reminded Amaziah that he was economically independent and did not need to be a prophet for financial gain, as some were in that time period. Nor was he on the payroll of the king, as was Amaziah. Then Amos informed Amaziah that his authority to speak truth came not from any king or political alliance but from God Almighty who roared like "a dangerous lion" and was "an agent who intend(ed) to restore justice in Israel."[19] Amaziah used his power gained through a close relationship to the throne of Jeroboam to effectively silence the voice of Amos. Most scholars believe that Amos only spent one year in prophetic activity in the Northern Kingdom of Israel, after which he most likely returned to Tekoa and his life there as a shepherd. The fact that Amos's words were recorded preserves his message of social justice and shows that God's voice cannot ultimately be silenced. Many years later the resurrection of Jesus of Nazareth would also witness to the inability of empires, kings, or even nationalistic religious leaders to quiet God's voice against injustice.

Today in Tekoa, the prophet's hometown, the voice of Amos continues to prophesy to Israel. On my visit to Tekoa I met Rabbi Menachem Froman. His long flowing white beard and his personal presence reminds one of a modern day Amos. Rabbi Froman was one of the early orthodox religious settlers in the West Bank of Palestine, eventually becoming the rabbi of the outpost settlement of Tekoa. Over time, though, he became convinced that the Bible calls for peace and justice. Froman has emerged as a courageous orthodox Jewish prophet of peace calling for the end of the occupation of Palestinian lands by the State of Israel. When I met Rabbi Froman, I noted that I was aware we were at the birthplace of Amos. The rabbi quoted Amos 9:7, "Are you not like the Ethiopians to me, O people of Israel? Says the Lord," to declare that God loves equally all of the people of the Holy Land. Froman believes that Israelis and Palestinians are equal in God's eyes and must learn to live together as neighbors. Rabbi Froman is already living as a neighbor with Palestinians and is willing as a Jew to become a citizen of a Palestinian state if and when that occurs. Amos is not silent. His voice is still heard.

The Role of the Prophet in Reconciliation

Martin Luther King Jr. said that Amos was "maladjusted."[20] The prophet would not adjust to or accommodate the injustice in society. King's friend Rabbi Abraham Heschel added, "The things that horrified the prophets are even now daily occurrences all over the world. There is no society to which Amos' words would not apply."[21] Amos was not silenced. He and the Hebrew prophets speak to us today reminding us to remain maladjusted to and horrified by injustice and oppression. In our efforts to propel reconciliation throughout society, the reconciler must embrace the role of the prophet. The prophet incessantly reminds people of the injustice and poverty found in the world. Abraham Heschel said that prophets are "some of the most disturbing people who have ever lived."[22] The prophet indicts those who create or benefit from oppression. The role of the prophet, as the old saying goes, is to afflict the comfortable and comfort the afflicted. Prophets express the anger of God at injustice while communicating God's compassion to the oppressed. Heschel wrote, "To us a single act of injustice . . . is slight; to the prophets, a disaster. To us injustice is injurious to the welfare of the people; to the prophets it is a deathblow to existence; to us an episode; to them, a catastrophe, a threat to the world."[23] Reconcilers are prophets of social justice.

Prophets speak hard and uncomfortable truths to those in power. Walter Brueggemann writes that the prophet's work "is nothing less than an assault on the consciousness of the empire, aimed at nothing less than the dismantling of the empire both in its social practices and its mythic pretensions."[24] Rizpah's prophetic actions spoke truth (without saying a word) and shamed

King David into acting justly. Jesus of Nazareth was a prophet of social justice who "interpreted what was happening to the people of Galilee who were being increasingly squeezed by colonial domination and internal exploitation."[25] Paul and leaders of the first-century church established prophetic communities that spoke truth to the power of Caesar by switching titles like Savior, Son of God, and Liberator used for the emperor and applying them to the resurrected Jesus. They aligned themselves with a Jesus who was crucified as an enemy of the state and took the side of oppressed people. Paul connected reconciliation with social justice calling for the liberation of colonized and marginalized people. Using the language of the postcolonialists, the truth teller "hurries on the break-up of the colonialist regime."[26] Prophets expose injustice in society. The preaching of Jeremiah Wright that the media portrayed as so offensive was simply him preaching like a biblical prophet telling the truth about injustice in the land of the United States. Reconcilers are prophetic truth tellers calling communities to public morality and responsibility for a just society.

The role of the prophet is not only one of exposing injustice and indicting the culprits. The prophet also envisions a just and reconciled future. The reconciler as prophet must have an "emancipatory imagination (that) soars out beyond the facts on the ground."[27] The reconciler envisions harmony, justice, and peace. Biblical scholar Walter Brueggemann describes this visionary capacity in *The Prophetic Imagination*, "The prophet does not ask if the vision can be implemented, for questions of implementation are of no consequence until the vision can be imagined. The *imagination* must come before the *implementation*. . . . The task of prophetic imagination and ministry is *to bring to public expression those very hopes and yearnings* that have been denied so long and suppressed so deeply that we no longer know they are there."[28] The table fellowship of Jesus produced a vision of what society could look like when everyone was included and invited to the table. First-century congregations were laboratories of justice and reconciliation where Romans, Greeks, and Jews, women and men, powerful and powerless, could experience reconciliation and envision what was possible in broader society. Reconcilers exercise a prophetic imagination for what God desires in society.

The Hebrew prophets spoke truth to oppressors so that they might repent and then become reconciled with those they had been oppressing. Fred Guyette writes, "Through the message He gives to the prophets, the

Lord also means to shake the conscience of the oppressors, to overturn their moral indifference. . . . His aim, however, is not their destruction. His desire is that they might change their ways; that they might be restored to the covenantal relationship with Him; that they might walk in the ways of justice. . . . the goal of justice in Amos is the formation of a beloved community that is faithful to the Lord."[29] This is consistent with the first-century church's attempt to reconcile colonizers with those they were colonizing. Bringing Romans into local congregations and healing them of the effects of colonialism led to truth telling in the Roman Empire. Reconcilers use prophetic truth telling to heal the powerful and privileged so that real reconciliation is possible.

Those who have taken on the mantle of social justice prophesying have not fared well. There are many examples of prophets in modern society silenced through rejection, persecution, imprisonment, and death. When prophets are silenced, injustice prevails. Yet, prophets are never truly silenced. *We just stop listening.* Jesus warned that, "Prophets are not without honor, except in their hometown, and among their own kin, and in their own house" (Mk 6:4). Reconcilers must accept the reality that they will not be honored when they take on the mantle of the prophet and speak truth to family, hometown, nation, congregation, institution, ethnic group, and the like.

New Testament scholar Ched Myers goes so far as to say that we are more comfortable with prophets after they are dead. They write, "The portrait we get in the Gospels—of an anointed man who ministered among the poor, relentlessly challenged the rich and powerful, and was executed as a political dissident—is a far cry from the stained-glass-window Christ we encounter in many churches. This seems to be a pattern in human culture: we are far more comfortable with the dead prophets than living ones. We honor them publicly only after they are safely disposed of, after which they are put on display in museums and shrines. Jesus understood this tendency well: 'Woe to you!' he exclaimed, 'For you build the tombs of the prophets whom your ancestors killed' (Lk 11:47)."[30] This is certainly true for Martin Luther King Jr. who after his death has been celebrated with a holiday. Retail stores now have their Martin Luther King Day sales. The Martin Luther King of the late 1960s who challenged the United States to address "the giant triplets of racism, materialism, and militarism" would not be useful for retail advertise-ments.[31] The disturbing nature of many other modern-day prophets has decreased as they have become subjects of history and veneration. Think of Sojourner Truth, César Chávez, Dorothy Day, Malcolm X, Nelson Mandela, and many others. When reconcilers become prophets of social justice, they will not be honored. They will be silenced.

Prophesying to the Reconcilers

In order for us to realize just societies, reconcilers must embrace the role of the prophet as truth teller in society and in the church. I want to expand our notion of the role of the prophet even further by asking the question, "Who prophesies the truth to the prophets?" This chapter began with the argument that the president of the United States needs a prophetic truth telling voice like Jeremiah Wright. In 2008 President Obama said he wanted to be a unifier. As a former community organizer in Chicago, he was familiar with the effects of injustice in society. Yet the demands and expectations of exercising power as president of the United States often contradict what is required for reconciliation and social justice. As I said earlier in the chapter, persons in power can easily be sidetracked or manipulated by their needs for power or by those around them with various agendas. They need truth tellers in order to stay on the straight path of God's justice and to persevere through to the end of the process of rec-onciliation. In order for justice and reconciliation to prevail, the hard words of prophets must be heard and implemented. What I said about persons in power I suggest is also true for those of us who are leaders in reconcilia-tion and social justice. We, too, can be sidetracked by our own needs and agendas. In order for us to have integrity and authenticity in our efforts at reconciliation, we need to invite truth tellers into our lives who can hold us accountable for embodying the values of social justice. Prophets ask hard questions and demand answers that lead to integrity. Following are some examples of questions those of us committed to reconciliation and social justice need to be asked.

How do money and connections to powerful people affect our work for reconcili-ation and social justice?

Do our social justice organizations empower women into positions of leadership?

Do our reconciliation organizations truly reflect the diversity of their constituency, community, and region, or do they settle for token representation?

Does our stated commitment to address racial injustice take on flesh in deep friendships and communal relationships with persons of different races and cultures?

Do we who are activists fighting poverty actually know any poor people?

Do we value all justice issues equally?

These questions are important for reconcilers to consider in order to remain authentic social change agents in society. We must invite hard honest questions of ourselves and our organizations. Regarding the effects of funding sources and connections to people in power, Incite! Women of Color Against Violence published a book titled *The Revolution Will Not be Funded*.[32] The premise of their book is that the funding sources of most nonprofit organizations have money to contribute because they benefit from the status quo in society. The book further notes that funding from government and foundations allows them to "monitor and control social justice movements."[33] Philanthropy can also serve as a form of appeasement or pacification for protesting communities by moderating the aims of groups committed to social change.[34] We need prophets asking us if whom we get our funding from affects how we do our work. Are we concerned that in order to keep our funding, we can, at the most, work for reform but not for full societal change? Lakota Nation elder Madonna Thunder Hawk writes about another way funding affects work for social justice. "People in non-profits are not necessarily thinking that they are 'selling out.' But just by trying to keep funding and pay everyone's salaries, they start to unconsciously limit their imagination of what they could do."[35] The challenge with the need for funding is it often means that you feel more accountable to your funders than to the constituency of persons facing injustice that you are in solidarity with.

The book also addresses who gets funded. Activists Tiffany Lethabo King and Ewuare Osayande note that race plays a role in funding even among social justice organizations. "Many white-led social justice nonprofits proclaim, in everything from their mission statements to their funding proposals, that they are committed to improving the social and economic conditions of the oppressed communities in which they operate. But alongside these proclamations exist a persisting hierarchy and circulation of capital within the social justice movement." In other words, white privilege equals access to white funders—which is a large majority of the funders.

People of color-led social justice nonprofits do not have the same access. They continue, "Given that white-led social justice groups, claiming to work on behalf of the oppressed and people of color, often rely on their existing and potential relationships with wealthy white people to sustain their organizations at best presents a serious conflict of interest."[36] Once again the question of whom we are accountable to, funders or those whom we work on behalf of, arises. So how do money and connections to powerful white people affect our work for reconciliation and social justice? It privileges white-led social justice and reconciliation organizations. Reconcilers must address this inequality in order to achieve true justice in society.

We need to invite such questions about the effects of fundraising on our commitment to reconciliation. The next questions challenge organizations to match their stated commitments in gender and racial/cultural diversity. If we make statements about our commitment to reconciliation, it should be evident in our staffing and programs. In organizations committed to social justice, it should be obvious that women are being empowered into leadership positions in the organization creating an egalitarian gender dynamic that affects the organization's mission, culture, strategies, and outcomes. Likewise in the area of racial and cultural diversity, organizations committed to reconciliation should be moving beyond the point where whites are in charge and persons of color have token positions. They should be at a place where top leadership positions and board appointments, at a minimum, reflect racial and cultural demographic realities.

Persons who have been marginalized or oppressed in society moving into positions of leadership with decision-making power does not by itself guarantee a more just and reconciled institution. More is required than just changing top leadership. The entire institution must be transformed. Women in leadership can make decisions that continue to privilege men. People of color in leadership can make decisions that continue to privilege whites. A person's experience of discrimination does not ensure that he or she will lead in a more just fashion. Also when white and/or male social justice activists gain positions of leadership in organizations, the feminist or the antiracist identity can disappear revealing an elitist side. Too often "embedded within (the) organizational strategy is an assumption of universal whiteness" (and maleness).[37] Reconciliation and social justice organizations with values and institutional structures that reflect maleness or whiteness (dominant culture) must become relics of the past. Reconciliation organizations should be multicultural and multiracial with gender partnership models. If reconciliation and social justice organizations (and churches) cannot achieve this, what hope is there for society? We need prophets speaking truth to social justice and reconciliation organizations.

Questions regarding our individual relational commitments are also vitally important. Far too many social justice leaders have the issues right but the relationships wrong. These relational questions cut to the heart of the reconciler. We can claim that we are committed to creating organizations that are diverse, but authenticity requires that there is evidence of diversity in our personal lives—actual lived experience of diversity. We can become "experts" on poverty but have no meaningful relationships with people experiencing poverty. The truth telling prophet challenges the reconciler to live a life that is consistent with her or his commitments. These relational connections with folks we advocate for actually offer us the truth telling voices we need to be effective. Reconcilers must be accountable to folks marginalized by poverty or who experience injustice.

The last question asked is how inclusive is our social justice and reconciliation agenda. That may seem like a strange question for a reconciler. But it is easy for us to identify one justice issue as most important. We can easily develop a hierarchy of issues where certain injustices are deemed more significant and needing to be addressed with greater priority. Allan Boesak saw this happen in the antiapartheid struggle in South Africa. He states, "What counted was the common struggle against white racism, economic exploitation, and political oppression." While strategically this no doubt made some sense, it allowed for other injustices to continue unaddressed, even within the antiapartheid movement itself. It also squelched any discussion of this reality. Boesak continues, "Few would dare raise questions of oppression internal to the struggle. Few would dare to 'confuse' the issue by raising questions about the insensitivity of the liberation movement to myriad issues pertaining to groups who felt themselves locked out, sat upon, disregarded, even as they marched and suffered with the rest of us. They were expected to subject their own, real pain to the greater suffering of 'the masses.' Gays knew it; women knew it; dissidents knew it; and so too those whose human rights were trampled underfoot in the military camps in the bush. . . . So no one speaks out." Boesak claims that it is the role of the prophet to speak out for all who are oppressed, "because God cares.

And here is the difference between prophecy and demagoguery."[38] Prophets speak the truth to reconcilers and liberators that there is no hierarchy of injustice—all human rights are equal.

There are more questions that must be asked. These are representative of the types of prophetic queries to put forth. Reconcilers need to invite truth tellers into their personal and work lives to pose challenging questions. When prophets are silenced, injustice prevails. Without prophetic preachers like Jeremiah Wright and truth tellers like Amos, injustice will continue to plague society. Governing authorities, power brokers, and religious institutions must be held accountable for what happens to those among us who experience injustice. Reconcilers must embrace the role of prophetic truth tellers. And those of us who claim the mantle of reconciliation must welcome truth tellers so that we might stay on the long road to reconciliation where just societies are realized.

Chapter 8

Subversive Piety
The Reradicalization of Desmond Tutu

Allan Aubrey Boesak

"Seventy Times Seven"

For the world, no one in South Africa is more identified with our process of reconciliation than Archbishop Desmond Tutu. More than that, he has, through his work as chair of our Truth and Reconciliation Commission (TRC), virtually become forgiveness personified. The TRC mandate came through an Act of a Parliament, from a decidedly secular government. Tutu, though, acted as though the commission's sessions were solemn Christian prayer meetings, with hymns and ritual candle lighting. He was unapologetically himself: a father confessor, presiding over the proceedings clad in his Archbishop's purple cassock, the very model of Christian piety.[1] What shaped his leadership at the TRC more than anything was not so much his politics or his understanding of international law. It was his Christian faith, his understanding of justice and his commitment to help make South Africa a reconciled community. Our fractured, divided, and painful past has been overcome; those who have struggled against apartheid have been vindicated "in the most spectacular fashion," but this victory was not just for the oppressed, it was "for all of us, black and white together—the rainbow people of God."[2] This new people would have a future but only if there was forgiveness.

Tutu does not trivialize apartheid: it *was* a crime against humanity. Neither does he seek excuses for the perpetrators of those crimes, but his theology would not allow him to see them as monsters, even if their evil deeds were monstrous:

131

The point is that if perpetrators were to be despaired of as monsters and demons then we were thereby letting accountability go out the window by declaring that they were not moral agents to be held responsible for their deeds . . . Theology says they still, despite the awfulness of their deeds, remain children of God with the capacity to repent, to be able to change . . . because our God is pre-eminently the God of grace . . . Ultimately, no person or situation in this theology is an irredeemable cause devoid of all hope.[3]

But accepting the perpetrator of apartheid crimes as a child of God meant reaching out with deep compassion, the victim placing herself in the shoes of the perpetrator, for "each of us has this capacity for the most awful evil—all of us. None of us could predict that if we had been subjected to the same influences, the same conditioning, we would not have turned out as these perpetrators." This was not to condone or excuse what they did, Tutu insists, "It is to be filled more and more with the compassion of God, looking on and weeping that one of His beloved had come to such a sad pass. We have to say to ourselves with deep feeling, not with cheap pietism, 'There but for the grace of God go I.'"[4]

One might legitimately ask how it is possible to weep for the perpetrator while the victims' own tears have not been recognized nor wiped away; their wounds are not seen, tended, or even wept over. But Christians "are constrained by the imperatives of this Gospel, the Good News of a God who had a bias for sinners contrary to the normal standards of the world."[5] This God, who offers us our salvation as a gift, whose love for us is "unchanging and unchangeable,"[6] compels us to forgive. And again Tutu pushes us to the brink: "Forgiving means abandoning your right to pay back the perpetrator in his own coin" and while it certainly is a loss to the victim, it is a loss that "liberates the victim."[7]

Forgiveness must not depend on the culprit's contrition and confession as precondition to forgive. It might help, but it is not "absolutely indispensable": "Jesus did not wait until those who were nailing Him to the cross had asked for forgiveness." He was ready even "as they drove in the nails to pray to His Father to forgive them." Not forgiving locks us up in a prison: "If the victim could forgive only when the culprit confessed, then the victim would be locked into the culprit's whim, locked into victimhood, whatever her own attitude or intention. That would be palpably unjust."[8]

Unconditional forgiveness is an act of justice to oneself as the victim. In the act of forgiveness, says Tutu, we do even more: "we are declaring our faith in the future of a relationship and in the capacity of the wrongdoer to make a new beginning on a course that will be different from the one that caused us the wrong."[9] Forgiveness is an act of faith. Then Tutu refers to the text in Matthew 18:22, "Not seven times, but, I tell you seventy times seven." Therein lies the future.

My point here is simply to show how beneficiaries and perpetrators of apartheid crimes, at least those who are willing to concede that wrongs have been done, would understandably react positively to the archbishop's words, seeing him reaching out to them in such life-saving Christian love. Indeed, it is as Charles Villa-Vicencio writes, "wonderful, soul-uplifting (and important) stuff . . . few of us are able to reach the heights that Archbishop Tutu has made part of his own life. The bar is simply too high."[10]

Desmond Tutu tells of the remarkable incident at the 1990 Rustenburg Conference where South African churches gathered to talk about reconciliation. Willie Jonker, Dutch Reformed Church (DRC) theologian from Stellenbosch University, took the unprecedented, unexpected, and courageous step of offering a public apology on his own behalf and that of his church and the Afrikaner people.[11] The public reactions afterwards were sometimes vicious, often bewildered, always emotional. In the hall that day, however, when Tutu strode to the podium, spoke into the stunned silence, and said, "We forgive you," he made this an unforgettable, historic moment. "The applause was deafening," remembers Frits Gaum, long-time senior official of the DRC; "tears of gratitude and forgiveness were flowing."[12] Gaum writes that this was forgiveness as Jesus would want: seventy times seven. This is the language that remade Desmond Tutu in the eyes of many whites; "redeemed" him is not too strong a word. He was such an impeccable foe of apartheid, and as a consequence, of the DRC, "a sworn enemy," Gaum calls him, who overwhelmed; they experienced this as "a moment of liberation." But they were now convinced that he had "proved in practice" that he meant what he said.[13]

It is therefore fair to say that for many whites, Desmond Tutu has become a redemptive presence in South Africa, the embodied forgiveness of whites, and simultaneously the embodied example of magnanimity for blacks. His was a piety that might be beyond the reach of most, but he personified the hope that a miracle was not impossible. And indeed, "mercifully and wonderfully," Tutu testifies, "as I listened to the stories of victims I marvelled at the magnanimity, that after so much suffering, instead of lusting for revenge they had this extraordinary willingness to forgive."[14]

This extraordinary phenomenon had little to do with politics, but everything with faith:

> For we who are Christians, the death and resurrection of Jesus Christ are proof positive that love is stronger than hate, that life is stronger than death, that light is stronger than darkness, that laughter, joy, compassion, gentleness and truth, all these are so much stronger than their ghastly counterparts. We were seeing this unfolding before our very eyes as we sat in the Commission.[15]

A Nonthreatening Spirituality?

While not all black people appreciated Desmond Tutu's theology and the consequences for reconciliation, from their point of view,[16] there is no doubt that Tutu's thinking and doings brought him new or renewed veneration in white circles. This might have come from a deeply felt sense of relief, perhaps even gratitude. Apartheid was a grave sin, and as its atrocities became known—although not nearly all of the truth came out—enough of it was revealed to make many whites shudder in shame, even though many also claimed that they did not know what was being done in their name.[17]

But the gratitude may go deeper still. In black people, Tutu's Christian piety actively dislodged much of the anger that leads only to bitter revenge and is slaked only by violent retribution; yet by the same token, it left little room for the righteous anger that should have been given a more respectful place.[18]

In the process though, white society and the largely white-owned and white-controlled media claimed ownership of Desmond Tutu's faith convictions and turned them into a nonthreatening spirituality, his piety into a harmless piousness, a purple wall of gentle forgiveness that stood between them and a terrifying black anger. The "rainbow nation" that was meant to express the vindication of those who struggled and won, black *and* white sharing in the victory, was turned into a protective cloak for white power and privilege. It was a slow but deliberate process of domestication.

We have seen these patterns before. Michael Eric Dyson explains how

Martin Luther King Jr. was appropriated by the status quo in America and how his legacy has become a foil for the most unseemly conservative plans to thwart the advancement of genuine racial equality and social justice in America.[19] It is not that white Americans genuinely love Dr. King. "By embracing King," Dyson writes, "many whites believed the threat of black insurrection could be contained, perhaps even shrewdly diverted."[20] Likewise, many whites in South Africa, by embracing Tutu and his dream of a rainbow nation, believe the threat of a revolution (which we mercifully escaped in 1994) could yet again be postponed. We remind ourselves of Elna Boesak's observation we met in chapter 6. For many white South Africans, she writes, "reconciliation has become a duty and a curse, not a voluntary choice and God-given calling. It is a political expedience divorced from their faith, emotional welfare and material prosperity."[21]

It is a domestication, the need for which is understandable, but it still remains strange that whites have so easily forgotten Desmond Tutu's role in the struggle, or disconnected him from the struggle itself, when he was, for them, an object of fear, hatred, and disdain. And he did fight apartheid with all his might. But that fighting spirit was a hunger and thirst for justice that flowed from his spirituality. Without it Tutu would have been indifferent, certainly less committed, perhaps completely uninvolved, more inclined to enjoy the relative comfort his status as bishop and later archbishop of the Anglican Church afforded him, busying himself with "church matters," staying away from politics and the wrath of the apartheid government and its supremacist supporters. But his was always a deep and genuine piety, springing from a spirituality of combative love that took him from the pulpit and the quiet of his prayer room to the struggle and from the crucifix on the wall to the streets where his people suffered on the crosses of racist oppression. His is a piety of liberation, rooted in God's compassionate justice for the poor and oppressed, and a deep love for all God's children.

Because it is a combative love, it is always subversive. It subverts the unjust status quo upheld by the powers of oppression and destruction. If you remove that combative love, it becomes a denuded, disconnected spirituality, a false piety no longer able to prophetically challenge the status quo, no longer willing, or simply unable to tell truth to power or to the people. "By default, coercion, or intention, it becomes the handmaiden of the false, patriotic piety, captive to the interests of the nation or the state," John de Gruchy says,[22] or, as Tutu himself laments, it does "what the prophet Jeremiah calls 'healing the hurt lightly' and (crying) 'Peace, peace, where there is no peace.'"[23]

This piety is subversive because it is neither sentimentalized nor privatized. Unlike the captivity of "false, patriotic piety," it is captive to God's inclusive love, compassionate justice, and the sacrificial solidarity and resistance of Jesus. False piety makes the poor voiceless and then presumes to speak on their behalf; subversive piety stands with the voiceless and enhances their cries for justice. False piety aligns itself with imperial power and succumbs to subservience; subversive piety resists imperial power and rises in obedience to God. False piety takes the Bible literally and becomes enslaved to the tyranny of fundamentalism; subversive piety takes the Bible seriously and becomes free to join in God's liberating, humanizing work in the world: "We were not inspired by political motives but by our faith. The Bible turned out to be the most subversive book imaginable in a situation of injustice and oppression."[24] This piety can never become the nonthreatening, bland, neutral, spirituality in which so many have tried to imprison Tutu.

Dyson makes the strong point that one of the ways Martin King has been domesticated is through the way his very words have been distorted, taken out of context, or selectively quoted in order to serve a perverted purpose. This is particularly the case, Dyson writes, with arguably King's most famous speech, "I Have a Dream."[25]

Tutu's words are similarly distorted, forgotten, or carefully selected. The overall result is twofold: one, that the radical intent of what he says is altered, faded, or completely lost and two, just as important, that Tutu's intentional connection between his personal piety and his public, political activism for justice is broken. When Frits Gaum quotes Tutu on Matthew 18:22, for instance, he does so in the context of Tutu's plea for, and acts of, forgiveness. He forgets, however, the context of Tutu's use of this text, which is the argument that in forgiving the wrongdoer, we are declaring our faith in the future of a relationship *and in the capacity of the wrongdoer to make a new beginning on a course that will be different from the one that caused us the wrong.* The "relationship" Tutu seeks cannot but be a relationship of equality, since without equality, reconciliation is not possible. While white South Africans hear only "forgiveness," Tutu speaks of conversion, repentance, and change: "According to Jesus we should be ready to do this not just once. Not just seven times, but seventy times seven—without limit— *provided, it seems Jesus says, your brother or sister who has wronged is ready to come and confess the wrong they have committed yet again."*[26]

Tutu's reading of the text requires that "provided," which too many conveniently forget. In fact, Tutu goes to some length to make sure we understand that for reconciliation to succeed, "Ultimately, acknowledgement by the culprit is almost indispensable. Acknowledgement of the truth, having wronged someone, is important in getting to the root of the breach."[27] True reconciliation is not cheap, and forgiving and being reconciled are not about "pretending that things are other than the way they are." True reconciliation "exposes the awfulness, the abuse, the pain, the degradation, the truth. It could even sometimes make things worse. It is a risky undertaking, but in the end it is worthwhile, because in the end there will be real healing from having dealt with the real situation. Spurious reconciliation can only bring spurious healing."[28]

Generally, that kind of conversation is not encouraged. Few whites can hear the truth about the "abuse, pain and degradation" without claiming that they are being "victimised." Tutu fervently hopes for remorse, "or at least some contrition or sorrow for that wrong, (which) should lead (the wrongdoer) to confessing the wrong he has done and asking for forgiveness."[29] In recognizing the "extraordinary magnanimity" of the black victims of apartheid crimes in their willingness to forgive, Tutu is clear that in forgiving, people are not being asked to forget. "On the contrary, it is *important* to remember, so that we should not let such atrocities happen again."[30] He explains the weight forgiveness carries for both the victim and the wrongdoer:

> Forgiveness does not mean condoning what has been done. It means taking what has happened seriously and not minimising it; drawing out the sting in the memory that threatens to poison our entire existence. It involves trying to understand the perpetrators and so have empathy, to try to stand in their shoes, and to appreciate the sort of pressures and influences that might have brought them to do what they did.[31]

Tutu firmly turns against the all too familiar demand from white South Africa that blacks must "let the past be the past," "move on," and that forgiving indeed means forgetting. Hence, this explains Tutu's immense disappointment in Mr. F. W. de Klerk, former president of South Africa, who has made this mantra his motto and has apologized for apartheid, but then, to Tutu's disgust, "qualified the apology out of existence . . . incapable of seeing apartheid for what it was—intrinsically evil."[32]

Also, forgiving is not condoning, going on with life as if nothing happened, but it is "taking the sting out of the memory." This means not obliterating it, but acknowledging the sanctity of it, keeping it holy before God, committing it to the grace of God, for that is the difference with nurturing it, allowing it to fester, poisoning the heart and mind, keeping the victim forever victimized. And it is when all this is done that room is created for empathizing with the oppressor's existential dilemma. "Confession, forgiveness, and reparation, wherever feasible, form part of a continuum."[33]

But here Desmond Tutu does not go nearly far enough. Reparations, as he himself acknowledges, can never compensate for the pain and humiliation, the suffering of loss on the side of the victim.[34] But this inherent inadequacy is precisely what prevents it from replacing justice. I should think one would have to insist, not on "reparations" as such, but rather on restitution and on the undoing of injustice and the doing of justice, by which I mean sustainable, systemic social justice, as an essential part of the continuum.[35] Reparations in the context of apartheid crimes cannot successfully rid themselves of condescension, of charity done out of somebody's largess. They cancel out the element of equality that is essential to making reconciliation real. Besides, reparations would have been paid by the government, out of public funds, rather than out of the ill-gained wealth of the beneficiaries of colonialism and apartheid. It is not the new democratic government that must make amends for apartheid crimes. Reparations mean a once-off amount that might acknowledge that the nation is "sorry," as Tutu says, but that can never be an acknowledgement of the centuries-long systemic, deliberate exploitation black South Africans were subject to and can never substitute for the systemic correction of the *systems* of exploitation that South Africa's choice for neoliberal capitalism continues to entrench, contributing vastly to the untransformed, and unreconciled, nature of our society.

Still, Desmond Tutu follows his trio of "confession, forgiveness, and reparation" with a paragraph that too many whites, in appropriating Desmond Tutu's piety for their own agenda of a comfortable, not costly, and transformation-resistant reconciliation, deliberately ignore. In South Africa, the archbishop writes,

> the whole process of reconciliation has been placed in considerable jeopardy by the enormous disparities between the rich, mainly the whites, and the poor, mainly the blacks. The huge gap between the haves and the have-nots, which was created and maintained by apartheid, poses the greatest threat to reconciliation and stability in our country. The rich provided the class from which the perpetrators and the beneficiaries of apartheid came and the poor produced the bulk of the victims. That is why I have exhorted whites to be keen to see transformation taking place in the lot of blacks. For unless houses replace the hovels and shacks in which most blacks live; unless blacks gain access to clean water, electricity, affordable health care, decent education, good jobs and a safe environment—all things which the vast majority of whites have taken for granted for so long—we can kiss goodbye to reconciliation.[36]

That we have not been able to make reconciliation "the concern of every South African"[37] is now a well-established, if infinitely sad, fact. Our discourse on reconciliation almost invariably begins with the desire "to move on" as if more than three centuries of oppression, exploitation, and dehumanization could be wiped out by the twin magic wands of political pietism and Christian quietism. And yet, Desmond Tutu was clear on this as well. "If we are going to move on and build a new kind of world community" he warned, "then there must be a way in which we can deal effectively with a sordid past."

> The most effective way I can think of is for the perpetrators *or their descendants* to acknowledge the horror of what happened and the descendants of the victims to respond by granting the forgiveness *they ask for,* providing something can be done, even symbolically, to compensate for the anguish experienced, whose consequences are still being lived through today . . . true forgiveness deals with the past, all of the past, to make the future possible.[38]

In the last few years an intense debate has been engendered by the insistence of white youth that they, since they were not responsible for apartheid, had nothing to apologize for, had no guilt to be repentant of, and had no responsibility for the plight of the victims of a regime they had never voted for. Desmond Tutu makes clear the *generational responsibility* of white South Africans regarding justice for what South Africans call the *historically disadvantaged*. Or perhaps the better term is *historically victimized*.

The matter is not as complex as it is made out to be. One distinction of racism is that it is not only systemic, or driven by the dynamics of power, but also that it creates *generational victims* just as it creates *generational beneficiaries*. Just as an example, the land that was stolen from the original South Africans in colonial times through dispossession and extermination, the legalization of land theft through the Land Acts of 1913 and 1936, the creation of the Bantustans, and the Group Areas Act is one long, vicious act of violence the tragic consequences of which whole communities have not yet recovered from. Yet the children and grandchildren of those who did this are still benefiting from this historic theft and are the inheritors of huge tracts of land in the rural areas and prime pieces of land in the urban areas. The TRC had a mandate that did not even recognize this as sustained, structural violence, and therefore a crime.

Precious little land restitution has been made or can be made, since our otherwise progressive Constitution guarantees the sanctity of private property as if it were on a par with the sanctity of life. The systemic economic exploitation has been generational and leaves white youth with a platform of wealth, privilege, and inherited confidence to build upon. I am not even speaking of the psychological damage that came with legalized and systemic dehumanization and the bewilderment that came from the destruction of communities, values, and culture always concomitant with colonization and domination. That creates, beyond apartheid's seemingly irreversible spatial arrangements and social engineering, a permanentization of structural injustice, a permanentization of *apartheid* that we have not even begun to address, since the economic and social arrangements brought into being by colonization and apartheid, and once again since 1994 created a "perpetuation of pauperization"[39] that continues to imprison generations of black South Africans. An older woman, a strong community leader/pastor from Botshabelo, the black township fifty kilometers from Bloemfontein, told our group in one of our *conversations on reconciled diversity*, "My pain and my anger are not from yesterday." If white youth want to disown any responsibility for apartheid and its disastrous consequences "because they did not vote for it," then the first thing they must do is to disown the inherited benefits of it.

Reconciliation and Prophetic Truth Telling

In my view, the public image of the deradicalized Desmond Tutu certainly has to do with the determination of white South Africans to create for themselves the perfect buffer between continued white power and privilege and black anger and disenchantment. In the United States they had one irresistible, noncontestable black icon: Martin Luther King Jr. In South Africa we have two: Desmond Tutu and Nelson Mandela.

But secondly, it has to do with a lack of understanding of radical black Christianity, as much as it has to do with not understanding the passion of the prophets of the Hebrew Bible, the point made with regard to Jeremiah Wright in the previous chapter. In radical black Christianity, a deep piety and a vibrant spirituality do not equate with a privatized, quietistic, noninvolved piousness. In black spirituality, as it is in genuine Reformed spirituality, faith totally dependent upon God and surrendered to the Holy Spirit is a faith totally committed to a public witness, a life *coram Deo* and *coram publicum*—before God and before the public. There is no dichotomy between our worship of God in the private space of our prayer life and our worship of God in public testimony for the sake of justice and on behalf of the voiceless.

Thirdly, it is a result of Desmond Tutu's own theological and political consistency. Tutu is as vocal and relentless a critic of the new African National Congress (ANC) regime as he was of apartheid. His prophetic voice lashes out as clearly when the ANC government fails to do justice, and he has spoken out persistently on a wide range of issues.[40] In our sometimes divisive and always racially driven politics, many whites have mistaken this prophetic integrity as "being on their side" and the angry responses of the ANC to Tutu's criticism as vindication of *their* political hostility. They fail to see this as not a stance *against* the ANC per se, but rather as a stance *for* justice and *against* injustice wherever it occurs.

Zionist supporters of the State of Israel, Jews and Zionist Christians alike, have discovered this as well. Tutu is passionate about justice for

Palestinians and about the ongoing Israeli occupation. He sees this as a continuation of the struggle against injustice, made worse by what he (like I, and millions the world over) has come to believe is a new emergence of apartheid. In a letter to the "Divestment Sponsors" at the University of California, Tutu writes, "It was with great joy that I learned of your recent 16-4 vote in support of divesting your university from companies that enable and profit from the injustice of the Israeli occupation of Palestinian land and violation of Palestinian rights. It is no more wrong to call out Israel in particular for its abuses than it was to call out the apartheid regime for its particular abuses."[41]

This stance has made Zionist supporters exceedingly angry. "Tutu is a black Nazi pig" was once spray painted on the wall of the St. George's Anglican Cathedral in Jerusalem in whose close Tutu was staying during a visit to the city.[42] As Tutu gets progressively more radical in his views, the pendulum has swung once again. But it is because there is no understanding of the consistent prophetic constraints of Tutu's faith and calling, no understanding of the prophetic tradition of solidarity and truth telling in which both Desmond Tutu and Jeremiah Wright stand. It is truth telling that has no borders, knows loyalties beyond skin color and culture, reaches beyond the struggles of "the race" to join the struggles of *the people*. For that reason, Desmond Tutu and Jeremiah Wright both struggle for justice for black people but also for Palestinians, women, gays, lesbians, bisexual, transsexuals, intersex persons, and oppressed groups the world over.[43]

I should say one more word about truth telling. Following Albie Sachs, Desmond Tutu speaks of "orders of truth," which do not mutually exclude one another. There is *forensic, factual truth*—verifiable and documentable; *social truth*—the truth of experience that is established through interaction, discussion and debate. Then there is *personal truth*, in the wonderful phrase of Judge Ismail Mahomed, "the truth of wounded memories." That was the "healing truth" Tutu strongly felt would have slipped through the cracks in a court of law with its rules and strict legal definitions and requirements and would have left many "who were frequently uneducated and unsophisticated, bewildered and even more traumatized than before." It was infinitely better for them to testify before the commission instead.[44]

Within the context of truth telling, however, I would like to suggest a fourth truth and that is *the truth of interrupted but resilient hope*. It is here that the prophet finds herself embedded both in the calling from God *and* in the struggle of the people. Prophet and people are bound together by that hope and the struggle for it; uplifted, envisioned, and emboldened by the reality of it. The struggle of the people for justice and liberation is a struggle in hope. Sanctified by the interruption of history in the death and resurrection of Jesus Christ, it reveals the violence and injustices at work in the systems of our world and calls for solidarity with those robbed of hope by brutal powers. That hope is frequently interrupted by the ruthlessness of the powers, by the suffering of the people, thwarted by the silencing of the prophets. Standing in and for that truth, that hope, through the faithfulness of the prophets, exposes that interruption and in turn interrupts the flow of history and the relentless works of evil, turns the world upside down, and shows to what extent our "reality" is in fact a lie.

That hope is fragile, for it is the hope of the vulnerable; but it is resilient, for it is a hope that is rooted in the promises of God, in the incarnation of Jesus Christ and the faithfulness of God's people. That truth, too, must be boldly proclaimed. It is a hope often brutally crushed but which remains resilient because it receives its life from the God "who executes justice for the oppressed" and who "lifts up those who are bowed down" (Ps 146:7, 8); from Jesus who "will proclaim justice to the Gentiles . . . who will not break a bruised reed or quench a smoldering wick until he brings justice to victory"—the One in whom the Gentiles shall put their hope (Mt 12:18, 20).

It is hope that is not seen (Rom 8:24)—that lives even though it is not evident through the tear gas and the tears, not so clearly defined in the prison cell or in the torture chamber, not always discernible in the deluge of the propaganda of the powerful, but kept alive by visions of justice and the sanctity of our humanity, empowering us to resistance and endurance. Every new struggle for justice renews that hope; every struggle for justice is renewed by that hope. Every stride toward freedom renews that hope, and every step in dignity is renewed by the audacity to hope.[45] The very audacity *of* that hope gives us the authority and freedom of the audacity *to* hope. The truth of interrupted but resilient hope enfolds and sanctifies the truth of wounded memories. It unmasks the false truth of ideology and pseudo piety. It inspires both prophet and people, and it helps us remember that while history may indeed be written by the victors, the future is fashioned by those who believe in it and nurture it with their hope. When that truth is spoken, the very gates of hell cannot prevail against it. *Nothing is more subversive than the truth of interrupted but resilient hope.*

The Reradicalization of Desmond Tutu

In 2003 Archbishop Tutu gave a strong indication of a growing impatience, indeed a returning radicality in his thinking:

> Can you explain how a black person wakes up in a sordid ghetto today, almost ten years after freedom? Then goes to work in town, which is still largely white, in palatial homes. And at the end of the day, he goes home to squalor? I don't know how those people don't just say, "To hell with peace. To hell with Tutu and the Truth Commission."[46]

There was, as far as I could tell, not much notice taken of this. But then, in August 2011, Tutu made his call for a wealth tax.[47] Apartheid, Tutu told his mainly white audience at Stellenbosch University, had left South Africans "riddled with self-hate" and was directly to blame for many of the ills our society still suffers from. Tutu was not sparing white sensitivities: "You all benefited from apartheid. Your children went to fancy schools, you lived in posh suburbs." He argued that a way for whites to show their seriousness with reconciliation was to pay a "wealth tax." "One per cent of their stock exchange holdings," he told a journalist at the event, "it's nothing."

The reactions were immediate and went on for weeks. They ranged from reasonable debate to the most vicious attacks, perhaps best summed up in the one-liner from a white male: "I hope he dies soon."[48] Some tried to bring reason to the debate. "The wealth tax idea is not something from a lunatic bishop," says Geoff Harris, lecturer in economics at the University of KwaZulu Natal. "It is something that many experts have proposed before. All it boils down to is making generosity a virtue," perhaps revealing once again that inability to resist the temptation to make Desmond Tutu more palatable, less radical than he actually is.[49] Harris goes on to point out that in 2008 the richest 10 percent of households received almost forty times more that the poorest 50 percent; the richest 10 percent currently earn 150 times more than the poorest 10 percent. "The dangers of such inequalities are there for all to see," he observes correctly. Indeed, it is not a matter of finding ways to make generosity a virtue; it is a matter of justice and equality. That calls for radical measures.

Tutu is, in fact, reiterating what the TRC has suggested in its report, and as we have seen, Tutu himself pointed out the dangers to reconciliation in *No Future without Forgiveness,* in 1999. Meanwhile the gap between the rich and the poor in this country has taken on disastrous proportions. South Africa, surpassing Brazil, is now the most unequal society on earth. "The worst example of the disparity between rich and poor," *Leadership Magazine* calls it, trying to put Tutu's call "in perspective."[50] Tutu, even in his passion, perhaps even anger, is still gentle: "My appeal is, do you think you might consider agitating for something akin to this?"[51]

Unusually instructive is the response of a young woman from Bloemfontein, writing in the provincial edition of a national Afrikaans paper.[52] Evidently widely distributed, and as widely applauded, it was sent to me in an e-mail under the title: "This Girl Should Go to Parliament!" Addressing the archbishop and setting out what white people are (still) doing for blacks (despite their unreasonableness), she writes in one long continuous paragraph:

> We GIVE! We take care (of them), we provide, we share, we cook soup and bake bread for them, empty our closets; we 'tip' the shop assistant who help us and the parking assistant and at the car wash. We pay for the funerals of their extended families to the third generation. We pay their school fees . . . We train our domestic servants, we knit jerseys, caps and gloves; we buy blankets, give our food away along the roads. We teach them to be neat, to pick up their trash, to cook, make clothes, to plant, to farm, to milk cows. We GIVE! We buy birthday cakes, medicine, pay their taxi fare, give our precious food to their hungry children. We stop the car and give them candy. We GIVE! We create jobs, we pity them, we pray, we pick up their babies from trash cans and bring them up, we organise parties at crèches in squatter camps . . . we give (our) hearts, livers, kidneys, lungs, and tongues. [Here she, in humorous profanity, adds a body orifice.] We GIVE! We are not racist, nor vengeful, (despite everything) we remain in

our country, we clean up after them, ferry them around. We comfort them, explain, remain calm, patiently waiting in long lines and smile . . . We GIVE! Did I say it already? We GIVE!

This does not need much commentary. It is, judging by the gleeful response, a word on behalf of many whites. She treats black people as help-less, wretched children, perpetual beggars, ingrates who scarcely deserve the charity white people dole out on a daily basis. There is not a clue that she understands that in South Africa, impoverishment of blacks and en-richment of whites are interdependent, active, continuing, deeply systemic processes, based on and bolstered by deliberate policies for over three cen-turies, designed to create victims and beneficiaries. But despite all this black wretchedness, whites "remain calm, not racist or vengeful." It is a clever letter: the condescending, sarcastic, mocking tone is hugely offensive and unbearably racist, but should black people react with anger, it is yet another sign of their ungratefulness, lack of a sense of humor, and their immaturity.

This young woman is a perfect example of what Paulo Freire identi-fies as the "false generosity of the powerful." It is not true generosity, but a generosity that seeks to obscure unjust orders, and fails to transform the world. Freire writes, "In order to have the continued opportunity to ex-press their 'generosity,' the oppressors must perpetuate injustice as well. An unjust order is the permanent fount of this 'generosity,' which is nourished by death, despair, and poverty. That is why its dispensers become desperate at the slightest threat to the source of that false generosity."[53]

This is the false generosity that needs to be destroyed, by replacing it with true generosity, and true generosity "consists precisely in fighting to destroy the causes which nourish false charity."[54] Radical reconciliation, I would argue, is a process whereby false generosity is destroyed, and true generosity is brought into being. False generosity feeds on the creation of what Freire calls "the rejects of life" extending their "trembling hands" in fearful supplication to the powerful who "GIVE!" Radical reconciliation, which calls for transformation and conversion of the powerless themselves, must turn those trembling hands into "human hands which work, and, by working, transform the world . . . by fighting for the restoration of their humanity, as individuals and as peoples, they will be attempting the resto-ration of true generosity."[55] Reconciliation with the "rejects of life" is not possible.

The archbishop did point out that the last seventeen years have seen unprecedented growth of wealth in black elite circles and our political aristocracy that has been created on the backs of the perpetual impoverishment of the poor and oppressed. The gap between rich and poor is no longer simply the gap between white and black. The wealthy black elite, too, are part of those whose "false generosity" should be challenged and changed.

Again we must reach deeper: a once-off tax or even an annual tax will not necessarily correct the systemic injustices we have embraced in neoliberal capitalism since 1994. We need meaningful policy adjustments in order to bring economic justice, in order to make meaningful reconciliation at the "secondary level," as Charles Villa-Vicencio calls it, possible.[56]

Theologian John de Gruchy's thoughtful and honest "Meditation on the Tutu Tax Proposal" is the exact opposite of the young woman's letter. Tutu's proposal is exactly the kind of thing one should expect from a true Christian prophet, for "apartheid is not dead," he writes. "Those of us who were the economic beneficiaries of apartheid remain its beneficiaries in many ways."

> For too long we felt entitled to the best schools, best medical care, best housing, best everything else in comparison to some of the worst education, health service, shacks, and everything else that has been the outcome not just of more recent government failures to deliver . . . but of centuries of colonial rule, land dispossession and racial discrimination.[57]

So in responding to Tutu, de Gruchy advises, "let us remember again what Jesus teaches us about economic justice, and only then pray—not just for the poor, but that our society will become less divided by wealth and poverty."

Forgiving the Unforgivable

As I write, South Africans are still struggling with the shock of what happened in a small town, Modimolle, in the province of Mpumalanga. Mr. Johan Kotze, estranged husband of Ms. Ina Bonnette, is alleged to have forced three laborers at gunpoint to gang rape and brutally mutilate her. He then tied her up and allegedly forced her to listen while her son Conrad begged for his life. Then he allegedly shot the boy three times, including a fatal shot to the head. Understandably this was big news, and, predictably, the media have taken to calling Johan Kotze "the Monster from Modimolle." The public want him condemned and destroyed.

In the middle of the media frenzy and the public outrage, Desmond Tutu stepped into the breach. In a letter to the press, Tutu called upon the media to stop calling Kotze a "monster." "These are dastardly deeds," he wrote, "barbaric and monstrous in extent and we are quite right to condemn them roundly, unequivocally." What is disturbing however, "is when our outrage leads us to dub the alleged perpetrator 'the Monster from Modimolle' as the media has been doing. He may indeed be guilty of inhuman, ghastly and monstrous deeds, but he is not a monster." Then Tutu returns to the argument he used at the TRC. "We are actually letting him off the hook . . . because monsters have no moral sense of right and wrong—and therefore cannot be regarded as morally blameworthy. No, Mr. Johan Kotze remains a child of God with the capacity to become a saint." In reference to the TRC and biblical examples, the archbishop concludes, "But we believed then, and I hope we still do, that it was possible for people to change for the better, that the worst criminal could become a good and virtuous person."[58] Perpetrators should be held accountable but not judged irredeemable.

More than a decade after the TRC, Desmond Tutu still calls us to account, holding onto his theology of forgiveness, confession, and change. This too, I submit, is an expression of the subversive piety we have been tracking throughout this chapter. Accountability with the intention to redeem is subversive of our natural inclination not just to judge, but to completely write off perpetrators. Therefore, it is also subversive of our resistance to reconciliation. The other person may have done monstrous deeds, Tutu argues, but is still "a child of God." That means that no human being can prescribe to God who might be acceptable as God's children, that before God our sins are grave enough for God to disclaim us all.

Tutu's piety subverts us in at least two more ways. First, it subverts us on a political level. Tutu reminds South Africans that at the TRC, we as a nation had been asked to forgive the most horrendous, inhumane acts by apartheid criminals, and we did, because it served a political purpose. If forgiveness were possible, then as a collective political act, why do we insist that this man is irredeemable? Is that not disturbingly hypocritical? Is it because our forgiveness of Kotze does not hold any political benefits for us?

But secondly, it subverts us on a theological level. Our common humanity brings a common vulnerability to culpability, no one is intrinsically better than the other: "There but for the grace of God go I." But, moreover, like Abraham in Genesis 18,[59] Tutu argues that it is not true, as we seem to think, that the holiness of God demands the vengeance of God, which, if we can have our way, we will execute on behalf of God. Rather the holiness of God demands mercy and forgiveness. Abraham finds it impossible to believe that a holy, just God can destroy the world because of the unjust and despite the presence of the righteous. The unjust should not cause the destruction of the world; rather, the just should guarantee the life of the world. For Tutu, Jesus, the Just One, is the guarantee of the life of the world, and in Jesus we are all forgiven, no matter the "monstrosity" of our sins. Abraham says, and Tutu argues, *can* God, *shall* God, if God is God and not some wilful, unstable tyrant, simply write off and destroy? Has God, like humans, fallen helplessly into a cycle of violent retribution and vengeance? Tutu refuses to believe that, and he calls upon South Africans to believe that with him. Tutu asks, Is it possible for us to be in solidarity with the victim and yet leave open the possibility for conversion, contrition, change in the perpetrator?

No one pretends that this is easy, but if reconciliation needs political forgiveness, reconciliation needs communal and personal forgiveness. For reconciliation to be genuine, we should allow ourselves to be subverted by the grace and mercy of God. Radical reconciliation requires less self-righteousness, less hypocrisy, less self-defensiveness, less judgmental arrogance. It requires more self-critical consciousness, more humility, more boldness, more piety—but of the subversive kind.

Conclusion
Beyond Political Pietism and Christian Quietism
Allan Aubrey Boesak and Curtiss Paul DeYoung

The Need for a "More Modest Reconciliation"

"They knew I was coming, and they must have been waiting for me."
Thus Allan Boesak begins the story of his encounter with five young people as he arrived for a meeting at the Apartheid Museum in Johannesburg, South Africa, in late 2001.[1] It turned out to be a discussion about reconciliation that, the young people felt, "was not working." They explained that what might be a good thing for white people was not such a good thing for blacks after all. "In the townships where we live," they explained, "nothing had come of it, and nothing was seen of it." They felt that white people "just did not care" and had not shown they understood what black people had suffered under apartheid, what it cost to offer the hand of friendship and forgiveness that was now being "slapped away." "We are being wasted," they said, meaning "we, as persons," their past, their struggle, their feelings, their willingness to make it work, their faith that it must work.

Feeling pressured, Allan finally asked them about President Nelson Mandela's wonderful example of forgiveness and reconciliation after his twenty-seven years in prison. They gave an answer he will never forget. "If I were made president of the country and given his millions," the spokesperson for the group answered, "I would also forgive everybody." This story is paradigmatic of the way the reconciliation process in South Africa has been experienced. The young people were not cynical, but they were disillusioned. Since then, that disillusionment has turned into anger. Since then, too, others, of an older generation, and much more fortunate than the black

151

youth from Soweto that night, have articulated the growing disenchantment with the reconciliation process.[2]

In South Africa, many have argued for what is now called "political
reconciliation." They dismiss what one can call "spiritual reconciliation." In
this book we have shown, especially through the influence of Archbishop
Desmond Tutu, how the South African reconciliation process acquired a
spiritual, especially Christian, emphasis. That this emphasis has had all sorts
of consequences is also clear. But it is this emphasis that has elicited some
critical response from those who felt that Archbishop Tutu's understanding of Christian forgiveness was setting the bar simply too high. There is,
therefore, a need for "a more modest notion of reconciliation that makes
its own set of demands." It involves, writes Charles Villa-Vicencio,

> Pardon, mercy, understanding and a willingness to seek ways to live
> with adversaries, despite past scars that refuse to go away. It involves
> political common sense rather than religious magnanimity; clear-head-
> edness rather than heroism; responsible living rather than monk-like-
> self-denial. It involves treating others in the kind of way we would like
> them to treat us. We do not necessarily have to forgive one another in
> order to live together in peaceful co-existence. We do have to respect
> one another and establish certain economic, social and political ground
> rules that enable this to happen. This level of political realism may be
> the only realistic political option we have, short of what John Vorster
> once called "an alternative too ghastly to contemplate."[3]

Villa-Vicencio is not the only one who argues this way. Former South
African president Thabo Mbeki and academic Jakes Gerwel both agree
with him.[4] Gerwel is adamant that we must avoid confusing politics and
theology in defining and determining the contours of reconciliation, which
is what a "spiritualization" of reconciliation will do. Notions of "love" and
"forgiveness" tend to "pathologize" a relatively healthy nation, taking us
back to "primitive" notions not suitable for modern societies. We no longer seek "for such idealistic denial or obfuscation of contradiction." The
"mechanisms of solidarity" of our contemporary society are no longer
"love for neighbor," but rather "commitment to consensus-seeking, cultiva-
tion of conventions of civility and respect for contracts."[5] These arguments
amount to a political pietism.[6]

"Something Lost in Translation"

While in South Africa reconciliation has been de-spiritualized into political pietism by many, in the United States reconciliation has been de-politicized into Christian quietism. Sociologists Michael Emerson and Christian Smith argue, in their 2000 book *Divided by Faith*, that "something (was) lost in translation" when the reconciliation discussion in the United States moved from the black community to the white community.[7] They write, "As the message of reconciliation spread to a white audience, it was popularized. The racial reconciliation message given to the mass audience is individual reconciliation. . . . Missing from the formula are the system-changing components of the original formulations. The more radical component of reconciliation espoused by the early black leaders and many of the current leaders—to challenge social systems of injustice and inequality, to confess social sin—is almost wholly absent in the popularized versions."[8] This created a privileged, evangelical, individualized reconciliation. We have argued in this book that also lost in translation was a biblical postcolonial reconciliation process that became an inauthentic form of reconciliation defined and dispatched from a womb of privilege. Both the South African "political reconciliation" and the U.S. evangelical "individualized reconciliation" seek to tame and defang radical reconciliation. Therefore, this so-called reconciliation has produced congregations that are diverse but not reconciled and institutions that address Reitz-like racism with modest coexistence rather than repentance or reparation.

Radical Reconciliation

In response to these efforts to translate radical reconciliation into political pietism or Christian quietism, it is necessary for us to make a few points. *One*, we must protest the oversimplification of the demand for Christian love and forgiveness as essential to reconciliation. Villa-Vicencio's language of juxtaposition is almost condescending: "political common sense" over against "religious magnanimity;" "clear-headedness" over against "heroism;" and "responsible living" over against "monk-like self-denial." Gerwel insists that the demand for radical Christian reconciliation is "pathologizing." (If it is "pathologizing," it is because it makes us "maladjusted" to injustice, as Martin Luther King noted.) We cannot approach reconciliation "purely on the basis of the biblical injunction to love one another," Thabo Mbeki writes. "Reconciliation has to be based on the removal of injustice."[9] The point in this book, however, is exactly to show that biblical reconciliation is *radical* reconciliation. Peace and justice, belong intrinsically, inextricably together. The God of justice calls for a love that transforms relationships, societies, indeed the world, so that justice and peace can embrace (Ps 85:11). *Reconciliation without social justice, equity, and dignity is not reconciliation at all.* Reconciliation and social justice are two sides of the same biblical coin. Reconciliation is translated into no more than political accommodation in which the "economic, social and political ground rules" of that accommodation are written by the rich and powerful, excluding the poor and powerless, while the powerless are expected simply to adhere to those rules, even while they work to the detriment of the poor.

If it is a "mechanism of solidarity" as Gerwel argues, in South Africa that mechanism has failed the poor miserably. Such an understanding of reconciliation is simply not enough, we argue. It is precisely the political pietism we are warning against. Radical reconciliation questions the assumption that justice can be served, social contracts honored, and solidarity enacted through politics and policies grounded in a neoliberal capitalism whose very survival depends on the exclusion of the powerless, the exploitation of the poor, and the nurturing of inequality the scale of which is devastatingly clear in South Africa as well as in the United States.[10]

Two, we have argued that forgiveness is not simply a matter of forgetting and "moving on" as if nothing has happened, or, indeed, nothing else has to be done. Forgiving is not forgetting, but holding the memory as holy before God, so that the victim is honored and the atrocity is never repeated again. *Reconciliation is holding the memory holy before God as a means of responding to God's demands for justice for the vulnerable and the powerless, the neglected, and the excluded.* There is nothing sentimental about it.

Three, Christian reconciliation is radical, costly reconciliation: not papering over the cracks, knowing it is not possible but between equals. It calls for systemic justice, a radical reordering of power relationships and sustained transformation of society. That it also calls for transformation of the heart and mind is not in contradiction to the call for justice. Rather, that is how reconciliation is sustained. While forgiveness may work differently for individuals who have to reconcile than for societies, the essential common denominator is the restoration of justice, equity, and dignity, of human contentment. *Radical reconciliation means that the deeply personal does not cancel out the thoroughly systemic.*

Four, we must protest the positing of our understanding of biblical reconciliation as if it moves in the realm of the unreal, the too idealistic, and hence the unattainable. There is nothing romantic about replacing unjust social and economic systems with policies of sustained economic justice bent toward equality. We fear that the "modest notion" of reconciliation, which must replace spiritual reconciliation, as Villa-Vicencio contends, is a dangerous modesty, damaging for the poor and powerless. It is a demand for modesty not of reconciliation but, in fact, of the poor: *they* must tone down their expectations of justice, for fear that their longing for the undoing of injustice and the doing of justice might "hold to ransom" the process of reconciliation to "moral . . . forms of idealism."[11] In the real world of politics, economics, and social structuring in the globalized world of the twenty-first century, it is the global poor who are held ransom by the wealthy and the powerful. *Reconciliation makes it incumbent on us to change this situation by liberating the global poor, and radically so.*

Fifth, reconciliation emerges from the margins and not from the centers of political or religious power. We hope we have made this abundantly clear as we rehearsed the story of Rizpah's silent prophetic encounter with King David, observed the truth-telling power of the outsider prophet Amos as he announced God's justice to the king and the high priest of Israel, and rediscovered the dramatic resistance of Jesus and a colonized, occupied first-century church to the Roman emperor and the religious authorities. Yet even then, the voices from the margins resounded with a reconciliation harmony calling forth also to those in power to join in a process meant to rehumanize all of God's children.

Relocating the Battleground

This book is not arguing that political reconciliation is not necessary. As the "litmus test of a successful political transition and peace endeavor,"[12] there certainly is a place for it. It is a necessary first step. But radical reconciliation calls for more. Even the defenders of political reconciliation themselves find it hard to avoid a language that is steeped in spirituality. Villa-Vicencio's use of "pardon" and "mercy" speaks of it, and "political forgiveness" still implies that there is something to forgive. And forgiveness, whichever way one describes it, is not naturally a secular, political word. One expects it at the end of a process of confession, repentance, and conversion, not at the end of a negotiated settlement. The best one can do there is to come to an understanding that it is better to find a way to accommodate each other's interests as best one can. Politics is, after all, the art of the possible. Forgiveness, by its very nature, belongs to the realm of the impossible, made possible only by the grace of God. Besides, he cannot act as if his reference to "doing unto others as we would have them do to us" (Mt 7:12) has nothing to do with Jesus. We are saying that Christians are called as agents of reconciliation, that that reconciliation is radical, and that the demands of that radical reconciliation should be made applicable to the political, social, and political realities within which they live and work. As such, Christians are suspicious of reconciliation as pure political accommodation, which secures only the world of the powerful, distrustful of a minimalist process that does not make compassionate justice and transformation the heart of its endeavor.

Theologian and antiapartheid activist Frank Chikane has made a point that is pertinent here. The process of equating reconciliation with negotiations and political settlements, he writes, is a "simplistic understanding" which "robs the word reconciliation of its deeper meaning." Negotiations can result from political pressures or from a mutual decision by parties to avoid a war because the costs are too great. This does not mean that the parties have had a change of heart—"they are simply relocating the battle ground to the negotiating table or parliament."[13]

In truth, though, the battleground is not shifted to parliament or the negotiating table, or even the board room table. Negotiations and political accommodation relocate the battleground to the townships and the streets, to the shacks and the hovels and the refugee camps, where people do daily battle with poverty and hunger and rats, and with the consequences of decisions made by political and economic elites who find it difficult to adequately represent the interests of the poor. It is shifted to poorly equipped schools in areas where children do battle with inferior education and the consequences of inadequately trained teachers. The battleground is relocated to the hearts of children who struggle with trampled dreams, fragmented hopes, and piecemeal joys; to the lives of young people, bewildered by disappointments and disillusionment, who face heavily armed soldiers in tanks with stones. It is relocated to violent streets where the generationally induced violence of colonialism and apartheid, slavery and genocide, still makes its victims by the millions. It is relocated to the wall in occupied Palestine where Israeli state-sponsored apartheid strips Palestinians of their rights, their ownership of their land, and their dignity through relentless checkpoints where hope is surrendered to the merciless tyranny of irrational fear and nationalistic egotism. The battle is relocated to cities in the United States where the lifespan of a young urban black man is as short as that of a peasant in Bangladesh and where the criminal justice system is the new Jim Crow.[14]

The battle is relocated to hospitals and clinics in poor communities in South Africa where there are never enough doctors or nurses, where medical equipment does not work properly, where clean bed sheets are an unbelievable luxury, where the infant mortality rates are frighteningly high, and where HIV-infected patients cannot take their medication because they do not have food to eat. It is relocated to the lives of the unemployed who do battle with political party promises, government statistics, and the grim realities of their own lives; to the hearts of the barely employed who do battle with waves of despair, remnants of hope, and elusive dignity. The battle is relocated to the rain forests of Bolivia where indigenous communities do battle with the carelessness of government and the untrammeled greed of international corporations. It is through those eyes and on these battlegrounds that we look for the realization of reconciliation, and it is these and other battles that make the call for radical reconciliation so urgent and indispensable.

Beyond Political Pietism and Christian Quietism

There is no doubt that cheap reconciliation is a great temptation. Its roots, however, are not biblical radicalism, but a quietistic piousness that does not see justice as the cause of Yahweh, as it was the cause of Jesus of Nazareth and the first-century church, as we have consistently argued. It concentrates on vague notions of repentance and forgiveness totally disconnected from the sinful realities of systemic injustice. It speaks of forgiveness in hymnal terms, but it leaves no room for the righteous anger of the victim, because it is itself incapable of feeling outrage at injustice. Cheap reconciliation, in pretending to be more and more like God, becomes less and less like God.

But the temptation of a politically pietistic reconciliation is just as great. It, too, is a form of cheap reconciliation, where it is not biblical reconciliation but indeed political accommodation that becomes a holy grail being pursued at the cost of justice, at the cost of the poor. Like Christian quietism, it appropriates the language of reconciliation, speaks of political forgiveness, social consensus and social contracts, civility and political correctness. But devoid of justice, equity, and dignity it remains an exclusionary pact amongst the powerful, not seeking genuine transformation driven by justice and in the process becomes the embodiment of the very contradictions it accuses Christian reconciliation of obfuscating and denying.

What the young people from Soweto, who encountered Allan at the Apartheid Museum, wanted was *radical reconciliation*. We invite you to move beyond political pietism and Christian quietism and join us on a journey that takes us from the radical solidarity of Rizpah, to the radical call for justice of the prophets, to the life and ministry of Jesus the radical reconciler. It is a revolutionary reconciliation that creates a new humanity where the powerful and powerless exchange places in order to find oneness through just social relationships. We hope we have opened perspectives on the kind of reconciliation we need, which indeed the world, for all its sacralized secularity, cannot do without. Amen!

Acknowledgements

From Allan:

This is my first effort at coauthorship, so initially somewhat daunted, somewhat nervous, I acceded to Curtiss DeYoung's request to write this book with him. It turned out to be a wonderful learning and altogether spiritual experience for which I am deeply grateful to Curtiss, certainly, but also to Orbis and Robert Ellsberg for making this possible.

Throughout 2011, I have had the immense privilege of leading a series of conversations, called "Conversations on Reconciled Diversity" with students at the University of the Free State (UFS) at Bloemfontein and with community and religious leaders from the black communities in the area. Those were some of the most enlightening and stimulating conversations I have had in a long time, and I am deeply indebted to the participants for their honesty, integrity, and wisdom, from which I have profited so much. They have grounded me firmly in our South African situation, as seen through the eyes of those "at the bottom of the well" (Derrick Bell), and helped to keep me on the right path whenever I was tempted to stray too far from the realities we have to confront in our quest for reconciliation. Thank you, too, to the International Institute for Studies in Race, Reconciliation and Social Justice at UFS who supported that work throughout the year.

Courtney Sampson and Charles Villa-Vicencio have read portions of the manuscript, and I was privileged to test the chapter on Rizpah at an international conference organized by Mitri Raheb in Bethlehem, Palestine. To all, my deep-felt thanks.

Much of the writing of this book took place during our summer vacation, traditional family time over Christmas and New Year's. I am therefore all the more overwhelmed by the love, patience, and understanding of my family during this time. Elna and our daughters, Sarah and Andrea, have been wonderful in not allowing my feelings of guilt to stand in the way of the urgency of this work.

Archbishop Desmond Tutu is an old friend and comrade, a spiritual father and mentor. It is a great privilege that you are willing to write the foreword to this book. Thank you!

From Curtiss:

As Allan said, it has been an immense pleasure to work on this book together. I so admire his sacrificial commitment to liberation and reconciliation. I deeply value our friendship. We are honored to have Robert Ellsberg and the Orbis team as our publishing partners in this venture.

I am grateful for the support of Bethel University during the writing of this book, which included a month study leave, and, in particular, my colleagues in the Department of Anthropology, Sociology, and Reconciliation Studies. I wish to thank Jonathan DeYoung and Lillie Gardner for research assistance. I have found conversations with friends, colleagues, students, and former students about the content of this book very helpful and encouraging. Particular appreciation goes to Robin Bell, Iwalani Kaai, Emmanuel Katongole, David Kim, Shawn Moore, Sindy Morales Garcia, Chris Rice, Chaun Webster, and Cecilia Williams. Three persons read and offered particularly helpful comments on portions of the manuscript—thanks to Neil Elliott, Michael Emerson, and Jeremiah Wright.

Finally, thanks to the ongoing support of my family: my dear wife, Karen, and much-loved children, Rachel, Jonathan, and Dane.

Endnotes

Introduction

[1] Allan Aubrey Boesak, *The Tenderness of Conscience: African Renaissance and the Spirituality of Politics* (Stellenbosch, South Africa: SUN Press, 2005). Curtiss Paul DeYoung, *Reconciliation: Our Greatest Challenge—Our Only Hope* (Valley Forge, PA: Judson Press, 1997).

[2] Curtiss Paul DeYoung, *Living Faith: How Faith Inspires Social Justice* (Minneapolis: Fortress Press, 2007). Allan A. Boesak, "What Dietrich Bonhoeffer Has Meant to Me," in Guy Carter, René van Eyden, Hans-Dirk van Hoogstraten, and Jurgen Wiersma, eds., *Bonhoeffer's Ethics: Old Europe and New Frontiers* (Kampen, Germany: Kok Pharos, 1991).

[3] Allan Aubrey Boesak, *Running with Horses: Reflections of an Accidental Politician* (Cape Town: Joho! Publishers, 2009).

[4] Curtiss Paul DeYoung, *Coming Together in the 21st Century: The Bible's Message in an Age of Diversity* (Valley Forge, PA: Judson Press, 2009).

Chapter 1

[1] Allan Aubrey Boesak, *The Tenderness of Conscience: African Renaissance and the Spirituality of Politics* (Stellenbosch, South Africa: SUN Press, 2005), 182.

[2] Ibid., 185–86.

[3] Ibid., 186.

[4] Ibid., 185–86.

[5] Willie James Jennings, *The Christian Imagination: Theology and the Origins of Race* (New Haven, CT: Yale University Press, 2010), 9–10.

[6] Richard Lischer, *The End of Words: The Language of Reconciliation in a Culture of Violence* (Grand Rapids: William B. Eerdmans Publishing Company, 2005), 5.

[7] John W. de Gruchy, *Reconciliation: Restoring Justice* (Minneapolis: Fortress Press, 2002), 21, quoting Dietrich Bonhoeffer, *Letters and Papers from Prison* (London: SCM Press, 1971), 300.

[8] De Gruchy, *Reconciliation*, 21.

[9] Many Pauline scholars do not accept Ephesians as written by Paul. They rather view it as composed by one of Paul's followers. While I believe there is merit for those arguments, I believe that the reconciliation sentiments in Ephesians 2 are consistent with Paul's comments elsewhere on the subject. Also, whoever the author of Ephesians was, the reconciliation reflections were composed under Roman colonization.

[10] For good overviews of the meanings of these words, see James Earl Massey, "Reconciliation: Two Bible Studies," in Timothy George and Robert Smith Jr., eds., *A Mighty Long Journey: Reflections on Racial Reconciliation* (Nashville: Broadman and Holman, 2000), 199–210 and Corneliu Constantineanu, *The Social Significance of Reconciliation in Paul's Theology: Narrative Readings in Romans* (London: T & T Clark International, 2010), 25–31.

[11] Massey, "Reconciliation," 204.

[12] De Gruchy, *Reconciliation*, 51.

[13] Massey, "Reconciliation," 205.

[14] Richard A. Horsley, "The Bible and Empires," in Richard A. Horsley, ed., *In the Shadow of Empire: Reclaiming the Bible as a History of Faithful Resistance* (Louisville, KY: Westminster John Knox Press 2008), 6.

[15] Wes Howard-Brook, *"Come Out, My People!" God's Call out of Empire in the Bible and Beyond* (Maryknoll, NY: Orbis Books, 2010), 18.

[16] Neil Elliott, "The Apostle Paul and Empire," in Horsley, ed., *Shadow of Empire*, 102.

[17] Richard A. Horsley, *Jesus and Empire: The Kingdom of God and the New World Disorder* (Minneapolis: Fortress Press, 2003), 28.

[18] Allan Aubrey Boesak, *Black and Reformed: Apartheid, Liberation and the Calvinist Tradition* (Maryknoll, NY: Orbis Books, 1984), 4. See also Allan Aubrey Boesak, *Farewell to Innocence: A Socio-ethical Study of Black Theology and Black Power* (Maryknoll, NY: Orbis Books, 1976), 27.

[19] Aimé Césaire, *Discourse on Colonialism*, rev. ed. (New York: Monthly Review Press, 1972, 2000), 42, 43.

[20] Frantz Fanon, *Black Skin, White Masks* (New York: Grove Press, 1967), 18.

[21] Albert Memmi, *The Colonizer and the Colonized* (Boston: Beacon Press, 1965), viii, 91.

[22] Fanon, *Black Skin, White Masks,* 17.

[23] W. E. B. DuBois, *The Souls of Black Folk* (New York: Barnes & Noble Classics, 1903, 2003), 9.

[24] L. Ann Jervis, "Reading Romans 7 in Conversation with Postcolonial Theory: Paul's Struggle toward a Christian Identity of Hybridity," in Christopher D. Stanley, ed., *The Colonized Apostle: Paul through Postcolonial Eyes* (Minneapolis: Fortress Press, 2011), 96, citing Leela Gandhi.

[25] Paulo Freire, *Pedagogy of the Oppressed* (New York: Seabury Press, 1970), 45.

[26] Memmi, *Colonizer and the Colonized,* 122.

[27] Fanon, *Black Skin, White Masks,* 98.

[28] I dropped verse 15a to respect the concerns by Pauline scholars that it contradicts Paul's strong Jewish identity in his undisputed epistles.

[29] See Constantineanu, *Social Significance of Reconciliation,* for extended discussion of the Damascus event.

[30] Constantineanu, *Social Significance of Reconciliation,* 65.

[31] John Dominic Crossan and Jonathan L. Reed, *In Search of Paul: How Jesus's Apostle Opposed Rome's Empire with God's Kingdom* (San Francisco: HarperSanFrancisco, 2004), 384.

[32] Neil Elliott, *Liberating Paul: The Justice of God and the Politics of the Apostle* (Minneapolis: Fortress Press, 1994, 2006), 110.

[33] Boesak, *Black and Reformed,* 17.

[34] Crossan and Reed, *In Search of Paul,* 280.

[35] Elliott, "The Apostle Paul and Empire," 103–04.

[36] De Gruchy, *Reconciliation,* 21, 54.

[37] Tat-siong Benny Liew, "Redressing Bodies in Corinth: Racial/Ethnic Politics and Religious Difference in the Context of Empire," in Stanley, ed., *The Colonized Apostle,* 137.

[38] Gustavo Gutiérrez, *A Theology of Liberation* (Maryknoll, NY: Orbis Books, 1973), 48.

[39] Ched Myers and Elaine Enns, *Ambassadors of Reconciliation, Volume 1: New Testament Reflections on Restorative Justice and Peacemaking* (Maryknoll, NY: Orbis Books, 2009), 5.

[40] Memmi, *Colonizer and the Colonized,* 52.

[41] Ibid., 22.

[42] Freire, *Pedagogy,* 46–47.

[43] Steve Biko, *I Write What I Like: Selected Writings* (Chicago: University of Chicago Press, 2002), 20.

[44] Curtiss Paul DeYoung, *Reconciliation: Our Greatest Challenge—Our Only Hope* (Valley Forge, PA: Judson Press, 1997), 74.

[45] Liew, "Redressing Bodies in Corinth," 137, 138.

[46] Curtiss Paul DeYoung, *Living Faith: How Faith Inspires Social Justice* (Minneapolis: Fortress Press, 2007), 100.

[47] Memmi, *Colonizer and the Colonized,* 40–41.

[48] Boesak, *Farewell,* 150.

[49] Freire, *Pedagogy,* 49.

[50] Richard B. Hays, *The Moral Vision of the New Testament: A Contemporary Introduction to New Testament Ethics* (San Francisco: HarperSanFrancisco, 1996), 32.

[51] Horsley, *Jesus and Empire,* 132–33.

Chapter 2

[1] Walter Brueggemann, *First and Second Samuel, Interpretation: A Bible Commentary for Teaching and Preaching,* James Luther Mays, Patrick D. Miller, Paul J. Achtemeier, eds. (Louisville, KY: John Knox Press, 1990), 336.

[2] Brueggemann, *First and Second Samuel,* 336. See also the discussion in Jin-Soo Kim, *Bloodguilt, Atonement and Mercy: An Exegetical and Theological Study of 2 Samuel 21:1–14, European University Studies* (Frankfurt am Main, Germany: Peter Lang), especially 230–232; Hans Willem Hertzberg, *I&II Samuel: A Commentary, Old Testament Library* (London: SCM Press, 1964), 381.

[3] Brueggemann offers his very insightful, in my view correct, "ironic" interpretation of the narrative in which he exposes David's *"Realpolitik."* "My judgment is that *Realpolitik* is crucial in this reported action of David . . . given this *interpretation,* the king who is presented as faithfully executing his office is in fact a ruthless, self-seeking king who takes desperate measures to secure his throne." The "reasons of state" given in the story that must justify David's actions are "palatable if they are couched in the language of piety and religious primitivism." And finally, "Believing David's rationale and the accusation against Saul requires innocent credulity." Brueggemann, *First and Second Samuel,* 336. Regrettably, he then leaves the story there and explores no further, completely leaving out Rizpah's response to David's actions, even though he gives more detailed commentary on the rest of the "intrusive" material in chapters 22 to 24. See also Carol A. Newsom and Sharon H. Ringe, eds., *The Woman's Bible Commentary, Expanded Edition* (Louisville, KY: Westminster John Knox Press, 1992), who ignore Rizpah. The more evangelical Catherine Clark Kroeger and Mary J. Evans, eds., *The IVP Women's Bible Commentary* (Downers Grove, IL: InterVarsity Press, 2002), mentions Rizpah's "devotion" without any attempt to explore any deeper meaning of the material, however: "By her lonely, gruesome vigil she brought about a shift in popular opinion and the behavior of the king." Ibid., 182. She is absent from otherwise important feminist writings; see, e.g., Vanessa L. Ochs, *Sarah Laughed: Modern Lessons from the Wisdom and Stories of Biblical Women* (New York: McGraw-Hill, 2005). Womanist authors too, have left her out; see, e.g., Renita J. Weems, *Just a Sister Away: A Womanist Vision of Women's Relationships in the Bible* (San Diego: LuraMedia, 1988).

[4] See, e.g., Joyce G. Baldwin, *1 and 2 Samuel, An Introduction and Commentary, Tyndale Old Testament Commentaries,* D. J. Wiseman, ed. (Leicester, UK: InterVarsity Press, 1988). The bloodguilt is caused by Saul: "In an incident unrecorded in the narrative about Saul, he had apparently been so rash as to break the covenant by putting Gibeonites to death." Ibid., 283. C. J. Goslinga, *Het Tweede Boek Samuel: Commentaar op het Oude Testament* (Kampen, Germany: Kok, 1962), 378ff: "Here we

see the lot of Saul's heirs, more correctly put: how Yahweh, in bloody fashion, has definitely dealt with the house of Saul, who has angered Him" (Boesak translation).

[5] Brueggemann, *First and Second Samuel,* 336.

[6] Ibid.

[7] A. A. Anderson, *2 Samuel: Word Biblical Commentary* (Dallas: Word Publishers, 1989), 248.

[8] Brueggemann, *First and Second Samuel,* 336.

[9] The German word "Wiedergutmachung" comes even closer in expressing the meaning of the word.

[10] Baldwin, *1 and 2 Samuel,* 284.

[11] See Richard A. Horsley, *Jesus and Empire: The Kingdom of God and the New World Disorder* (Minneapolis: Fortress Press, 2003), 28–31.

[12] See, e.g., Hertzberg, *I&II Samuel,* 381; Goslinga, *Het Tweede Boek Samuel,* 378ff.

[13] See, e.g., Robert D. Bergen, *1,2 Samuel: An Exegetical and Theological Exposition of Holy Scripture, The New American Commentary* (Nashville: Broadman & Holman Publishers, 1996), 444.

[14] Brueggemann, *First and Second Samuel,* 337.

[15] Hertzberg, *I & II Samuel,* differs: "The historical question whether the sons of Saul did not die 'very opportunely' for David . . . is quite another matter. The narrative is not concerned with this. It deals with two other things, the affliction of the famine and the Gibeonite blood-vengeance." Ibid., 381–82.

[16] Brueggemann, *First and Second Samuel,* 337.

[17] See Allan Aubrey Boesak, *Die Vlug van Gods Verbeelding, Bybelverhale van die Onderkant* (Stellenbosch, South Africa: Sun Media, 2005), 63–64.

[18] Baldwin, *1 and 2 Samuel,* 284. It was not David, Goslinga argues, that had a quarrel with Saul. "Now that it had become clear that Yahweh had the quarrel with Saul . . . David could, and should not have, resisted this (act of God)." *Het Tweede Samuel Boek,* 388.

[19] "It is . . . not important how the men are killed, but that their bodies should be exposed," making this a particularly "humiliating death." Hertzberg, *I&II Samuel,* 383.

[20] Jin-Soo Kim, *Bloodguilt,* 230.

[21] J. Cheryl Exum, *Tragedy and Biblical Narrative: Arrows of the Almighty* (New York: Cambridge University Press, 1992), 110.

[22] See John J. Walters, "Who Was Hagar?" in Cain Hope Felder, ed., *Stony the Road We Trod: African American Biblical Interpretation* (Minneapolis: Fortress Press, 1991), 187–205; John H. Otwell, *And Sarah Laughed: The Status of Women in the Old Testament* (Philadelphia: Westminster Press, 1977); Margaret Wold, *Women of Faith and Spirit: Profile of Fifteen Biblical Women* (Minneapolis: Augsburg, 1987);

Renita Weems, *Just a Sister Away;* Allan A. Boesak, *Die Vlug van Gods Verbeelding,* 1–28.

[23] Mario Costa, Catherine Keller, and Anna Mercedes, "Love in Times of Empire," in Bruce Ellis Benson and Peter Goodwin Heltzel, eds., *Evangelicals and Empire: Christian Alternatives to the Political Status Quo* (Grand Rapids: Brazos Press, 2008), 294.

Chapter 3

[1] Richard A. Horsley, "Introduction: The Bible and Empires," in Richard A. Horsley, ed., *In the Shadow of Empire: Reclaiming the Bible as a History of Faithful Resistance* (Louisville, KY: Westminster John Knox Press, 2008), 7.

[2] Richard A. Horsley, *Jesus and Empire: The Kingdom of God and the New World Order* (Minneapolis: Fortress Press, 2003), 21.

[3] Ibid., 15, 30, 34.

[4] Howard Thurman, *Jesus and the Disinherited* (New York: Abingdon-Cokesbury Press, 1949), 18.

[5] William R. Herzog II, *Parables as Subversive Speech: Jesus as Pedagogue of the Oppressed* (Louisville, KY: John Knox Westminster Press, 1994), 17.

[6] Richard B. Hays, *The Moral Vision of the New Testament: A Contemporary Introduction to New Testament Ethics* (San Francisco: HarperSanFrancisco, 1996), 127.

[7] John Dominic Crossan, *God & Empire: Jesus Against Rome, Then and Now* (San Francisco: HarperSanFrancisco, 2007), 117.

[8] Neil Elliott, "The Bible and Empire," in Curtiss Paul DeYoung, Wilda C. Gafney, Leticia A. Guardiola-Sáenz, George Tinker, and Frank M. Yamada, eds., *The Peoples' Bible, New Revised Standard Version with the Apocrypha* (Minneapolis, Fortress Press, 2008), 94.

[9] Hays, *Moral Vision,* 163.

[10] Allan Aubrey Boesak, *Black and Reformed: Apartheid, Liberation and the Calvinist Tradition* (Maryknoll, NY: Orbis Books, 1984), 12.

[11] Andries van Aarde, *Fatherless in Galilee: Jesus as the Child of God* (Harrisburg, PA: Trinity Press International, 2001), 64, 74.

[12] Richard A. Horsley, *Galilee: History, Politics, People* (Valley Forge, PA: Trinity Press International, 1995), 238–45; Roberto W. Pazmiño, "Double Dutch: Reflections of an Hispanic North-American on Multicultural Education," in Justo L. Gonzales, ed., *Voces: Voices from the Hispanic Church* (Nashville: Abingdon Press, 1992), 138–39.

[13] Brian K. Blount, "The Apocalypse of Worship: A House of Prayer for ALL the Nations," in Brian K. Blount and Leonora Tubbs Tisdale, eds., *Making Room at the Table: An Invitation to Multicultural Worship* (Louisville, KY: Westminster John Knox Press, 2001), 20.

[14] Horsley, *Jesus and Empire*, 35.

[15] Marcus J. Borg and John Dominic Crossan, *The Last Week: A Day-by-Day Account of Jesus's Final Days in Jerusalem* (San Francisco: HarperOne, 2006), 2–5. See also Curtiss Paul DeYoung, "From Resistance to Reconciliation," in Michael G. Long, ed., *Resist! Christian Dissent for the 21st Century* (Maryknoll, NY: Orbis Books, 2008), 12–13.

[16] Ibid., 2.

[17] Ibid., 4.

[18] Elliott, "Bible and Empire," 94.

[19] Horsley, *Shadow of Empire*, 5.

[20] Vincent Harding, "Black Power and the American Christ," in Floyd B. Barbour, ed., *The Black Power Revolt: A Collection of Essays* (Boston: P. Sargent, 1968), 86, quoted in Allan Aubrey Boesak, *Farewell to Innocence: A Socio-Ethical Study on Black Theology and Power* (Maryknoll, NY: Orbis Books, 1976), 42.

[21] See Curtiss Paul DeYoung, *Coming Together in the 21st Century: The Bible's Message in an Age of Diversity* (Valley Forge, PA: Judson Press, 2009), 50–72.

[22] Thurman, *Jesus*, 29.

[23] See Cain Hope Felder, *Troubling Biblical Waters: Race, Class and Family* (Maryknoll, NY: Orbis Books, 1989), 37; and DeYoung, *Coming Together in the 21st Century*, 53–54.

[24] Van Aarde, *Fatherless*, 6. These were Jesus son of Phabet, who was robbed of the high priesthood; Jesus son of Ananus; Jesus also called Jason; Jesus son of Sapphias; Jesus the brother of Onias, who was robbed of the high priesthood by Antiochus Epiphanes; Jesus son of Gamaliel, who was proclaimed high priest; Jesus the oldest priest after Ananus; Jesus son of Damneus, who was proclaimed high priest; Jesus son of Gamala; Jesus son of Saphat, who was the leader of a band of robbers; Jesus son of Thebuthus, a priest; Jesus son of Josedek.

[25] Mt 27:11; Mk 15:2; Lk 23:3; Jn 18:33.

[26] Lk 4:18–19.

[27] Richard A. Horsley and John S. Hanson, *Bandits, Prophets, and Messiahs: Popular Movements in the Time of Jesus* (Minneapolis: Winston Press, 1985), 48. "Social bandits emerge from incidents and circumstances in which what is dictated by the state or local rulers is felt to be unjust or intolerable. Underlying such incidents, however, are general social economic conditions in which many peasants are marginal and vulnerable." Ibid., 49.

[28] See van Aarde, *Fatherless,* 58ff.

[29] See ibid., 61ff; on the allusions to Jesus in the rabbinic writings, see note 50, also 110–11; see also his references to Jane Schaberg, *The Illegitimacy of Jesus: A Feminist Theological Interpretation of the Infancy Narratives* (San Francisco: Harper & Row, 1987).

[30] Van Aarde, *Fatherless,* 75; Obery M. Hendricks, *Politics of Jesus: Rediscovering the True Revolutionary Nature of Jesus' Teachings and How They Have Been Corrupted* (New York: Doubleday, 2006), 52, 70–71.

[31] See, e.g., Joerg Rieger, *Christ & Empire: From Paul to Postcolonial Times* (Minneapolis: Fortress Press, 2007), 23.

[32] See Warren Carter, *Matthew and Empire: Initial Explorations* (Harrisburg, PA: Trinity Press International, 2001), chap. 2. The poet Statius described Emperor Domitian as "Lord of the earth," "ruler of the nations and mighty sire of the conquered world, hope of men and beloved of the gods"; and for Martial, Domitian was "the world's sure salvation," its "blest protector and savior," its "chief and only welfare." Carter, *Matthew and Empire,* 25.

[33] Van Aarde, *Fatherless,* 7.

[34] James Cone, *God of the Oppressed* (Maryknoll, NY: Orbis Books, 1975), 33.

[35] Kelly Delaine Brown, "God Is as Christ Does: Toward a Womanist Theology," *JRT* 46 (1989): 12.

[36] Cone, *God of the Oppressed,* 126.

[37] See Brian Bantum, *Redeeming Mulatto: A Theology of Race and Christian Hybridity* (Waco, TX: Baylor University Press, 2010).

[38] See, for example, the growing literature by scholars such as Richard Horsley, *Jesus and Empire;* Warren Carter, *Matthew and Empire* (see note 6); John Dominic Crossan, *The Historical Jesus: The Life of a Mediterranean Jewish Peasant* (San Francisco: HarperSanFrancisco, 1991); K. C. Hanson and Douglas E. Oakman, *Palestine in the Time of Jesus: Social Structures and Social Conflicts* (Minneapolis: Fortress Press, 1998). Equally important are the studies on Paul and the imperial context; see, e.g., Richard A. Horsley, ed., *Paul and Politics: Ekklesia, Israel, Imperium, Interpretation, Essays in Honor of Krister Stendahl* (Harrisburg, PA: Trinity Press International, 2000); Richard A. Horsley, ed., *Paul and Empire: Religion and Power in Roman Imperial Society* (Harrisburg, PA: Trinity Press International, 1997).

[39] Horsley, *Jesus and Empire,* 6–9. Horsley continues to examine and expose, in my view, quite convincingly, the de-politicization of both Galilee and the Roman Empire, 9–14; see Nicholas Wolterstorff, *Justice: Rights and Wrongs* (Princeton, NJ: Princeton University Press, 2010), 96ff.

[40] See A. A. Boesak, "The Divine Favour of the Unworthy—When the Fatherless Son Meets the Black Messiah," *HTS Teologiese Studies/Theological Studies* 67, no. 1: art. # 933, 9 pages. DOI:10.4102/hts.v67i933.

[41] See Horsley, *Jesus and Empire,* 103; William R. Herzog II, *Prophet and Teacher: An Introduction to the Historical Jesus* (Louisville, KY: Westminster John Knox Press, 2005) and William R. Herzog II, *Parables as Subversive Speech: Jesus as Pedagogue of the Oppressed* (Louisville, KY: Westminster John Knox Press, 1994). Jesus certainly is much more socially and politically radical than Marcus Borg's "religious

revolutionary"; see Marcus Borg, *Jesus: Uncovering the Life, Teachings and Relevance of a Religious Revolutionary* (New York: Harper Collins, 2006).

⁴² Van Aarde, *Fatherless,* 75.

⁴³ Hendricks, *Politics of Jesus.*

⁴⁴ Ibid., 5–6. Hendricks then sets out throughout his book to prove this thesis. He speaks of Jesus "Messiah and Tactician" and Jesus' political strategies, from "treating the people's needs as holy," giving "voice to the voiceless," exposing "the workings of oppression," calling "the demon by name," to how Jesus saved his anger "for the mistreatment of others," never for himself, taking "blows without returning them," in which he focuses on Jesus' nonviolent stance, to Jesus' practical politics: "Don't just explain the alternative—show it." Ibid., 99–188. I find his line of reasoning entirely convincing.

⁴⁵ Ibid., 129.

⁴⁶ Horsley, *Jesus and Empire,* chapters 4 and 5.

⁴⁷ Ibid., 130.

⁴⁸ Miguel A. de la Torre, *Liberating Jonah: Forming an Ethics of Reconciliation* (Maryknoll, NY: Orbis Books, 2007), 81.

Chapter 4

¹ Miguel A. de la Torre, *Liberating Jonah: Forming an Ethic of Reconciliation* (Maryknoll, NY: Orbis Books, 2007), 81.

² Howard Thurman, *Jesus and the Disinherited* (New York: Abingdon-Cokesbury Press, 1949), 13.

³ See Allan Aubrey Boesak, *The Fire Within: Sermons from the Edge of Exile* (Cape Town: New World Foundation, 2004), 75–84.

⁴ Nicholas Wolterstorff, *Justice: Rights and Wrongs* (Princeton, NJ: Princeton University Press, 2010), 116–17.

⁵ Ibid., 117.

⁶ Obery M. Hendricks, *The Politics of Jesus: Rediscovering the True Revolutionary Nature of the Teachings of Jesus and How They Have Been Corrupted* (New York: Doubleday, 2006), 7, 8.

⁷ Wolterstorff, *Justice,* 123.

⁸ To understand fully the prophet's intention, we should read this word as both a noun and a verb. The Bible's intention is not to convey a concept, but an act.

⁹ Wolterstorff, *Justice,* 123.

¹⁰ Ibid., 123.

¹¹ Ibid., 123, 124.

¹² See Allan Aubrey Boesak, "And Zacchaeus Remained Sitting in the Tree," in Curtiss Paul DeYoung, ed., *Coming Together in the 21st Century: The Bible's Message in an Age of Diversity* (Valley Forge, PA: Judson Press, 2009), 143–47.

[13] See also the way South African politicians themselves speak of reconciliation in South African politics: Allan Aubrey Boesak, *The Tenderness of Conscience: African Renaissance and the Spirituality of Politics* (Stellenbosch, South Africa: Sun Press, 2005), chap. six, "A Nation at Peace with Itself."

[14] Desmond Tutu, *No Future Without Forgiveness* (London: Rider, 1999), 86.

[15] See Jakes Gerwel, "National Reconciliation: Holy Grail or Secular Pact," in Charles Villa-Vicencio and Wilhelm Verwoerd, eds., *Looking Back, Reaching Forward: Reflections on the Truth and Reconciliation Commission of South Africa* (Cape Town: University of Cape Town Press, 2000), 277–86, who fears that "spiritualization" of the reconciliation process might "pathologize a nation in relatively good health by demanding a perpetual quest for the Holy Grail of reconciliation." For him the "secular pact" reached between the two former enemies is already remarkable enough. Charles Villa-Vicencio asserts that in our situation, moral demands "that are too high," such as notions of repentance, forgiveness, and restitution, are often "politically unhelpful;" see Boesak, *Tenderness,* 177.

[16] See Wolterstorff, *Justice,* 109.

[17] For much of the information on tax collectors, sinners, and the rituals of eating I am indebted to I. H. Marshall, A. R. Milard, J. I. Packer, and D. J. Wiseman, eds., *New Bible Dictionary,* 3rd ed. (Leicester, UK: InterVarsity Press, 2003); William R. Herzog II, *Prophet and Teacher: An Introduction to the Historical Jesus* (Louisville, KY: Westminster John Knox Press, 2005); K. C. Hanson and Douglas E. Oakman, *Palestine in the Time of Jesus: Social Structures and Social Conflicts* (Minneapolis: Fortress Press, 1998), *passim;* and Richard A. Horsley, *Jesus and Empire.*

[18] See Herzog, *Prophet and Teacher,* 194–99.

[19] Ernest van Eck writes, "Taxation was exploitative: Rome assessed its tribute and then left Antipas and the temple elite free to exploit the land to whatever degree they saw fit. The elite thus lived at the expense of the non-elite." See E. van Eck, "When Neighbors Are Not Neighbors: A Social-Scientific Reading of the Parable of the Friend at Midnight (Lk 11:5–8)," *HTS Teologiese Studies / Theological Studies* 67, no. 1 (2011): art. # 788, 14 pages, DOI:10.4102/hts.v67i1.788, p. 222. See also the informative discussion on the question of taxes and tributes in Herman C. Waetjen, *A Reordering of Power: A Socio-Political Reading of Mark's Gospel* (Minneapolis: Fortress Press, 1989), 5, 7–9.

[20] Walter Wink, *When the Powers Fall: Reconciliation in the Healing of Nations* (Minneapolis: Fortress Press, 1998), 7.

[21] See Charles Villa-Vicencio, *Walk with Us and Listen: Political Reconciliation in Africa* (Cape Town: University of Cape Town Press, 2009), 6, 7.

[22] "For this reason," writes Karl Barth, "in the relations and events in the life of people, God always takes his stand unconditionally and passionately on this side and on this side alone: against the lofty and on behalf of the lowly; against those

who already enjoy right and privilege and on behalf of those who are denied and deprived of it"; see Karl Barth, _Church Dogmatics,_ II/I (Edinburgh, Scotland: Clarke, 1957), 386.

[23] The TRC Amnesty Hearings uncovered horrific accounts of torture and killings of black activists by black policemen called "Askari's" under the supervision of white commanders; see Tutu, _No Future,_ 95–98; see also Antjie Krog, _Country of My Skull_ (Johannesburg: Random House, 2002), 85–88.

[24]Waetjen, _Reordering of Power,_ 90.

Chapter 5

[1] Cover of _Time Magazine,_ January 11, 2010.

[2] David Van Biema, "The Color of Faith," _Time Magazine,_ January 11, 2010, 38–41. Statistics in the article are from Michael Emerson, sociologist at Rice University in Houston, Texas. In an e-mail from Emerson on December 25, 2011, he confirmed these statistics as his analysis of the National Congregations Survey of 2007.

[3] Curtiss Paul DeYoung, Michael O. Emerson, George Yancey, and Karen Chai Kim, _United by Faith: The Multiracial Congregation as an Answer to the Problem of Race_ (New York: Oxford University Press, 2003), 2–3.

[4] Ibid., 2.

[5] Bill Hybels, the senior pastor of Willow Creek Community Church, provided an endorsement for the book, "The book was a huge gift to me. It filled in several more pieces to the puzzle we've been working on at Willow, as we move with great internationality toward becoming a multi-cultural, Acts 2 church."

[6] Martin Luther King, Jr., "An Address Before the National Press Club," in James M. Washington, ed., _A Testament of Hope: The Essential Writings of Martin Luther King, Jr._ (San Francisco: Harper and Row, 1986), 101.

[7] Richard N. Pitt, "Fear of a Black Pulpit? Real Racial Transcendence Versus Cultural Assimilation in Multiracial Churches," _Journal for the Scientific Study of Religion_ 49, no. 2 (2010): 220.

[8] Korie L. Edwards, _The Elusive Dream: The Power of Race in Interracial Churches_ (New York: Oxford University Press, 2008), 8.

[9] Ibid.,117.

[10] DeYoung et al., _United by Faith,_ 37.

[11] In _United by Faith_ (ibid., 29–33) we suggested that Paul went first to Jews and then to Gentiles due to differences in cultural practices. It would have been difficult for many observant Jews of the time to share communal meals and be in fellowship with uncircumcised Gentiles. This reality was certainly a factor in their strategy when initiating faith communities in the Roman Empire. Yet, I am arguing here that the primary reality being addressed was colonization and reconciliation.

[12] Paulo Freire, *Pedagogy of the Oppressed* (New York: Seabury Press, 1970), 43–69.

[13] Ched Myers and Elaine Enns, *Ambassadors of Reconciliation, Volume 1: New Testament Reflections on Restorative Justice and Peacemaking* (Maryknoll, NY: Orbis Books, 2009), 8–9.

[14] Freire, *Pedagogy*, 44.

[15] Myers and Enns, *Ambassadors*, 9.

[16] Willie James Jennings, *The Christian Imagination: Theology and the Origins of Race* (New Haven, CT: Yale University Press, 2010), 269.

[17] Ibid., 271.

[18] Tat-siong Benny Liew, "Redressing Bodies in Corinth: Racial/Ethnic Politics and Religious Difference in the Context of Empire," in Christopher D. Stanley, ed., *The Colonized Apostle: Paul through Postcolonial Eyes* (Minneapolis: Fortress Press, 2011), 129.

[19] Ibid.

[20] Ibid., 133.

[21] Neil Elliott, *The Arrogance of Nations: Reading Romans in the Shadow of Empire* (Minneapolis: Fortress Press, 2008), 134.

[22] Richard B. Hays, *The Moral Vision of the New Testament: A Contemporary Introduction to Christian Ethics* (San Francisco: HarperSanFrancisco, 1996), 53.

[23] Mimi Haddad, "Reading the Apostle Paul through Galatians 3:28," in Curtiss Paul DeYoung, ed., *Coming Together in the 21st Century: The Bible's Message in an Age of Diversity* (Valley Forge, PA: Judson Press, 2009), 74. See also ibid., 82–84.

[24] Hays, *Moral Vision*, 132. Obviously some folks contest the idea of Paul as committed to gender equality. His writings have been used against women. For an argument for Pauline egalitarianism that includes even the disputed epistles, see Mimi Haddad, "Reading the Apostle Paul," 73–93.

[25] It is possible the debate about circumcision was concerned with maintaining Jewish culture as the church became demographically more Gentile.

[26] Myers and Enns, *Ambassadors*, 85.

[27] Richard A. Horsley, *Jesus and Empire: The Kingdom of God and the New World Disorder* (Minneapolis: Fortress Press, 2003), 133.

[28] See DeYoung et al., *United by Faith*, 42–61, for discussion of the racial segregation of the church in the United States.

[29] Brian Bantum, *Redeeming Mulatto: A Theology of Race and Christian Hybridity* (Waco, TX: Baylor University Press, 2010), 141.

[30] Soong-Chan Rah, *The Next Evangelicalism: Freeing the Church from Western Cultural Captivity* (Downers Grove, IL: IVP Books, 2009), 22, 147.

[31] Edwards, *Elusive Dream*, 35, 6.

[32] For a full description of the ways in which multiracial churches must cater to whites to stay diverse, even when the pastor is African American, read Korie Edwards, *Elusive Dream*. She discusses this in some detail, and her central case study is of a multiracial congregation with a senior pastor who is African American.

[33] Edwards, *Elusive Dream*, 6.

[34] See Curtiss Paul DeYoung, "The Power of Reconciliation: From the Apostle Paul to Malcolm X," *CrossCurrents* 57 (Summer 2007): 203–08, for a discussion of how reconciliation provides healing to cultural identity.

[35] Pitt, "Black Pulpit," 222–23.

[36] Albert Memmi, *The Colonizer and the Colonized* (Boston: Beacon Press, 1965), 20.

[37] Edwards, *Elusive Dream*, 117.

[38] Rah, *Next Evangelicalism*, 162.

[39] Freire, *Pedagogy*, 60.

[40] This idea of the importance of the African American church for the formation of multiracial churches is one I have had for some time. The language of going through the black church came in a conversation with Korie Edwards at "Divided by Faith: A Decade Retrospective," Indiana Wesleyan University, Marion, Indiana, October 15, 2010.

[41] Rah, *Next Evangelicalism*, 12.

[42] See DeYoung, *Coming Together in the 21st Century*, 56–63, for a discussion of the effects of white images of Jesus Christ.

[43] Edwards, *Elusive Dream*, 80.

[44] Martin Luther King, Jr., "Facing the Challenge of a New Age," in Washington, ed., *Testament of Hope*, 140.

[45] Bantum, *Redeeming Mulatto*, 184, 192.

[46] Jean Bernabé, Patrick Chamoiseau, and Raphaël Confiant, *Éloge de la Créolité / In Praise of Creoleness,* Édition Bilingue (Paris: Gallimard, 1993), 75.

[47]Ibid., 112.

Chapter 6

[1] Pronounced "Raits." The students lived in a residence named after a well-loved nineteenth-century president of the Orange Free State when it was still a Boer republic and hugely popular for his championing of the cause of Afrikaner nationalism.

[2]"Reitz Four Want R1million to Talk," *City Press,* February 27, 2011. http://www.citypress.co.za/SouthAfrica/News/Reitz-four-want-R1m-to-talk-20110226 (accessed May 2, 2011).

[3] Ibid.

[4] Jonathan Jansen, "Reconciliation as an institutional matter" in Fanie du Toit and Erik Doxtader, eds., *In the Balance: South Africans Debate Reconciliation,* Institute for Justice and Reconciliation (Johannesburg: Jacana Media, 2010), 126.

[5] *Mail and Guardian Online,* February 21, 2011, http://mg.co.za/article/2011-02-26-varsity-puts-reitz-four-incident-to-rest (accessed March 1, 2012).

[6] Jansen, "Reconciliation," 126, original emphasis. This assertion might be true, but it certainly does not negate the fact that racism remains an evil, if sometimes perhaps a more subtle presence on all university campuses in South Africa, as it does in all of South African society, despite the denials of those who believe that a "post-apartheid" society equals a society free of racism. In South Africa the president of a university bears the title Rector and Vice-Chancellor.

[7] Jansen, "Reconciliation," 127.

[8] See Allan Aubrey Boesak, *Running with Horses: Reflections of an Accidental Politician* (Cape Town: JoHo! Publishers, 2009), 264–67.

[9] Jansen, "Reconciliation," 132.

[10] *City Press,* "Reitz Four Want R1m to Talk," February 27, 2011.

[11] Jansen, "Reconciliation," 128.

[12] The colloquium was held as part of the *Volksblad* Arts Festival in July 2008, six months after the exposure of the Reitz event, on the campus of the UFS.

[13] Elna Boesak, "Tussen Reitz en 'n Rots: Wat het Verkeerd Geloop?" unpublished paper, *Volksblad* Arts Festival, University of the Free State, Bloemfontein, July 10, 2008, 1, 2.

[14] Ibid., 2.

[15] Ibid.

[16] Ibid., 3.

[17] Ibid., 5, 6.

[18] Ibid., 8.

[19] See Xolela Mangcu, *On the Brink: The State of Democracy in South Africa* (Scottville, South Africa: University of KwaZulu Natal Press), 2008, 5.

[20] *Invictus* was a movie made of the 1996 Rugby World Cup, especially the final match won by South Africa, and at the end of which Nelson Mandela endeared himself even more to the (mostly) white rugby-crazy public and the nation by coming on to the field, donning the captain's no. 6 jersey and a Springbok cap, and claiming the victory for the nation as a whole. In its portrayal of race relations and reconciliation, the movie is indeed simplistic and heavily romantic.

[21] Elna Boesak, "Tussen Reitz en 'n Rots," 9.

[22] The complete text of the Belhar Confession can be found in Allan Boesak, "To Stand Where God Stands: Reflections on the Confession of Belhar," in *Studia Historiae Ecclesiasticae* 34, no. 1 (July 2008): 141–72. The confession was adopted in 1986 and since then by several denominations within the worldwide Reformed communion.

23 The text of the confession refers to Ps 146; Lk 4:16–19; Rom 6:13–16; Am 5.

24 Jansen, "Reconciliation," 125.

25 Ibid, 127.

26 It is a supposedly a term of endearment, much like "Uncle" and "Aunt" in the slave-holding and Jim Crow Southern United States, a generic South African term referring to those women who work in the white households as "maids." Many white people apparently find it puzzling that black people experience this as racist and deeply offensive.

27 "As the abused workers sat in my office, I saw my parents, my colleagues, my people." Jansen, "Reconciliation," 126.

28 See Steve Biko, *I Write What I Like: A Selection of his Writings* (Johannesburg: Ravan Press, 1996).

29 "But what did we expect from students wrapped-up in all-white residences?" Jansen asks, in continuation of his "institutional" argument. Jansen, "Reconciliation," 128.

30 Ibid., 126.

31 *Skollie* is South African slang for what Americans call a "gangbanger." The *skollie* is always black.

32 Jonathan Jansen, "Don't Look Back in Anger," *The Times,* August 12, 2010, 7.

33 Jansen, "Reconciliation," 128.

34 Ibid., 130.

35 Quoted in Wilhelm Verwoerd, "Forgiving the Torturer but Not the Torture," *Sunday Independent,* December 14, 1998; see also Allan Aubrey Boesak, *The Tenderness of Conscience: African Renaissance and the Spirituality of Politics* (Stellenbosch, South Africa: Sun Press, 2005), 196.

36 Boesak, *Tenderness,* 196. See also John W. de Gruchy, *Reconciliation: Restoring Justice* (Minneapolis: Fortress Press, 2002), 164–70.

37 Jansen, "Reconciliation," 130.

38 Ibid.

39 See Mahmood Mamdani, "Beyond Kempton Park: Reflections on Nuremberg and the Question of Justice," public lecture at Africa Memorial Day conference, University of the Free State, Bloemfontein, July 14, 2010, 7. Apartheid was a crime against humanity, and black South Africans, seeing the horrific consequences of that crime, fully had the right to claim legal redress. Stepping away from historic precedent to give up the right to legal justice is an act of national magnanimity too easily taken for granted.

40 Desmond Tutu, *No Future without Forgiveness* (London: Rider, 1999), 90, 91. Tutu's book is replete with moving examples of forgiveness from blacks but also includes moving examples from whites, albeit not many, who genuinely showed remorse. Hence his plea for a like generosity of spirit from whites, "to contribute to national unity and reconciliation."

[41]　Ibid., 91.

[42]　Jody Kollapen, "Reconciliation: engaging with our fears and expectations," du Toit and Doxtader, *In the Balance,* 20, 21.

Chapter 7

[1]　Curtiss Paul DeYoung, "A Lifting of the Burden," in Marvin A. McMickle, ed., *The Audacity of Faith: Christian Leaders Reflect on the Election of Barack Obama* (Valley Forge, PA: Judson Press, 2009), 60. See also "Race & Obama: What's Changed," in *Christian Century,* December 30, 2008.

[2]　"The Nobel Peace Prize 2009—Press Release." Nobelprize.org. January 12, 2012. http://www.nobelprize.org/nobel_prizes/peace/laureates/2009/press.html (accessed February 28, 2012).

[3]　Barack Obama, *The Audacity to Hope: Thoughts on Reclaiming the American Dream* (New York: Random House, 2006). See also Jeremiah A. Wright Jr., "The Audacity to Hope," in Jeremiah A Wright Jr., *What Makes You So Strong: Sermons of Joy and Strength,* Jini Kilgore Ross, ed. (Valley Forge, PA: Judson Press, 1993), 97–110.

[4]　Clarence E. Walker and Gregory D. Smithers, *The Preacher and the Politician: Jeremiah Wright, Barack Obama, and Race in America* (Charlottesville: University of Virginia Press, 2009), 34–35.

[5]　Ibid., 9, 26.

[6]　Ibid., 9–10.

[7]　Martin Luther King Jr., "A Time to Break Silence," in James M. Washington, ed., *A Testament of Hope: The Essential Writings and Speeches of Martin Luther King, Jr.* (San Francisco: HarperCollins, 1991), 233.

[8]　Richard Lischer, *The Preacher King: Martin Luther King, Jr. and the Word that Moved America* (New York: Oxford University Press, 1997), 35.

[9]　Taylor Branch, *Parting The Waters: America in the King Years 1954–63* (New York: Simon and Schuster, 1988), 12, 22, 24.

[10]　Walker and Smithers, *Preacher and Politician,* 37.

[11]　For description of visit, see Curtiss Paul DeYoung, *Homecoming: A "White" Man's Journey through Harlem to Jerusalem* (Minneapolis: Jezi Press, 2009), 124–26.

[12]　James Luther Mays, *Amos: A Commentary* (Philadelphia: Westminster Press, 1969), 2.

[13]　Abraham J. Heschel, *The Prophets* (New York: HarperCollins Publisher, 2001), 8, 9.

[14]　Willy Schottroff, "The Prophet Amos: A Socio-Historical Assessment of His Ministry," in Willy Schottroff and Wolfgang Stegemann, eds., *God of the Lowly: Socio-Historical Interpretations of the Bible* (Maryknoll, NY: Orbis Books, 1984), 40.

[15]　Thomas L. Leclerc, *Introduction to the Prophets: Their Stories, Sayings, and Scrolls* (New York: Paulist Press, 2007), 133.

16 Ted Grimsrud, "Healing Justice: The Prophet Amos and a 'New' Theology of Justice," in Ted Grimsrud and Loren L. Johns, eds., *Peace and Justice Shall Embrace: Power and Theopolitics in the Bible* (Telford, PA: Pandora Press U.S., 1999), 71.

17 Neil Elliott, "The Bible and Empire," in Curtiss Paul DeYoung, Wilda C. Gafney, Leticia A. Guardiola-Sáenz, George "Tink" Tinker, and Frank M. Yamada, eds., *The Peoples' Bible: New Revised Standard Version with the Apocrypha* (Minneapolis: Fortress Press, 2008), 90.

18 Robert Martin-Achard, "The End of the People of God," in Robert Martin-Achard and S. Paul Re'emi, *Amos & Lamentations: God's People in Crisis* (Grand Rapids: Wm. B. Eerdmans Publishing Co., 1984), 57.

19 Fred Guyette, "Amos the Prophet: A Meditation on the Richness of 'Justice,'" *Jewish Bible Quarterly*, 36, no. 1 (January–March 2008): 15.

20 Martin Luther King Jr., "The American Dream," in Washington, ed., *Testament*, 216.

21 Heschel, *Prophets*, 3.

22 Ibid., xxi.

23 Ibid., 4.

24 Walter Brueggemann, *The Prophetic Imagination, Second Edition* (Minneapolis: Fortress Press, 2001), 9.

25 William R. Herzog II, *Jesus, Justice, and the Reign of God: A Ministry of Liberation* (Louisville, KY: Westminster John Knox Press, 2000), 67.

26 Frantz Fanon, *The Wretched of the Earth* (New York: Grove Press, 1963), 50. See also Dylan Rodriguez, "The Political Logic of the Non-Profit Industrial Complex," in Incite! Women of Color Against Violence, eds., *The Revolution Will Not Be Funded: Beyond the Non-Profit Industrial Complex* (Cambridge: South End Press, 2007), 39.

27 Walter Brueggemann, *Out of Babylon* (Nashville: Abingdon Press, 2010), 69.

28 Brueggemann, *Prophetic Imagination*, 40, 65.

29 Guyette, "Amos," 19.

30 Ched Myers and Elaine Enns, *Ambassadors of Reconciliation, Volume 1: New Testament Reflections on Restorative Justice and Peacemaking* (Maryknoll, NY: Orbis Books, 2009), 19.

31 Martin Luther King Jr., "A Time to Break Silence," 240.

32 Incite! Women of Color Against Violence, eds., *The Revolution Will Not be Funded* (Cambridge: South End Press, 2007).

33 Andrea Smith, "Introduction: The Revolution Will Not be Funded," in Incite! Women of Color Against Violence, eds., *The Revolution Will Not Be Funded*, 3.

34 For an example, see Robert L. Allen, "From Black Awakening in Capitalist America," in Incite! Women of Color Against Violence, eds., *Revolution*, 53–62.

[35] Madonna Thunder Hawk, "Native Organizing Before the Non-Profit Industrial Complex," in Incite! Women of Color Against Violence, eds., *Revolution* 105.

[36] Tiffany Lethabo King and Ewuare Osayande, "The Filth on Philanthropy: Progressive Philanthropy's Agenda to Misdirect Social Justice Movements," in Incite! Women of Color Against Violence, eds., *Revolution*, 81, 82.

[37] Ana Clarissa Rojas Durazo, "'We Were Never Meant to Survive': Fighting Violence against Women and the Fourth World War," in Incite! Women of Color Against Violence, eds., *Revolution*, 115.

[38] Allan Aubrey Boesak, *The Fire Within: Sermons from the Edge of Exile* (Cape Town: New World Foundation, 2004), 81.

Chapter 8

[1] Desmond Tutu, *No Future without Forgiveness* (London: Rider, 1999), 72.

[2] Ibid., 77

[3] Ibid., 74–75.

[4] Ibid., 76.

[5] Ibid., 74.

[6] Ibid., 75.

[7] Ibid., 219.

[8] Ibid., 220.

[9] Ibid., 220. In chapter 6 I have set out my argument on the question of reversed victimhood, and it is not my intention to repeat the argument here. But I refer also to what I have said on victimhood in chapter 2.

[10] Charles Villa-Vicencio, "Reconciliation and Bloemfontein," unpublished paper, University of the Free State, February 25, 2011, 1.

[11] Tutu, *No Future,* 223–25.

[12] Laurie Gaum and Frits Gaum, *Praat verby Grense* (Cape Town: Umuzi, 2010), 82, 83.

[13] Gaum & Gaum, *Praat,* 84.

[14] Tutu, *No Future,* 76.

[15] Ibid., 76.

[16] Ibid., 224–25. Tutu writes about the markedly different reaction from many of the black delegates at the Rustenburg conference.

[17] Ibid., 217. Tutu rejects this: "For those with eyes to see there were accounts of people dying mysteriously in detention. For those with ears to hear there was much that was disquieting and even chilling. But, like the three monkeys, they chose neither to hear, nor see, nor speak of evil."

[18] See chapter 6, and Allan Aubrey Boesak, *The Tenderness of Conscience: African Renaissance and the Spirituality of Politics* (Stellenbosch, South Africa: Sun Press, 2005), 195–96.

[19] Michael Eric Dyson, *I May Not Get There With You: The True Martin Luther King Jr.* (New York: Touchstone Books, 2000), xv, 234–41, and *passim*.

[20] Ibid., 6.

[21] Elna Boesak, "Tussen Reitz en 'n Rots: Wat het Verkeerd Geloop?", unpublished paper, Volksblad Arts Festival, University of the Free State, Bloemfontein, July 10, 2008, 5–6.

[22] John de Gruchy, "Prayer, Politics, and False Piety," in Allan Aubrey Boesak and Charles Villa-Vicencio, eds., *When Prayer Makes News* (Philadelphia: Westminster Press, 1986), 104.

[23] Tutu, *No Future*, 218.

[24] Ibid., 11.

[25] Dyson, *I May Not Get There With You*, 11–29.

[26] Tutu, *No Future*, 220–21, emphasis mine.

[27] Ibid., 218.

[28] Ibid.

[29] Ibid. It is important to note here that in stating this, Desmond Tutu goes considerably beyond the legal mandate of the TRC. The brief of the TRC required only that the truth be revealed about atrocities for the perpetrator to be given amnesty. Tutu's talk of "remorse," "contrition," "confession," and "change" is Gospel talk that raises the bar for genuine reconciliation high above what was legally required.

[30] Ibid., 219.

[31] Ibid., 221.

[32] Ibid., 202–03. As a result, Tutu calls de Klerk "a small man, lacking magnanimity and generosity of spirit."

[33] Ibid., 221

[34] Ibid., 54–57. "It would be acknowledged that it was merely symbolic rather than substantial." Ibid., 57.

[35] See Allan Aubrey Boesak, *Running with Horses: Reflections of an Accidental Politician* (Cape Town: JoHo! Publishers, 2009), 258–83, where I speak of reconciliation as restitution; of justice as the restoration of integrity, human dignity, and human contentment.

[36] Tutu, *No Future*, 221.

[37] Ibid., 222.

[38] Ibid., 226, my emphasis.

[39] See Sampie Terreblanche, "From White Power to White Wealth: The Unresolved Moral Crisis of White South Africans," unpublished paper, November 1, 2007, 5, 6.

[40] From greed to government incompetence to the lack of clear policies to combat poverty, Tutu has continued to speak out where the churches, as institutional bodies, have mostly remained silent. He has been relentlessly vocal on the

more sensitive issues as well, such as the arms deal scandal, which at last is being probed by an independent judicial Commission of Inquiry.

[41] "Issue the Same in Palestine as it was in South Africa." http://mondoweiss.net/2010/04/tutu-issue-is-the-same-in-palestine-as-it-was-in-south-africa-equality.html (accessed January 25, 2012).

[42] Tutu, *No Future,* 215–16.

[43] See, for example, "Good News for Homosexuals," in Jeremiah Wright, *Good News, Sermons of Hope for Today's Families,* Jini Kilgore Ross, ed. (Valley Forge, PA: Judson Press, 1995), 73–86.

[44] Tutu, *No Future,* 33.

[45] Jeremiah Wright, "The Audacity to Hope," *What Makes You so Strong? Sermons of Joy and Strength,* Jini M. Kilgore, ed. (Valley Forge, PA Judson Press, 1993), 97–110.

[46] Joseph Nevins, "Truth, Lies and Accountability: In Search of Justice in East Timor," *Boston Review,* January/February, 2007, cited in Mamphela Rampele, *Laying Ghosts to Rest: Dilemmas of the Transformation in South Africa* (Cape Town: Tafelberg, 2008), 66.

[47] http://www.iol.co.za/news/politics/tutu-calls-for-wealth-tax-on-whites-1.1116744 (accessed January 5, 2012). A month later, on September 16, 2011, I sat in an audience, again in Stellenbosch and again mostly white, and heard Tutu expound the most delightful, radical liberation theology, picking up on all the themes liberal theology in South Africa has proclaimed as "passé" and as "the romantization of the poor."

[48] http://www.iol.co.za/news/politics/tutu-calls-for-wealth-tax-on-whites-1.1116744 (accessed January 5, 2012).

[49] Press release Diakonia Council of Churches, Durban, KwaZulu Natal, http://anisa.org.za/news/20110902/tutu's_wealth_tax_not_bad_idea_–_prof_geoff_harris (accessed January 5, 2012), Anabaptist Network in South Africa.

[50] "Putting Tutu in Perspective," http://www.leadershiponline.co.za/articles/other/1523 (accessed January 5, 2012). The "perspective" is in light of a similar call in Germany by respected economist Jakob Augstein writing in Der Spiegel magazine, making a case "Why Germany's Rich Must Pay Higher taxes." "Germany," Augstein writes, "is a land of inequality… If we are serious about saving German democracy, we have to raise taxes on the rich."

[51] *Leadershiponline,* "Putting Tutu in Perspective."

[52] This letter, having appeared in *Die Volksblad,* was sent to me by the same young Christian college lecturer cited above, in that same exchange of e-mails.

[53] Paulo Freire, *Pedagogy of the Oppressed* (New York: Penguin Books, 1972), 21.

[54] Ibid.

[55] Ibid., 22.

[56] See note 10.

[57] http://kairossouthernafrica.wordpress.com/2011/08/25/john-de-gruchy-meditation-on-the-tutu-tax-proposal (accessed January 30, 2012).

[58] The appeal appeared as an article in the *Cape Times,* January 18, 2012, 1. I am working from the original document sent to me by Archbishop Tutu.

[59] I have spelled out my thinking, which I am following here, in a sermon on Genesis 18:16–33, see Allan Boesak, "Try God: Be Bold," in Allan Aubrey Boesak, *The Fire Within: Sermons from the Edge of Exile* (Cape Town: New World Foundation, 2004), 25.

Conclusion

[1] See Allan Aubrey Boesak, *Running with Horses: Reflections of an Accidental Politician* (Cape Town: Joho! Publishers, 2009), 258–59.

[2] Former World Bank official Mamphela Ramphele for instance, speaks of "the miracle that never was"; see Mamphela Ramphele, *Laying Ghosts to Rest: Dilemmas of the Transformation in South Africa* (Cape Town: Tafelberg, 2008), 28. See also the references to economist Sampie Terreblanche in chapter 8.

[3] Charles Villa-Vicencio, "Reconciliation in Bloemfontein," unpublished paper, University of the Free State, February 25, 2011, 1.

[4] See Thabo Mbeki, *Africa: The Time Has Come* (Cape Town: Tafelberg/Mafube, 1998), 55; Jakes Gerwel, "National Reconciliation: Holy Grail or Secular Pact," in Charles Villa-Vicencio and Wilhelm Verwoerd, eds., *Looking Back, Reaching Forward* (Cape Town: UCT Press and London: Zed Books, 2000), 277–86.

[5] Gerwel, "National Reconciliation," 283–84.

[6] Allan responds at length to these arguments in Allan Aubrey Boesak, *The Tenderness of Conscience: African Renaissance and the Spirituality of Politics* (Stellenbosch, South Africa: SUN Press, 2005), 177–94.

[7] Michael O. Emerson and Christian Smith, *Divided by Faith: Evangelical Religion and the Problem of Race in America* (New York, Oxford University Press, 2000), 66.

[8] Ibid., 67.

[9] Mbeki, *Africa,* 55.

[10] See Christi van der Westhuizen, *White Power & The Rise and Fall of the National Party* (Cape Town: Zebra Books, 2007), 240–46; Sampie Terreblanche, "From White Power to White Wealth: The Unresolved Moral Crisis of White South Africans," unpublished paper, response to van der Westhuizen's book, November 1, 2007. In South Africa the political reconciliation process is an essential part of the 1994 Elite Pact, "driven by global corporatism and by the Washington ideology of market fundamentalism," writes economist Sampie Terreblanche, and "the entrenchment of neo-liberal capitalism during the transition has translated into the continuation of apartheid and colonialism's legacy of extreme inequality," argues

Christi van der Westhuizen. What we have indisputably, and painfully, learned over the last thirty years is that the Washington Consensus does not include the consent of the global poor and powerless.

[11] See Charles Villa-Vicencio, *Walk With Us and Listen: Political Reconciliation in Africa* (Cape Town: University of Cape Town Press, 2009), 2.

[12] Ibid., 1.

[13] Cited by Mahmood Mamdani, "Reconciliation Without Justice," *Southern African Review of Books* 46 (November/December 1996); see also Boesak, *Tenderness*, 178.

[14] The life expectancy comparison is found in Christopher J. L. Murray, Sandeep Kulkarni, and Majid Ezzati, "Eight Americas: New Perspectives on U.S. Health Disparities," *American Journal of Preventive Medicine*, 29, no. 5, Suppl. 1 (2005): 6. The new Jim Crow comes from Michelle Alexander, *The New Jim Crow: Mass Incarceration in the Age of Colorblindness* (New York: New Press, 2010).

Bibliography

Alexander, Michelle. *The New Jim Crow: Mass Incarceration in the Age of Colorblindness*. New York: New Press, 2010.

Allen, Robert L. "From Black Awakening in Capitalist America." In *The Revolution Will Not Be Funded: Beyond the Non-Profit Industrial Complex,* Incite! Women of Color Against Violence, eds., 53–62. Cambridge: South End Press, 2007.

Anderson, A. A. *2 Samuel: Word Biblical Commentary.* Dallas: Word Publishers, 1989.

Baldwin, Joyce, G. *1 and 2 Samuel: An Introduction and Commentary, Tyndale Old Testament Commentaries,* D.J. Wiseman, ed. Leicester, UK: InterVarsity Press, 1988.

Bantum, Brian. *Redeeming Mulatto: A Theology of Race and Christian Hybridity.* Waco, TX: Baylor University Press, 2010.

Barth, Karl. *Church Dogmatics, II/I,* Edinburgh, Scotland: Clarke, 1957.

Bergen, Robert D. *1,2 Samuel: An Exegetical and Theological Exposition of Holy Scripture, The New American Commentary.* Nashville: Holman Reference, 1996.

Bernabé, Jean, Patrick Chamoiseau, and Raphaël Confiant. *Éloge de la Créolité / In Praise of Creoleness,* Édition Bilingue. Paris: Gallimard, 1993.

Biko, Steve. *I Write What I Like: Selected Writings.* Johannesburg: Ravan Press, 1996; Chicago: University of Chicago Press, 2002.

Blount, Brian K. "The Apocalypse of Worship: A House of Prayer for ALL the Nations." In *Making Room at the Table: An Invitation to Multicultural Worship,* Brian K. Blount and Leonora Tubbs Tisdale, eds., 16–29 Louisville, KY: Westminster John Knox Press, 2001.

Boesak, Allan Aubrey. *Farewell to Innocence: A Socio-ethical Study of Black Theology and Black Power.* Maryknoll, NY: Orbis Books, 1976.

Boesak, Allan Aubrey. *Black and Reformed: Apartheid, Liberation and the Calvinist Tradition.* Maryknoll, NY: Orbis Books, 1984.

Boesak, Allan Aubrey. *Comfort and Protest: The Apocalypse from a South African Perspective.* Philadelphia: Westminster Press, 1987.

Boesak, Allan Aubrey. "What Dietrich Bonhoeffer Has Meant to Me." In *Bonhoeffer's Ethics: Old Europe and New Frontiers,* Guy Carter, René van Eyden, Hans-Dirk van Hoogstraten, and Jürgen Wiersma, eds., 21–29. Kampen, Germany: Kok Pharos, 1991.

Boesak, Allan Aubrey. *The Fire Within: Sermons form the Edge of Exile.* Cape Town: New World Foundation, 2004.

Boesak, Allan Aubrey. *Die Vlug van Gods Verbeelding: Bybelverhale van die Onderkant.* Stellenbosch, South Africa: SUN Press, 2005.

Boesak, Allan Aubrey. *The Tenderness of Conscience: African Renaissance and the Spirituality of Politics.* Stellenbosch, South Africa: SUN Press, 2005.

Boesak, Allan Aubrey, "To Stand Where God Stands: Reflections on the Confession of Belhar." *Studiae Historiae Ecclesiasticae,* 34, no. 1 (July 2008): 141–72.

Boesak, Allan Aubrey. "And Zacchaeus Remained Sitting in the Tree." In *Coming Together in the 21st Century: The Bible's Message in an Age of Diversity,* Curtiss Paul De Young, ed., 143–47. Valley Forge, PA: Judson Press, 2009.

Boesak, Allan Aubrey. *Running with Horses: Reflections of an Accidental Politician.* Cape Town: Joho! Publishers, 2009.

Boesak, Elna. "Tussen Reitz en 'n Rots: Wat het Verkeerd Geloop?" Unpublished paper, *Volksblad* Arts Festival, University of the Free State, Bloemfontein, July 10, 2008.

Borg, Marcus. *Jesus: Uncovering the Life, Teachings and Relevance of a Religious Revolutionary.* New York: Harper Collins, 2006.

Borg, Marcus J., and John Dominic Crossan. *The Last Week: A Day-by-Day Account of Jesus's Final Days in Jerusalem.* San Francisco: HarperOne, 2006.

Branch, Taylor. *Parting The Waters: America in the King Years 1954–63.* New York: Simon and Schuster, 1988.

Brown, Kelly Delaine. "God Is as Christ Does: Toward a Womanist Theology." *JRT* 46 (1989).

Brueggemann, Walter. *First and Second Samuel: Interpretation, A Bible Commentary for Teaching and Preaching,* James Luther Mays, Patrick D. Miller, and Paul J. Achtemeier, eds. Louisville, KY: John Knox Press, 1990.

Brueggemann, Walter. *The Prophetic Imagination, Second Edition.* Minneapolis: Fortress Press, 2001.

Brueggemann, Walter. *Out of Babylon.* Nashville: Abingdon Press, 2010.

Carter, Warren. *Matthew and Empire: Initial Explorations.* Harrisburg, PA: Trinity Press International, 2001.

Césaire, Aimé. *Discourse on Colonialism,* rev. ed. New York: Monthly Review Press, 1972, 2000.

Clark Kroeger, Caroline, and Mary J. Evans, eds. *The IVP Women's Bible Commentary.* Downers Grove, IL: Intervarsity Press, 2002.

Constantineanu, Corneliu. *The Social Significance of Reconciliation in Paul's Theology: Narrative Readings in Romans.* London: T & T Clark International, 2010.

Costa, Maria, Catherine Keller, Anna Mercedes, "Love in Times of Empire." In *Evangelicals and Empire: Christian Alternatives to the Political Status Quo,* Bruce Ellis Benson and Peter Goodwin Heltzel, eds., 291–305. Grand Rapids: Brazos Press, 2008.

Crossan, John Dominic. *The Historical Jesus: The Life of a Mediterranean Jewish Peasant.* San Francisco: HarperSanFrancisco, 1991.

Crossan, John Dominic. *God & Empire: Jesus Against Rome, Then and Now.* San Francisco: HarperSanFrancisco, 2007.

Crossan, John Dominic, and Jonathan L. Reed. *In Search of Paul: How Jesus's Apostle Opposed Rome's Empire with God's Kingdom.* San Francisco: HarperSanFrancisco, 2004.

De Gruchy, John W. "Prayer, Politics, and False Piety." In *When Prayer Makes News,* Allan Aubrey Boesak and Charles Villa-Vicencio, eds., 97–112. Philadelphia: The Westminster Press, 1986.

De Gruchy, John W. *Reconciliation: Restoring Justice.* Minneapolis: Fortress Press, 2002.

De la Torre, Miguel A. *Liberating Jonah: Forming an Ethic of Reconciliation.* Maryknoll, NY: Orbis Books, 2007.

DeYoung, Curtiss Paul, *Coming Together: The Bible's Message in an Age of Diversity.* Valley Forge, PA: Judson Press, 1995.

DeYoung, Curtiss Paul. *Reconciliation: Our Greatest Challenge—Our Only Hope.* Valley Forge, PA: Judson Press, 1997.

DeYoung, Curtiss Paul. *Living Faith: How Faith Inspires Social Justice.* Minneapolis: Fortress Press, 2007.

DeYoung, Curtiss Paul. "The Power of Reconciliation: From the Apostle Paul to Malcolm X." *CrossCurrents* 57 (Summer 2007): 203–08.

DeYoung, Curtiss Paul. "From Resistance to Reconciliation." In *Resist! Christian Dissent for the 21st Century,* Michael G. Long, ed., 3–18. Maryknoll, NY: Orbis Books, 2008.

DeYoung, Curtiss Paul. *Coming Together in the 21st Century: The Bible's Message in an Age of Diversity.* Valley Forge, PA: Judson Press, 2009.

DeYoung, Curtiss Paul. "A Lifting of the Burden." In *The Audacity of Faith: Christian Leaders Reflect on the Election of Barack Obama,* Marvin A. McMickle, ed., 60–63. Valley Forge, PA: Judson Press, 2009.

DeYoung, Curtiss Paul. *Homecoming: A "White" Man's Journey through Harlem to Jerusalem.* Minneapolis: Jezi Press, 2009.

DeYoung, Curtiss Paul, Michael O. Emerson, George Yancey, and Karen Chai Kim. *United by Faith: The Multiracial Congregation as an Answer to the Problem of Race.* New York: Oxford University Press, 2003.

DeYoung, Curtiss Paul, Wilda C. Gafney, Leticia A. Guardiola-Sáenz, George

"Tink" Tinker, and Frank M. Yamada, eds. *The Peoples' Bible: New Revised Standard Version with the Apocrypha.* Minneapolis: Fortress, 2008.

DuBois, W. E. B., *The Souls of Black Folk.* New York: Barnes & Noble Classics, 1903, 2003.

Dyson, Michael Eric. *I May Not Get There With You: The True Martin Luther King Jr.* New York: Touchstone Books, 2000.

Edwards, Korie L. *The Elusive Dream: The Power of Race in Interracial Churches.* New York: Oxford University Press, 2008.

Elliott, Neil. *Liberating Paul: The Justice of God and the Politics of the Apostle.* Minneapolis: Fortress Press, 1994, 2006.

Elliott, Neil. "The Apostle Paul and Empire." In *In the Shadow of Empire: Reclaiming the Bible as a History of Faithful Resistance,* ed. Richard A. Horsley, 97–116. Louisville, KY: Westminster John Knox Press, 2008.

Elliott, Neil. *The Arrogance of Nations: Reading Romans in the Shadow of Empire.* Minneapolis: Fortress, 2008.

Elliott, Neil. "The Bible and Empire." In *The Peoples' Bible: New Revised Standard Version with the Apocrypha,* eds. Curtiss Paul DeYoung, Wilda C. Gafney, Leticia A. Guardiola-Sáenz, George "Tink" Tinker, and Frank M. Yamada, 85–98. Minneapolis: Fortress, 2008.

Emerson, Michael O., and Christian Smith. *Divided by Faith: Evangelical Religion and the Problem of Race in America.* New York: Oxford University Press, 2000.

Exum, J. Cheryl. *Tragedy and Biblical Narrative: Arrows of the Almighty.* New York: Cambridge University Press, 1992.

Fanon, Frantz. *The Wretched of the Earth.* New York: Grove Press, 1963.

Fanon, Frantz. *Black Skin, White Masks.* New York: Grove Press, 1967.

Freire, Paulo. *Pedagogy of the Oppressed.* New York: Seabury Press, 1970; New York: Penguin Books, 1972.

Gaum, Laurie, and Frits Gaum. *Praat verby Grense.* Cape Town: Umuzi, 2010.

Gerwel, Jakes. "National Reconciliation: Holy Grail or Secular Pact." In *Looking Back, Reaching Forward,* Charles Villa-Vicencio and Wilhelm Verwoerd, eds., 277–86. Cape Town: UCT Press and London: Zed Books, 2000.

Goslinga, C.J. *Het Tweede Boek Samuel: Commentaar op het Oude Testament.* Kampen, Germany: Kok, 1962.

Grimsrud, Ted. "Healing Justice: The Prophet Amos and a 'New' Theology of Justice." In *Peace and Justice Shall Embrace: Power and Theopolitics in the Bible,* Ted Grimsrud and Loren L. Johns, eds., 64–85. Telford, PA: Pandora Press U.S., 1999.

Gutiérrez, Gustavo. *A Theology of Liberation.* Maryknoll, NY: Orbis Books, 1973.

Guyette, Fred. "Amos the Prophet: A Meditation on the Richness of 'Justice.'" *Jewish Bible Quarterly* 36, no. 1 (Jan–Mar 2008): 15–21.

Haddad, Mimi. "Reading the Apostle Paul through Galatians 3:28." In *Coming Together in the 21st Century: The Bible's Message in an Age of Diversity,* Curtiss Paul DeYoung, ed., 73–93. Valley Forge, PA: Judson Press, 2009.

Hanson, K. C. and Douglas E. Oakman. *Palestine in the Time of Jesus: Social Structures and Social Conflicts.* Minneapolis: Fortress Press, 1998.

Harding, Vincent. "Black Power and the American Christ." In *The Black Power Revolt: A Collection of Essays,* Floyd B. Barbour, ed. Boston: P. Sargent, 1968.

Hays, Richard B. *The Moral Vision of the New Testament: A Contemporary Introduction to New Testament Ethics.* San Francisco: HarperSanFrancisco, 1996.

Hendricks, Obery M. Jr. *The Politics of Jesus: Rediscovering the True Revolutionary Nature of Jesus' Teachings and How They Have Been Corrupted.* New York: Doubleday, 2006.

Hertzberg, Hans Willem. *I&II Samuel: A Commentary: Old Testament Library.* London: SCM Press, 1964.

Herzog II, William R. *Parables as Subversive Speech: Jesus as Pedagogue of the Oppressed.* Louisville, KY: John Knox Westminster Press, 1994.

Herzog II, William R. *Jesus, Justice, and the Reign of God: A Ministry of Liberation.* Louisville, KY: Westminster John Knox Press, 2000.

Herzog II, William R. *Prophet and Teacher: An Introduction to the Historical Jesus.* Louisville, KY: Westminster John Knox Press, 2005.

Heschel, Abraham J. *The Prophets.* New York: HarperCollins Publisher, 2001.

Horsley, Richard A. *Galilee: History, Politics, People.* Valley Forge, PA: Trinity Press International, 1995.

Horsley, Richard A., ed. *Paul and Empire: Religion and Power in Roman Imperial Society.* Harrisburg, PA: Trinity Press International, 1997.

Horsley, Richard A., ed., *Paul and Politics: Ekklesia, Israel, Imperium, Interpretation, Essays in Honor of Krister Stendahl.* Harrisburg, PA: Trinity Press International, 2000.

Horsley, Richard A. *Jesus and Empire: The Kingdom of God and the New World Disorder.* Minneapolis, Fortress Press, 2003.

Horsley, Richard A. *In the Shadow of Empire: Reclaiming the Bible as a History of Faithful Resistance,* ed. Louisville, KY: Westminster John Knox Press, 2008.

Horsley, Richard A. "Introduction: The Bible and Empires." In *In the Shadow of Empire: Reclaiming the Bible as a History of Faithful Resistance,* ed., Richard A. Horsley, 1–7. Louisville, KY: Westminster John Knox Press, 2008.

Howard-Brook, Wes. *"Come Out, My People!" God's Call out of Empire in the Bible and Beyond.* Maryknoll, NY: Orbis Books, 2010.

Incite! Women of Color Against Violence, eds. *The Revolution Will Not be Funded.* Cambridge: South End Press, 2007.

Jansen, Jonathan, "Reconciliation as an institutional matter." In *In the Balance, South Africans Debate Reconciliation,* Institute for Justice and Reconciliation,

Fanie du Toit and Erik Doxtader, eds., 125–32. Johannesburg: Jacana Media, 2010.

Jennings, Willie James. *The Christian Imagination: Theology and the Origins of Race.* New Haven, CT: Yale University Press, 2010.

Jervis, L. Ann. "Reading Romans 7 in Conversation with Postcolonial Theory: Paul's Struggle toward a Christian Identity of Hybridity." In *The Colonized Apostle: Paul through Postcolonial Eyes*, ed. Christopher D. Stanley, 95–109. Minneapolis: Fortress Press, 2011.

Katongole, Emmanuel, and Chris Rice. *Reconciling All Things: A Christian Vision for Justice, Peace and Healing.* Maryknoll, NY: IVP Press, 2009.

Kim, Jin-Soo. *Bloodguilt, Atonement, and Mercy: An Exegetical and Theological Study of 2 Samuel 21:1–14, European University Studies.* Frankfurt am Main, Germany: Peter Lang, 2007.

King Jr., Martin Luther. "A Time to Break Silence." In *A Testament of Hope: The Essential Writings of Martin Luther King; Jr.,* James M. Washington, ed., 231–44. San Francisco: Harper and Row, 1986.

King Jr., Martin Luther. "An Address Before the National Press Club." In *A Testament of Hope: The Essential Writings of Martin Luther King; Jr.,* James M. Washington, ed., 99–105. San Francisco: Harper and Row, 1986.

King Jr., Martin Luther. "The American Dream." In *A Testament of Hope: The Essential Writings of Martin Luther King; Jr.,* James M. Washington, ed., 208–16. San Francisco: Harper and Row, 1986.

King, Tiffany Lethabo, and Ewuare Osayande. "The Filth on Philanthropy: Progressive Philanthropy's Agenda to Misdirect Social Justice Movements." In *The Revolution Will Not Be Funded: Beyond the Non-Profit Industrial Complex,* Incite! Women of Color Against Violence, eds., 71–89. Cambridge: South End Press, 2007.

Kollapen, Jody. "Reconciliation: engaging with our fears and expectations." In *In the Balance, South Africans Debate Reconciliation,* Institute for Justice and Reconciliation, Fanie du Toit and Erik Doxtader, eds., 17–26. Johannesburg: Jacana Media, 2010.

Krog, Antjie. *Country of My Skull.* Johannesburg: Random House, 2002.

Leclerc, Thomas L. *Introduction to the Prophets: Their Stories, Sayings, and Scrolls.* New York: Paulist Press, 2007.

Liew, Tat-siong Benny. "Redressing Bodies in Corinth: Racial/Ethnic Politics and Religious Difference in the Context of Empire." In *The Colonized Apostle: Paul through Postcolonial Eyes*, ed. Christopher D. Stanley, 127–45. Minneapolis: Fortress Press, 2011.

Lischer, Richard. *The Preacher King: Martin Luther King, Jr., and the Word that Moved America.* New York: Oxford University Press, 1997.

Lischer, Richard. *The End of Words: The Language of Reconciliation in a Culture of Violence.* Grand Rapids: William B. Eerdmans Publishing Company, 2005.

Mahajan, Rahul. *The New Crusade: America's War on Terrorism.* New York: Monthly Review Press, 2002.

Mamdani, Mahmood. "Beyond Kempton Park; Reflections on Nuremberg and the Question of Justice," public lecture, Africa Memorial Day, University of the Free State, Bloemfontein, July 14, 2010.

Mangcu, Xolela. *On the Brink: The State of Democracy in South Africa.* Scottville, South Africa: University of KwaZulu Natal Press, 2008.

Marshall, I. H., A. R. Milard, J. I. Packer, and D. J. Wiseman, eds. *New Bible Dictionary,* 3rd ed. Leicester, UK: InterVarsity Press, 2003.

Martin, Ralph P. *Word Biblical Commentary, Volume 40, 2 Corinthians.* Waco, TX: Word, 1986.

Martin-Achard, Robert. "The End of the People of God." In *Amos & Lamentations: God's People in Crisis,* Robert Martin-Achard and S. Paul Re'emi, eds., 1–71. Grand Rapids: Wm. B. Eerdmans Publishing Co., 1984.

Massey, James Earl. "Reconciliation: Two Biblical Studies." In *A Mighty Long Journey: Reflections on Racial Reconciliation,* eds., Timothy George and Robert Smith, Jr., 199–222. Nashville: Broadman and Holman, 1999.

Mays, James Luther. *Amos: A Commentary.* Philadelphia: Westminster Press, 1969.

Mbeki, Thabo. *Africa: The Time Has Come.* Cape Town: Tafelberg/Mafube, 1998.

Memmi, Albert. *The Colonizer and the Colonized.* Boston: Beacon Press, 1965.

Murray, Christopher J. L., Sandeep Kulkarni, and Majid Ezzati, "Eight Americas: New Perspectives on U.S. Health Disparities." *American Journal of Preventive Medicine,* 29, no. 5 (Suppl. 1): 4–10.

Myers, Ched, and Elaine Enns. *Ambassadors of Reconciliation, Volume I: New Testament Reflections on Restorative Justice and Peacemaking.* Maryknoll, NY: Orbis Books, 2009.

Newsom, Carol A., and Sharon H. Ringe, eds. *The Women's Bible Commentary,* Expanded Edition. Louisville, KY: Westminster John Knox Press, 1992.

Obama, Barack. *The Audacity to Hope: Thoughts on Reclaiming the American Dream.* New York: Random House, 2006.

Ochs, Vanessa L. *Sarah Laughed: Modern Lessons from the Wisdom and Stories of Biblical Women.* New York: McGraw-Hill, 2005.

Otwell, John H. *And Sarah Laughed: The Status of Women in the Old Testament.* Philadelphia: Westminster Press, 1977.

Pazmiño, Roberto W. "Double Dutch: Reflections of an Hispanic North-American on Multicultural Education." In *Voces: Voices from the Hispanic Church,* Justo L. Gonzales, ed., 137–45. Nashville: Abingdon Press, 1992.

Pitt, Richard N. "Fear of a Black Pulpit? Real Racial Transcendence Versus

Cultural Assimilation in Multiracial Churches." In *Journal for the Scientific Study of Religion* 49, no. 2 (2010): 218–23.

Rah, Soong-Chan. *The Next Evangelicalism: Freeing the Church from Western Cultural Captivity.* Downers Grove, IL: IVP Books, 2009.

Ramphele, Mamphela. *Laying Ghosts to Rest: Dilemmas of the Transformation in South Africa.* Cape Town: Tafelberg, 2008.

Rieger, Joerg. *Christ & Empire: From Paul to Postcolonial Times.* Minneapolis: Fortress Press, 2007.

Rodriguez, Dylan. "The Political Logic of the Non-Profit Industrial Complex." In *The Revolution Will Not Be Funded: Beyond the Non-Profit Industrial Complex,* Incite! Women of Color Against Violence, eds., 21–40. Cambridge: South End Press, 2007.

Rojas Durazo, Ana Clarissa. "'We Were Never Meant to Survive': Fighting Violence Against Women and the Fourth World War." In *The Revolution Will Not Be Funded: Beyond the Non-Profit Industrial Complex,* Incite! Women of Color Against Violence, eds., 113–28. Cambridge: South End Press, 2007.

Schaberg, Jane. *The Illegitimacy of Jesus: A Feminist Theological Interpretation of the Infancy Narratives.* San Francisco: Harper & Row, 1987.

Schottroff, Willy. "The Prophet Amos: A Socio-Historical Assessment of His Ministry." In *God of the Lowly: Socio-Historical Interpretations of the Bible,* Willy Schottroff and Wolfgang Stegemann, eds., 27–46. Maryknoll, NY: Orbis Books, 1984.

Smith, Andrea. "Introduction: The Revolution Will Not be Funded." In *The Revolution Will Not Be Funded: Beyond the Non-Profit Industrial Complex,* Incite! Women of Color Against Violence, eds., 1–18. Cambridge: South End Press, 2007.

Stanley, Christopher D., ed. *The Colonized Apostle: Paul through Postcolonial Eyes.* Minneapolis: Fortress Press, 2011.

Terreblanche, Sampie. "From White Power to White Wealth: The Unresolved Moral Crisis of White South Africans." Unpublished paper, November 1, 2007.

Thunder Hawk, Madonna. "Native Organizing Before the Non-Profit Industrial Complex." In *The Revolution Will Not Be Funded: Beyond the Non-Profit Industrial Complex,* Incite! Women of Color Against Violence, eds., 101–06. Cambridge: South End Press, 2007.

Thurman, Howard. *Jesus and the Disinherited.* New York: Abingdon-Cokesbury Press, 1949.

Tutu, Desmond. *No Future without Forgiveness.* London: Rider, 1999.

Van Aarde, Andries. *Fatherless in Galilee: Jesus as the Child of God.* Harrisburg, PA: Trinity Press International, 2001.

Van Biema, David. "The Color of Faith." *Time Magazine,* January 11, 2010, 38–41.

Van der Westhuizen, Christi. *White Power & The Rise and Fall of the National Party.* Cape Town: Zebra Books, 2007.

Van Eck, Ernest. "When Neighbours Are Not Neighbours. A Social-Scientific Reading of the Parable of the Friend at Midnight, (Luke 11:5–8)." *HTS Teologiese Studies/Theological Studies* 67, no. 1: art. # 788, 14 pages, DOI:10,4102/hts/v67il.788.

Verwoerd, Wilhelm. "Forgiving the torturer but not the torture." *Sunday Independent,* December 14, 1998.

Villa-Vicencio, Charles. *Walk with Us and Listen: Political Reconciliation in Africa.* Cape Town: University of Cape Town Press, 2009.

Villa-Vicencio, Charles. "Reconciliation and Bloemfontein." Unpublished paper, University of the Free State, Bloemfontein, February 25, 2011.

Waetjen, Herman C. *A Reordering of Power: A Socio-Political Reading of Mark's Gospel.* Minneapolis: Fortress Press, 1989.

Walker, Clarence E., and Gregory D. Smithers. *The Preacher and the Politician: Jeremiah Wright, Barack Obama, and Race in America.* Charlottesville: University of Virginia Press, 2009.

Walters, John J. "Who Was Hagar?" In *Stony the Road We Trod: African American Biblical Interpretation,* Cain Hope Felder, ed., 187–205. Minneapolis: Fortress Press, 1991.

Weems, Renita. *Just a Sister Away: A Womanist Vision of Women's Relationships in the Bible.* San Diego: LuraMedia, 1988.

Wink, Walter. *When the Powers Fall: Reconciliation in the Healing of Nations.* Minneapolis: Fortress Press, 1998.

Wold, Margaret. *Women of Faith and Spirit: Profile of Fifteen Biblical Women.* Minneapolis: Augsburg Press, 1987.

Wolterstorff, Nicholas. *Justice: Rights and Wrongs.* Princeton, NJ: Princeton University Press, 2010.

Wright, Jeremiah A. Jr. *What Makes You so Strong? Sermons of Joy and Strength.* Jini M. Kilgore, ed. Valley Forge, PA: Judson Press, 1993.

Wright, Jeremiah A. Jr. *Good News: Sermons of Hope for Today's Families.* Jini Kilgore Ross, ed. Valley Forge, PA: Judson Press, 1995.

Index

African National Congress, 141
Amaziah, 120–21
Amos, 61, 118–22, 155
anger, reconciliation and, 107–8, 134–35
apartheid, 2, 14, 20; effects of, 138–41, 144–47, 151–53; and Reitz incident, 93–111. *See also* South Africa
Audacity to Hope, The (Obama), 116
Augustus, 43–44

Bantum, Brian, 85, 90
Belhar Confession, 101–2, 108
Bernabé, Jean, 90–91
Biko, Steve, 20
Blount, Brian, 47
Boesak, Allan, biography of, 2–3
Boesak, Elna, 98–101, 103, 110, 135
Bonhoeffer, Dietrich, 2, 10–11
Borg, Marcus, viii–ix, 48
Britz, Dolf, 110
Brown, Kelley Delaine, 53
Brueggemann, Walter, 25, 26, 28, 122, 123

Césaire, Aimé, 14
Chamoiseau, Patrick, 90–91

Chikane, Frank, 156
colonialism, 13–15; and apartheid, 14; and crucifixion, 13–14, 17–18; Jesus and, 11, 16–18, 21–22, 45–55; Paul and, 11–12, 14–23; Roman Empire and, 11, 13–15, 64–66
colonized/colonizer relationship. See oppressed/oppressor relationship
Coming Together in the 21st Century (DeYoung), 3
Cone, James, 53
Confiant, Raphaël, 90–91
congregations: multicultural, 79–85; multiracial U.S., 77–79, 85–91
Constantineanu, Corneliu, 16
Creoleness, 90–91
Crossan, John Dominic, 16–17, 45, 48, 54
crucifixion: as colonial punishment, 13–14, 17–18; of Jesus, 13–14, 16–17, 37, 48–49, 54

David, King, 25–39, 69
de Gruchy, John W., 10–11, 12, 18–19, 135–36, 147
de Klerk, F.W., 9, 138
de la Torre, Miguel, 57

DeYoung, Curtiss, biography of, 2–3
Divided by Faith (Emerson and Smith),
    153
DuBois, W. E. B., 15
Dutch Reformed Mission Church,
    101, 133
Dyson, Michael Eric, 134–35, 136

Edwards, Korie, 78–79, 86, 87, 88, 90
Elliott, Neil, 17–18
Elusive Dream, The (Edwards), 78–79
Emerson, Michael, 77–78, 153
End of Words, The (Lischer), 10
Ephesians, 16, 19, 22, 44
Exum, Cheryl, 31

Fanon, Frantz, 14–15
1 Corinthians, 19, 21
forgiveness: reconciliation and, 63–64,
    97, 107, 132–34, 136–38, 154,
    156; TRC and, 63–64, 97, 107
Freire, Paulo, 15, 20, 22, 80, 81, 146
Froman, Menachem, 121–22

Galatians, 19
Galilee, 11, 45, 47–48, 52
Gaum, Frits, 133, 136
Gerwel, Jakes, 152, 153, 154
"Great Myth", in South Africa,
    99–101, 110
Grimsrud, Ted
Gutiérrez, Gustavo, 19
Guyette, Fred, 123–24

Haddad, Mimi, 84
Harding, Vincent, 49–50, 57
Harris, Geoff, 144–45
Hays, Richard B., 84
Hebrews, Letter to the, 44
Hendricks, Obery M., 54–55, 60

Herod, 44, 64
Heschel, Abraham, 119, 122
Horsley, Richard A., 13, 22, 44, 48–49,
    54, 55

Incite! Women of Color
    Against Violence, 126
In Praise of Creoleness, 90–91
Isaiah: Jesus' use of, 18, 45–46, 57,
    60–61; reconciliation and,
    18, 57–62
Israel, and Palestinian occupation,
    35, 43–44, 121-22, 141–42

Jansen, Jonathan, 95–96, 97, 98,
    102–3, 104–6, 107, 108–9
Jennings, Willie, 10, 81, 82
Jericho, 64
Jeroboam II, 119–21
Jesus: as black, 53-54; and colonialism,
    11, 16–18, 21–22, 45–55;
    crucifixion of, 13–14, 16–17,
    37, 48–49, 54; fatherlessness of,
    46–47, 52; and Isaiah, 18, 45–46,
    57, 60–61; ministry of, 45–55;
    as prophet, 123, 124; and race,
    49–50, 53–54; and Roman
    Empire, 16–18, 21–22, 43–46,
    48–51; and women, 46–47, 84
Jesus and the Disinherited (Thurman), 45
Jews: and colonialism, 12–14, 43–45;
    and multicultural congregations,
    79–85
Johns, Vernon, 117
Jonker, Willie, 133
Josephus, 51
justice: reconciliation and, 18–19,
    58–62, 67–74, 101-8, 137-
    47, 153–54; and TRC, 63–64;
    in Zaccheus story, 67-74

King, Martin Luther, Jr., 78, 90, 115, 117, 122, 124–25, 134–35, 136
King, Tiffany Lethabo, 126
Kim, Karen Chai, 77–78
Koko, Emma, 93, 110–11
Kollapen, Jody, 110
Kotze, Johan, 147–49

Lakewood Church, 77
liberation theology, 53–54
Liew, Tat-siong Benny, 19, 21, 82
Lischer, Richard, 10
Living Faith (DeYoung), 2
Luke, Gospel of, 43–44, 45–46, 57, 58, 60–61, 62; Zaccheus story in, 63–74

Mahomed, Ismail, 142
Mandela, Nelson, 9, 97, 109, 141, 151
Mark, Gospel of, 47–48
Masitha, Moses, 110–11
Massey, James Earl, 12
Matthew, Gospel of, 43–44, 52, 59
Mbeki, Thabo, 152, 153–54
Memmi, Albert, 14, 15, 20, 21, 81–82
multiracial congregations, 77–79, 85–91. *See also* race
Myers, Ched, 20, 80–81, 124

No Future without Forgivenes (Tutu), viii, 145

Obama, Barack, 115–18, 125
oppressed/oppressor relationship, 19–22, 79–83
Osayunde, Ewuare, 126

Palestine, Israeli occupation of, 35, 43–44, 121–22, 141–42

Paul: as colonial subject, 14–23; on reconciliation, 11–12, 15–23
Pitt, Richard, 78, 87–88
Pontius Pilate, 48, 65
Preacher and the Politician, The (Walker and Smithers), 117, 118
Prophetic Imagination, The (Brueggemann), 123
prophets: Hebrew, 117–124; Jesus as, 123, 124; and reconciliation, 122–29; Wright as, 117–18, 123, 125

race: Jesus and, 49–50, 53–54; and multiracial congregations, 77–79, 85–91; and Reitz incident, 93–111
Rah, Soong-Chan, 85, 88–89
reconciliation: and anger, 107–8, 134–35; definition of, 10–12, 15–22; and forgiveness, 63–64, 97, 107, 132–34, 136–38, 154, 156; and justice, 18–19, 58–62, 67–74, 101–8, 137–47, 153–54; and multicultural congregations, 77–91; Paul on, 11–12, 15–23; and prophets, 122–29; and race, 85–91; and Reitz incident, 93–111; Rizpah story and, 36–39, 122–23, 155; in South Africa, 9–11, 93-111; Zaccheus story and, 67–74
Reconciliation (de Gruchy), 18–19
Reconciliation (DeYoung), 2
Reed, Jonathan, 16–17
Reitz incident, 93–111
Revolution Will Not Be Funded, The (Incite!), 126
Rizpah story (2 Sam), 25–39, 122–23, 155

Roman Empire, 11, 12–22; Jesus and, 16–18, 21–22, 43–46, 48–51; taxation under, 64–66
Roosevelt, Eleanor, 105
Running with Horses (Boesak), 2

Sachs, Albie, 142
Saul, in Rizpahh story, 27–30
2 Corinthians, 15–17, 18, 69
2 Samuel, Rizpah story in, 25–39
Smith, Christian, 153
Smithers, Gregory D., 117, 118
solidarity, 34
South Africa: "Great Myth" in, 99–101, 110; and justice, 101–8, 137–47; reconciliation in, 9–11, 93–111, 131–41, 144–49, 151–54; Reitz incident in, 93–111

taxation: under Roman Empire, 64–66
tax collectors, 65–66, 72–73
Tekoa, 118, 119, 121–22
Tenderness of Conscience, The (Boesak), 2
Thunder Hawk, Madonna, 126
Thurman, Howard, 45, 50, 58
Truth and Reconciliation Commission (TRC): and forgiveness, 63–64, 97, 107; and justice, 63–64; origins of, 9–10; Tutu and, 63–64, 97, 109, 131, 148

Tutu, Desmond Mpilo, vii–x, 131–49; domestication of, 134–38; on Palestinian occupation, 141–42; and TRC, 10, 63–64, 97, 109, 131, 148
Twin Cities Urban Reconciliation Network, 2

United by Faith, 77–78, 79
United Democratic Front, 2
University of the Free State, 93–111

van Aarde, Andries, 46–47, 51, 52–53, 54, 55
victimhood, 105–7; Rizpah story and, 32, 37–38
Villa-Vicencio, Charles, 133, 147, 152, 153, 155–56

Waetjen, Herman, 73
Walker, Clarence E., 117, 118
Willow Creek Community, 77, 78
Wink, Walter, 69
Wolterstorff, Nicholas, 54, 60, 61–62
women, Jesus and, 46–47, 84
Women's Bible Commentary, 26
Wright, Jeremiah, Jr., 116–18, 123, 125, 141

Yancey, George, 77–78

Zaccheus story (Luke), 63–74